Land of Fair Promise

Politics and Reform in Los Angeles Schools, 1885-1941

Judith Rosenberg Raftery

Land of Fair Promise

Politics and Reform in Los Angeles Schools, 1885-1941

Stanford University Press *1992*
Stanford, California

Published with the assistance of the
Edgar M. Kahn Memorial Fund

Stanford University Press
Stanford, California

Printed in the United States of America

CIP data appear at the end of the book

To my children, Daniel, Jennifer, and John,
and to the memory of my mother and my father,
Ruth and Rudolph Rosenberg

Acknowledgments

Many friends and colleagues devoted time and effort to reading and criticizing this manuscript through its various stages, and I happily extend my thanks and appreciation to them. I am particularly pleased to thank four friends who offered their astute insight and suggestions: Eric Monkkonen directed my graduate research at UCLA and has continued to guide me; Martin Ridge nudged and prodded me to sharpen my ideas; Joseph Conlin generously gave his time and his great gift of criticism. To Lewis O. Saum, on whose intelligence, acumen, and support I have learned to rely, I owe special thanks. He has read this material almost as often as I have and has encouraged me at every step of the way. Without the help of such friends, this book would never be in print.

For financial support I am very grateful to the John Randolph Haynes and Dora Haynes Foundation and the Henry E. Huntington Library, San Marino, California, for fellowships in 1986 and 1989. I am also grateful to California State University, Chico, for a University Summer Scholarship, the university's Humanities and Fine Arts Research Council and Dean Donald Heinz for three Summer Research Grants, and Graduate School Dean Elaine Wangberg for three Affirmative Action grants that provided money for computer services to prepare the manuscript. I thank Nancy Riley for her copy editor's eye, and Carolyn Livingston and Kathie Pendo for their typing and technical skills. Also, I thank Dara Thornton for her cheerfulness as well as her typing skill, and Joy Hansen and the secretarial staff at the California Institute of Technology's Humanities and Social Science Division for the support they gave from 1984 to 1986.

Chapters 2 and 4 contain materials published earlier in different form, in "Progressivism Moves into the Schools: Los Angeles Public Schools, 1905–1918," *California History*, 46 (June 1987): 94–103. A section of Chapter 5 appeared in "Missing the Mark: Intelligence Testing in Los Angeles Public Schools, 1922–1932," *History of Education Quarterly*, 28 (Spring 1988): 73–93. I am grateful to the editors of these journals for permission to draw on this material.

The majority of the information for this book comes from the following institutions: the University Research Library and the Education and Psychology Library at the University of California, Los Angeles; the Los Angeles Board of Education's Secretariat Office, where I had the support of several dedicated workers, particularly Rachel Tucker; and the Henry E. Huntington Library. The list of people I wish to thank at the Huntington Library is considerable because I have spent so many wonderful hours working there and sharing school stories with friends. I thank Directors Robert Middlekauff and Robert Skotheim; Director of Research Martin Ridge; Reader Services staff Virginia Renner, Leona Schonfeld, Elsa Sink, and Doris Smedes; Mary Wright who oversees the Rare Books section; Brita Mack, the Photo Archivist; Alan Jutzi, Curator of Rare Books; and Susan Naulty, the Ephemera Collection Archivist.

I visited other libraries while working on this study, and I thank the hard-working librarians who assisted me at the Bancroft Library, University of California, Berkeley; the Hoover Institution, Stanford University; and the Suzzallo Library, University of Washington. I also owe thanks to Janet Jenks, Humanities and Social Science Librarian at the California Institute of Technology, for her help and friendship over the years. At Meriam Library, California State University, Chico, Reference Librarian Henrietta Lo and Sylvia J. Jones in Inter-Library Loan made my work easier.

Several people read and criticized all or sections of the manuscript during its several stages, and I am grateful for their help.

Gerald Grob read the manuscript twice, and each time offered encouragement and assistance. My good friends Karen Blair, Karen Lystra, Bettyann Kevles, and Mary Elizabeth Perry helped in every way. Paul Zall willingly shared his knowledge on many long walks in the Huntington Gardens, and John P. Reid answered my legal questions with good humor. I also benefited from the help of Sara Alpern, Pam Aschbacher, Abraham Hoffman, Dan Kevles, Sue Ridyard, Rita Roberts, Armstead Robinson, Steven L. Schlossman, Sarah Stage, and Tanis Thorne. Among my colleagues at California State University, Jacqueline Barnhart, Lawrence and Marcia Bryant, Clarence MacIntosh, and especially Joanna Cowden gave their time and effort each time I asked, and I am grateful to them.

Many people provided me with food and comfort during these years "on the road." Mary and Howard Berg, Sandi and Allen Brune, Barbara and Alan Donagan, Helen and Bob Grubs, Elizabeth and John James, Betsy and Ralph Perry, and especially Lynne Costain, Joanne and Virgil Grillo, and Evonne Phillips. I thank my brother and sister-in-law, Joel and Judy Rosenberg, and my nieces, Jana and Stephanie, for making their home my home in the Bay Area. To my aunts and uncles and cousins—the Dretzins, Glickmans, Levines, Merlins, Miroffs, Palmers, Ratners, and Tobeys—many of whom attended Los Angeles public schools and whose gatherings have always created an atmosphere of intellectual stimulation, I offer thanks. Also thanks to Don, Bev, and Brad Armstrong and the parents of Little League ball players and car-poolers in Pasadena and in Chico who have carted, housed, and fed John while allowing his mother to work.

I owe a debt of gratitude to Associate Director Norris Pope at Stanford University Press, who has had faith in this project and facilitated its publication, and to Associate Editor Karen Brown Davison. Finally, I want to thank William W. Freehling and Kenneth M. Stampp. Though they have had no direct part in this work, I am much in their debt for introducing me to the exciting world of historical scholarship years ago at UC, Berkeley.

My father, Rudolph Rosenberg, died before this work was completed, but his humanity, his quest for truth, and his intellectual curiosity have inspired me. I dedicate this work to his memory and to that of my dear mother; and most importantly, to my three children, who have grown up with this study, and to my new daughter-in-law, Ana.

J.R.R.

Contents

Land of Fair Promise

Politics and Reform in Los Angeles Schools,

1885-1941

Introduction

Here English stalk and there flit Japanese
    And Chinese glide where Buddha's shrine appears;

    Here Western girls, Italians, Portuguese,
There humbled relicts of Spain's haughty years—
    All marching, marching in Los Angeles,
    Souled by the spirit of the pioneers!

—*Lee Shippey*

No longer a pueblo, Los Angeles in 1885 still had a frontier look. But the frontier look was fading, and the city was growing fast, faster than any urban area in the West. Its population, little more than 11,000 in 1880, jumped to 50,000 in 1890. By 1920 Los Angeles had replaced San Francisco as the largest city west of the Rockies and by 1930, with a population over a million, it had surpassed Boston to become the fourth-largest city in the United States. The city's schools reflected that growth. The one-room schoolhouse had disappeared by the turn of the century, and in its place stood a modern urban school system.

This study traces the development of modern schooling in a Far Western city. It explores the changing school policy brought about by rapid population growth and the recognition that large numbers of school children were either nonwhite or non–English speaking. It begins in the Progressive Era, when industrialization, immigration, and urbanization contributed to immense social and economic problems.* In towns and cities reformers felt compelled to reestablish order and end political corruption. They wanted to turn back the clocks to a less com-

*I have capitalized Progressive throughout the text to indicate a particular group of reformers who believed optimistically in progress and turned to local, state, and federal government to help rectify society's ills. Some of these Progressives would later join the political party of that name, others would not.

plicated era. In Los Angeles, and elsewhere, they drew on the ideas of Jane Addams and John Dewey to help them recreate a small-town setting in what had become a bustling metropolis.

The reformers worked at retaining a sense of community but with mixed goals in mind. On the one hand they wished to make a uniform, homogeneous society and to use the most advanced, scientific methods to that end. On the other, they hoped to retain enough local community spirit so that the old, small-town atmosphere could survive.[1] These goals were difficult to reconcile and often resulted in conflict.

Schools became the center for the Progressives' reforming spirit, in part, because of the newness of the notion that politics and education could be separated.[2] Throughout the nation a major area of reform focused on professionalization and its concomitant, efficiency. This led to streamlined school boards based on a corporate model where, in the ideal, the boards made decisions that were then carried out by professional educators, the superintendents. Yet ideal and reality are often far apart. Conflicts erupted when the desires of one did not mesh with those of the other, or when one or the other, or both, ran up against powerful influences from the outside.

Many of the Los Angeles reformers were women who had influenced school policies before suffrage. After 1911, when California women won full citizenship, these reformers expanded their campaigns for social change. Some of them had risen to prominence as clubwomen; others were working women, teachers who had begun to see themselves as professional educators. But professionalization proved to be a double-edged sword. Better trained than their predecessors, they nevertheless had to fight to hold on to their status as the system became more efficient, more structured, more impersonal, and at the same time, more professional.

By linking these themes, the study provides a context in which to study policy change and school reform. Ever since Michael Katz offered his analysis of public schooling as rigid and undemocratic, historians have been constructing a new conceptual framework for education history. David Tyack moved beyond the earlier, positive interpretations of Lawrence Cremin and beyond Katz's views, to argue that in their drive for efficiency and homogeneity, urban elites and "professional" educators succeeded only at the sacrifice of democratic principles. Diane Ravitch was mainly interested in refuting Katz and the revisionists; nevertheless, she offered an early challenge. Later works by Maris Vinovskis, Paul E. Peterson, Wayne Urban, William J. Reese, Ira Katznelson and Margaret Weir, Julia Wrigley, David Hogan, Paula Fass, and Ronald Cohen have contributed to a fuller picture of American education.[3]

This book has been shaped by these historians and others. While continuing to ask their questions, I have widened the circle to reach a better understanding of the complexities in this period. The work began as a chronological study of Americanization and the imposition of middle-class Protestant culture on immigrant children in Los Angeles public schools. But as it evolved, certain subjects overlapped, providing a thematic as well as a chronological structure.

As I read the minutes of the Board of Education, I was struck by the number of petitions from immigrant groups. Many of these were requests for additional services, such as rooms to conduct native language classes, after-school playgrounds, or auditoriums for national celebrations, and in most cases, the board granted the requests. These newcomers had learned how to assert themselves with surprising ease. Their sophisticated use of the Board of Education prompted me to look for other ways in which minorities expressed their self-determination.

I looked for answers to perplexing questions. In what ways did reformers impose Americanization, and how did immigrant communities react to the imposition? As I studied the politics of reform, I used the themes of political and professional self-interest to explain the motivations behind many reforms, and I have asked questions that seem central to this study. Were school policy changes solely the work of elites? Were the poor victims of social process, or were they in some way agents of change? A close look at the role of both the initiators and the targets of school reforms reveals complicated issues. Reformers were interested in both reform and social control because of their mixed feelings of concern for the newcomers and mistrust of them. At times immigrants were unwilling recipients; at others they played active parts in reform. They at once criticized institutions and used them to their advantage. In this study of over fifty-five years of Los Angeles school history, I have analyzed how these often contradictory aims led to friction within the schools, and the methods employed to divert conflicts.

I begin with a discussion of the Western Progressives who established social services within the schools—the penny-lunch programs, after-hour playgrounds, day-care centers, and kindergartens—to offset the poverty in the homes of newly arrived immigrants and to help their transition from foreigner to American. Next, as the immigrant population grew, reformers organized classes to teach English and American culture, including such innovations as home classes for shut-in mothers. Meanwhile, as more attempts were made to establish cultural conformity, the ethnic groups began to chart their own course. Significantly, they petitioned the schools to provide after-school facilities to perpetuate their own languages and cultures.

The stakes over who controlled the schools were high. The politics of reform led to open battles in which various groups of reformers lined up on either side. Reformers wanted to rid the city and the schools of corruption, separate both from politics, and move into the twentieth century in a modern, efficient way—in a motorcar rather than in a horse and buggy. Disagreements arose over the manner and importance of reform, the cost, and the ultimate value to society.

Conflicts also developed between what reformers expected of the school and what immigrants wanted. The results laid bare major problems with the reforms themselves. This happened after the introduction of the California Home Teacher Act of 1915. Although not always apparent, educators' self-interest often accompanied reform. Again, we find an example in the Home Teacher Act, which offered a group of female teachers a unique position, and for a few, entree into the educational hierarchy: a chance for more women teachers to gain acceptance in state administration.

The First World War and the Red Scare encouraged changes in school policy that reflected the prevailing intolerant attitudes toward pluralism. These changes came in the form of federal and state pressure to Americanize immigrants. During the 1920's educators searched for conformity within the schools and society. They hired experts to teach new methods and techniques, and the district created the Department of Psychology and Educational Research. Psychologists believed IQ measurement would bring homogeneity to the schools. Many Los Angeles educators, from classroom teachers to superintendents, found mental testing unreliable and looked for alternative methods to evaluate the abilities of children. In several instances lower-level administrators, counselors, principals, and teachers asserted themselves and found that the mental testing program allowed them to influence school policy.

In the end the city's schools reflected society's biases. Angelenos demanded conformity, but at the same time they did not necessarily want to commingle. Many neighborhoods, for example, saw nonwhites as threats to their sense of community, and in certain districts, residents exerted pressure on the board to segregate the schools. In some instances the board gave in; in others it withstood the pressure. Nevertheless, by the early 1930's, the patterns of racial segregation had been set.

Despite the seeming ambiguities and conflicts, many reformers and ethnic groups shared similar goals. Similar but not the same: just as reformers wanted to keep a sense of community, so many immigrants wanted to develop their own sense of community. In pursuit of their goals, reformers and educators worked assiduously to modify the immigrants' social behavior, using the public schools as their tools. Sometimes immigrants shared their ideas, and sometimes they did not, but together they reshaped American education. They built a new social fabric, a patchwork put together by the unrelenting realities of twentieth-century America. Los Angeles schools became a paradigm of Progressive reform. As the story unravels, there were few heroes, few villains, just people willing to make trade-offs and accommodate each other.

I

Background of an American City

> Wonderful Southern California . . .
> land of fair promise
>
> —*Louise Ward, 1906*

Shortly after the turn of the century, schoolgirl Louise Ward wrote New York relatives from her new hometown, Los Angeles, in "wonderful Southern California," the "land of fair promise."[1] She had much to tell. Everyone she saw seemed "rushing to and fro with a kind of energetic" vigor. "Plentiful" automobiles added to the excitement, as did the mix of people, "lean and fat, white, brown, black all shapes and sizes" filling the streets. She told of new projects going up everywhere, and she pointed out that in contrast to the East, Angelenos constructed their buildings and homes low, "because of the dread earthquakes." To complete the picture, she added images Easterners had come to expect from California: "Oh, you should see the fruit, the most magnificent berries, red raspberries, strawberries and blackberries" and "flowers, flowers, flowers."[2]

Ward's letters, like thousands of others, echoed the themes of excitement and growth amidst pleasant surroundings: the themes that inspired and beckoned newcomers to Los Angeles. Yet a few years earlier, only astute observers ventured bets on Los Angeles becoming a "land of fair promise." By the mid-1880's the Southern Pacific and Santa Fe railroads arrived, providing Southern California with two rail links to the rest of the nation. Still, few people could have predicted the spectacular transformations that were about to take place on the banks of the Los Angeles River.

Unlike the northern part of the state, Los Angeles had retained many of the vestiges of a Spanish outpost long after Spanish and Mexican officials departed. The Gold Rush that played so significant a role in the rapid growth of San Francisco and Sacramento had comparatively little effect on Los

Angeles. Nevertheless, more non-Spanish-speaking immigrants trickled in after 1848, bringing new institutions and cultures. For a few years after statehood town officials conducted business in English and Spanish, and instruction in two of the four public schools was in Spanish.[3] But English quickly displaced Spanish both in the halls of government and in the schools, and American traditions overshadowed Hispanic. Accounts of the Centennial Parade of 1876 described typical American pageantry, no different from what one would encounter in almost any small town of the time, without the religious overtones that characterized nineteenth-century Spanish or Mexican festivals. Major H. M. Mitchell and his aides led the ensemble. Next came "the Opera band, followed by the officers of the 1st Division. . . . They were followed by the Los Angeles Guard. . . . Next came the magnificent car appropriated to the Goddess of Liberty, who was personated in a very queenly manner by Miss Carrie Cohn. She was attended by Miss Lulu Lehman, representing Peace, and Miss Ally Carpenter, representing Plenty."[4] Most of the town's fraternal orders, benevolent organizations, artisans, and merchants, along with a bevy of young ladies, marched along behind Major Mitchell.

A California combination of Abilene and Sioux City, Los Angeles mixed the cow-town ambiance of saloons, gunslingers, and vigilantes with the ambiance of a farming center of vineyards and orange groves. Sometimes the balance clearly favored the cow town, particularly in 1871, when a shooting in Chinatown exploded into the murder of nineteen Chinese men. That episode marked the end of unrestrained disregard for law and order. The days of the frontier came to an end as modernization and the iron horse moved west.[5]

The railroads transformed the region. Competition between the Santa Fe and the Southern Pacific soon resulted in grand-scale rate wars and equally grand-scale land speculation as travel in and out of Los Angeles became ridiculously inexpensive. Fares from cities along the Mississippi River to Southern California were under twenty-five dollars, and for a short time in March 1886, the Kansas City–Los Angeles ride cost as little as one dollar.[6]

The low rates helped persuade many Easterners and Midwesterners to take a chance in Southern California. Migrants brought with them their Protestant values, values that soon became the basis of cultural hegemony in Los Angeles. Whatever remnants of a frontier town one might have encountered in the 1870's vanished under the onslaught of these transplants from the east. The population expanded from 1,610 in 1850 to 11,183 in 1880; by 1890, over 50,000 people resided in the city.[7] Southern California had already achieved a reputation as a health spa; now travel advertisers glorified it as a Garden of Eden, an agricultural paradise. Charles Nordhoff, the most widely read of the publicists, proclaimed the area "the finest part of the state and the best region in the United States for farmers." Charles Dudley Warner told readers of the *Atlantic Monthly* that "Southern California should be called a garden rather than a region because of its lushness."[8]

The city's vitality was undeniable, though some had reservations about it. Edwards Roberts, a popular travel writer who toured the Southwest in the 1880's, preferred Pasadena and Santa Barbara in both looks and style to bustling Los Angeles. Disappointed that he found few reminders of Spanish culture beyond some street names, he saw little distinction between Los Angeles and eastern cities. Yet Roberts felt its energy. In his column in the *Chicago Daily News*, he noted that Los Angeles stood as "a city of tender age, young, untried, rough, and awkward but with great strength of purpose, prosperous, progressive, and altogether something of a phenomenon." And he added that "a stranger may fret and . . . may get cross at the newsboys and bootblacks and flies which meet one at every corner [but] there is business here, and that is what acts as a balm."[9]

Roberts captured the spirit of the city. The combination of boosters, cheap travel, and seemingly abundant resources brought thousands of Americans to the "land of sunshine."* Their arrival signaled the beginning of new lives as citrus, grape, melon, and walnut growers or as chicken ranchers. The influx

***Land of Sunshine* was the title of a magazine edited by Charles Fletcher Lummis, writer and promoter of the West, the Spanish missions, and above all, himself.

of immigrants eager for land caused land values to skyrocket and opened opportunities for speculators, who happily bought up chunks of property in the hope of turning a quick profit. Unfortunately, for the less ambitious, as with any boom, the Southern California land boom could not last long, and by 1887 many a Cornhusker or Hoosier had lost both savings and hopes. Few had anticipated that farming or ranching in California required expertise and the same bit of luck as it had in Nebraska or Indiana. Some packed their bags and returned east; thousands stayed, sadder but wiser.[10]

Many of those who remained determined to make Los Angeles and the surrounding area one of the most progressive regions in the country. The boom had spurred the growth of many institutions, and they continued to expand under the watchful eye of conservative businessmen like Isaias W. Hellman, founder of the city's first bank.[11] Newspapers and journals increased in number and circulation. By 1890 the southland published 160 of them, including the *Los Angeles Times.* Harrison Otis and his wife, Elizabeth Ann Otis, arrived in the city in 1882 and almost immediately took over the floundering *Daily Times*, renamed it after their adopted city, and turned it into the region's leading newspaper.[12] Interurban transportation also expanded far beyond what most had imagined. From eleven miles of track in 1880 to over eighty miles in 1889, the Los Angeles basin was on its way to becoming a region of trolleys. In 1910, when Henry E. Huntington sold his shares in the Pacific Electric Railway Company to E. E. Harriman, president of the Southern Pacific, the new owner inherited over a thousand miles of track.[13]

Industrial development had lagged simply because the boom had featured land speculation rather than manufacturing. The discovery of oil by Edward L. Doheny in 1892, however, gave Los Angeles the economic underpinnings for industrial growth. Oil gave the region its first heavy industry, along with the need for a deep-water port. The location of the harbor turned out to be an issue not easily resolved. Collis Huntington, president of the Southern Pacific until his death in 1900, favored Santa Monica, where his railroad had acquired land and a right-of-way. Other groups favored San Pedro. Those who opposed Huntington's heavy-handed politics included Otis and his *Times*, U.S. Senator Stephen M. White, and the powerful Los Angeles Chamber of Commerce under the adroit leadership of Charles Dwight Willard. Together with other Southern Californians, they formed the Free Harbor League to fight Huntington. League members believed that the San Pedro location promised them freer access than they would have in a port so heavily under Southern Pacific control as the Santa Monica one would be.[14] The vigorous lobbying campaign of the pro–San Pedro forces and general public distrust of railroad monopolies as personified by Huntington and his line led Congress to throw the federal government's support behind the San Pedro site.

The harbor and other economic concerns were a continuing preoccupation as the boom came and went. Just as important, however, was the community's impulse to make Southern California a model of eastern respectability. The mixture of boosterism and the infusions of reform-minded Republicans—mostly Protestants from America's heartland—created a new civic pride that sponsored park commissions, community halls, and educational institutions. In no area were the new city leaders more concerned than in education. One college had existed in Los Angeles before 1880, the Jesuit College of St. Vincent, but the rapidly growing population demanded non-Catholic institutions as well. Under the auspices of the Methodist Episcopal Church, the astute business acumen of Robert M. Widney, and three local donors, Ozro W. Childs (a Protestant), John G. Downey (a Catholic), and Isaias W. Hellman (a Jew), the University of Southern California opened in 1880. Other institutions added to the air of permanence. The State Normal School, later the University of California, Los Angeles, was founded in 1881; it was followed, in quick succession, by Occidental College and Whittier College in 1887, Pomona College in 1888, and Throop Institute, renamed the California Institute of Technology, in 1891.[15]

The growth of the public schools mirrored the city's growth. The Reverend Henry Weeks had opened the first English-speaking school in 1850, and within five years the city built three schoolhouses. But this marked the end of the school-building effort for several years. It started up again in 1872, with the erection of another schoolhouse, and in the following year, construction on a high school began. Then came the explosion. The boom years nearly tripled school attendance. Nineteen teachers taught 1,262 students in 1876; by 1884 the city employed sixty-six teachers for 3,417 students. According to the Board of Education's annual report for that year, school enrollments had increased an average of 40 percent and, to keep up with this rapid growth, the number of teachers had been increased by 35 percent.[16]

Though the schools made valiant attempts to provide newcomers with public education, these rapid increases made life difficult for those in charge. The superintendent, L. D. Smith, reported that the crowded conditions were creating such serious problems that he was faced with the possibility of having to refuse admission to some children. The lack of scholastic uniformity was also a serious problem. Appealing to the Board of Education, Smith told of children who came "from all parts of the country, from schools of all grades," and "all varying greatly in their courses of study." He warned of the danger of the newcomers disturbing the "uniformity of grading," but he was hopeful that with considerable time and much hard work, these children could be harmonized and assimilated. Finally, there was the ever-pressing problem for educators—"the cramped financial condition."[17] Smith reminded the board that his budget, based on the population counts from the previous year, had been thrown out of whack by the sudden jump in students. Naturally he hoped that the next year's appropriation would be higher.

But the preceding year's counts could not keep up with the rapidly growing school population, and in the ensuing decades the problem of greater demands for limited resources forced many schools to go on half-day sessions. The *Los Angeles Express* noted on January 2, 1906, that 400 new students had enrolled that year, resulting in the overcrowding of classrooms.[18] The pattern continued, and by 1916 the number of pupils in Los Angeles had jumped to 54,796.[19]

By then, not only had the numbers changed substantially;

so had the ethnic make-up of the student body. In the nineteenth century the majority of new settlers had come from other regions of the United States, and most of them spoke English. By 1900, out of a total of 102,479 city residents, 19,964 were foreign-born; most had come from northwestern Europe (12,135) or Canada (2,897, including 214 French speakers). There was a substantial Chinese population (2,111) and a few Japanese (151), but the census data made no distinction in this case between the foreign- and native-born. At any rate, the Chinese were the second-largest nonwhite minority group after black Americans (2,131), at least according to the census. Conceivably, both were outnumbered by Mexican Americans, for some recent studies place their numbers around then at between 3,000 and 5,000.[20] But until 1930, when a special designation appeared on the census forms, Mexicans were recorded as white, so there is no way to know their exact population share; 817 Mexicans appear in the 1900 census under the foreign-born category.[21]

After 1900 the origins of immigrants in Los Angeles, as in the rest of the country, underwent profound changes. Better economic and political conditions in Western Europe had made emigration less attractive, while declining circumstances in Eastern and Southern Europe, Japan, and Mexico encouraged migration to the United States. Los Angeles did not become an immigrant center in the fashion of New York or San Francisco, at least not until much later; the overall percentage of foreign-born remained almost the same between 1900 and 1920. But Northern Europeans no longer predominated. The Central, Southern, and Eastern European population increased from 13,557 in 1910 to over 30,000 in 1920, and though Northern Europeans continued to come in, the rate of increase, from 32,046 to 39,382, had slowed. Over that period the Mexican community grew from 5,632 to 21,598, the Japanese community from 4,238 to 8,536, and the black community from 7,599 to 15,579.[22]

Los Angeles was not noticed as an immigrant city because its foreign-born population was so small compared with the huge numbers of immigrants flooding into New York (with a 40-percent share of foreign-born in 1910 and 35 percent in 1920), Chicago (36 percent and 30 percent), and San Francisco (31 percent and 28 percent). Los Angeles held at 19 percent.[23] But the numbers alone do not convey the immensity of the demographic changes occurring in Los Angeles. The minutes of the Los Angeles Board of Education give a different impression. The problems created by the influx of immigrants was a major concern to school personnel. Most of the foreign-born lived in the old section of the city, commonly known as the "foreign district." In an area stretching from the original pueblo, across the river, east to Boyle Heights, then running along the railroad tracks down Central Avenue and San Pedro Street, the newly arrived established their societies and expanded their neighborhoods.

To be sure, not all foreigners lived in this district and not all those who did live there were non–English speakers. Some black Americans lived in the "foreign district," and many immigrants lived in scattered pockets throughout the city. Commercial fishing in San Pedro attracted Croatians, Italians, Mexicans, and some Japanese. Other Japanese established a fishing community on Terminal Island and farmed in the Hawthorne-Gardena area; and a Mexican farming community was well established in the San Fernando Valley before the city annexed most of the area in 1917.[24]

For reformers, educators, and service groups, both public and private, the problems of new arrivals like these became an overriding concern. Throughout the nation and throughout the period under study, they worked to mitigate the hardship of the immigrants' life and at the same time assimilate them into American society. Reformers, often motivated by self-interest or at least by an interest in promoting some pet project, fashioned changes designed to benefit larger society as well as themselves. Their attempts to restore civil order symbolized their eagerness for efficiency as much as their interest in reform, the canons of Progressivism. In short, reformers wanted to put things right. It was not long before their pursuit of that goal led them to settle in on the public schools.[25]

2

Progressivism Moves into the Schools

> The cooperative Commonwealth is, . . . after all, the ultimate hope for which we all must work. Now that women have begun to take an active interest in affairs, who can tell? The greatest hindrance to progress has been ignorance and prejudice. Women's minds are opening now and events will move rapidly.
>
> —*Caroline Severance, 1912*

At the turn of the century many middle-class Americans were thinking in terms of reestablishing order in a society transformed by modernization and its concomitants: immigration, urbanization, industrialization, and labor unrest. The political and social movement that grew out of their unease became known as Progressivism, and the period in which their views dominated American political life as the Progressive Era.[1]

Progressivism featured the optimistic premise that, guided by people of goodwill, progress and growth went hand in hand with order and stability. But before progress could proceed, attention had to be paid to some of society's glaring inadequacies. Progressives turned to government to assist them in reordering society and in protecting America from the selfish special-interest groups that they viewed as having caused the disarray.

Progressive impulses moved in several directions: first, a belief in humanitarian reform; second, an equally strong belief in the need for organizational reform based on business models; and third, a belief in the need for political reform, a belief that at times incorporated both principles. Unfortunately, reformers also often differed bitterly on methods and procedures, and their compromises resulted in actions that reflected their self-interest as often as legitimate reform.

No institution was more altered by these impulses than the public school. The persuasiveness of humanitarian Progressives and organizational Progressives was so intense, and their reforms so successfully imposed, that their influences have continued to affect schooling to this day.[2]

A new elite emerged in the late nineteenth century composed of public administrators, efficiency experts, professional managers, and social scientists captivated by the vision of a scientifically managed society. Influenced by national figures who combined ardent social and spiritual idealism, reform took on particular urgency. From the pulpit, the Protestant theologians Washington Gladden and Walter Rauschenbusch provoked passionate responses to their call for a social gospel to help the poor. And from the classroom and settlement house, John Dewey and Jane Addams provided communities of like-minded reformers guidelines for reshaping the nation's social institutions. They persuaded better-off Americans to help the poor, particularly the foreign-born, to become healthy, useful Americans—under the watchful eye of reformers, of course.

The Restructuring of Political Power

In Los Angeles the reformers' first preoccupation was to stop corruption and create efficient government by changing the city's election process from the ward system to a system of citywide representation. That they succeeded in doing in 1903.[3] But the campaign to end machine politics and the political control of the monopolistic Southern Pacific railroad had begun years before, in 1895, when young reform-minded businessmen and professionals led by Dr. John Randolph Haynes, a physician turned businessman, founded the Direct Legislative League. By 1900 the league had introduced three items that were to have national appeal—the initiative, recall, and referendum. Working with like-minded reformers, they persuaded Los Angeles voters to pass a new city charter in 1903. The new charter included their proposal for direct legislation, provided for a Board of Civil Service Commissioners—based on the federal model and designed to regulate city jobs through competitive examination—and mandated a reorganization of the Board of Education.[4]

Reform of the school board had been under consideration for

several years. The city's rapid growth during the 1880's land boom had increased the number of school board members from five to nine, one for each city ward. Not many years later, in 1897, several members came under suspicion for accepting bribes and "general dishonesty."[5] Certain members were further accused of extorting money from teachers and janitors to safeguard their positions. A full-blown investigation was ordered.

The newspapers had a field day. The *Los Angeles Daily Herald* editorialized on the "promised sensation" sure to come from the investigation. The superintendent of school buildings "made a clean breast of his connection with the charges of extortion and blackmail" and implicated two of the board members.[6] One was arrested, and the other resigned. To the chagrin of many, the jury acquitted the arrested member. Outraged at the acquittal, the *Daily Herald* remarked that the verdict was "not unexpected": "Nor will it change the opinion of the great majority of the community regarding the accused man's guilt."[7] Other resignations followed, and the newspaper called for a new election process to ensure responsible representatives.[8]

The scandal was not forgotten, and five years later the 1903 city charter reduced the number of board members to seven, all elected from the city at large. As one educator wrote, the new board consisted of the type of people Los Angeles voters wanted. "We have a non-partisan Board of Education, in fact as well as in name; and we are getting toward the next step in the development, that is, toward what is better than non-partisan–a non-personal administration of public school affairs."[9]

In pushing their charter through, the Progressives succeeded in doing more than merely ousting corrupt officials. They also succeeded in streamlining and centralizing both the city government and the school board. The smaller, nonpolitical school board they fought for placed Los Angeles squarely in the movement toward centralized school systems. Centralization, proposed soon after the Civil War by the Boston educator and early prophet of standardized education John Philbrick, became standard reform procedure during the Progressive period. The initial cry for reform often came after a discovery of corruption, as in this case. Reformers believed that centralization would allow the schools to be administered more efficiently by noncorruptible, nonpartisan, and in some cases, "non-personal administration."[10]

The new charter meant that the board members' role became more administrative. The board made policy and the school superintendent carried it out. The superintendent took on greater responsibility for the day-to-day activities, and he in turn had assistant superintendents who saw to the details. The certification of teachers became more standardized; to protect them from the whims of the board, their merit ratings were based on examination. Board members no longer visited classrooms on a regular basis and, ostensibly anyway, lost their say in the hiring and firing of teachers.[11] But as Wayne Urban has ably demonstrated, some teachers resisted these reforms, fearful of a loss of income and status if promotions and pensions were based on examination and education rather than on seniority. Older, less-educated teachers resented examinations to test their competency. In Los Angeles some of these problems had been settled by state-mandated pensions in 1895 and a system in which promotion was based on a combination of examination and service.[12]

Also in 1903 the California legislature enacted a compulsory school act, and shortly thereafter the city appointed a truant officer. Compulsory attendance had been a concern of school officials for some time. In his annual report of 1896–97, Superintendent James A. Foshay bemoaned the "many cases of truancy" that had come with the growth of the population. "We must have the children in school, not occasionally, but regularly, if they are to be educated." He hoped for a special school for habitual truants, "thus [to] teach them, through proper discipline, entirely different habits from those which some seem to be acquiring at the present time."[13]

Not everyone in Los Angeles viewed compulsory education as a blessing. Some saw it as an unwarranted intrusion into family life. Many ethnic groups saw extended schooling as unnecessary or frivolous, a way for children to avoid paid work that the family needed to support itself. In one instance a teacher told of two immigrant women passing by the school and asking a boy from their neighborhood, "Why do you still go to school like a baby?" In another, a parent told an interviewer that soon after the act went into effect, fathers would go to jail because they kept their children home on religious holidays. "If our children are absent a few days," he noted, "the truant officer comes around."[14] But in general, as Paul E. Peterson has shown, working-class parents complied with and supported compulsory education laws in the conviction that they precluded the exploitation of children and had "the salutary side effect of decreasing the size of the labor force, thereby raising the price of unskilled labor."[15]

Reform coincided with the growth of the city's non-English-speaking communities, and the change that reformers hoped would bring nonpartisan representation could, at the same time, work against the least assimilated newcomers. In many cities partisan ward politicians provided the link between immigrants and municipal institutions, often as directly as locating jobs and housing and distributing food in particularly difficult times. Therefore, from the immigrants' perspective, the new reforms might set up barriers and work against any chance they might have to influence ward-elected members. Nevertheless, as familiar avenues closed with the termination of the ward system, others opened. Minority groups found ways to effect change through their network of voluntary associations and the public schools.

Volunteerism and Women in the Progressive Age

In the earliest stages of the Progressive Era, volunteers led the path to reform. To no greater degree did their reforming impulse manifest itself than in school reform, and perhaps in no other area did reform so reflect the self-interest of the reformers. Those volunteers, many of whom were women, combined their role as moral guardian with their experience from religious and charity work, and from social settlements. During this period women entered public life in larger numbers than ever before. Their increased access to higher education, participation in the professions, and experience in women's organizations gave women a larger sense of public purpose. Moreover, many women identified cities as extensions of their homes and believed they had the experience and nurturing powers to reestablish order. Industrialization had polluted society, and they saw it as their responsibility to clean it up. They did not plan to disrupt social structure; they believed that the working class should keep in its place. Nor did they threaten men's positions; they created positions for women that were extensions of their domestic sphere. Women took up the cause of public education in Los Angeles, asserted their middle-class values, and became the backbone of the school welfare programs.[16]

Female reformers began defining their public posture through social reforms. Empowered by their organizational experiences in women's clubs, settlement houses, and charity work, areas in metaphor and fact known as "women's sphere," women were no longer content to sit on the sidelines and let others carry out reforms.[17] It was the volunteers, usually upper-middle-class women, such as Caroline Severance, who led the way. But gradually as more women held college degrees, and in California where women won suffrage in 1911, working women, such as Bessie D. Stoddart, also exerted themselves. Many of these working women began to see themselves as professionals, either in education or in related fields, as qualified as any to have their say in policy matters.

Kathryn Kish Sklar's study of Florence Kelley and Hull House illustrates that the Chicago settlement created a real community and gave female reformers a secure base for their operations.[18] It comes as no surprise that many of the Los Angeles female reformers lived or worked in settlement houses based on the Hull House model and relied on their settlement community for moral substance. Stoddart, who figures prominently in this chapter, and Amanda Mathews Chase, whom we meet in the next, launched their reform work from College Settlement. Some traded on their professional credentials and reforming talents to gain political positions. Stoddart became a member of the Board of Education, and Chase worked with the California Commission of Immigration and Housing and became the state's first home teacher.

The combination of upper- and middle-class reformers brought a wide range of experience and an even wider agenda for social change to their work in school reform. It also brought a variety of largely self-interested actions. Many female reformers had publicly fought for suffrage; some had taught school; and others had participated in settlement houses. Most reformers were Protestants, and although the school reforms they instituted were secular, there was little deviation from the Protestant ethos.

At times reformers collaborated for specific reforms and worked together to push through one project or another; at others their interests clashed. In 1917, for instance, in an attempt to sponsor refined and uplifting cultural events for schoolchildren, the Friday Morning Club subsidized a performance of Shakespeare's *The Tempest.* A last-minute change resulted in the troupe substituting *The Merchant of Venice*. Some, but not all, Jewish club members objected, and a few prominent members threatened to resign if the play was performed in the public schools.* The threats went unheeded, and the play was performed. Even for groups of wealth and social status, American genteel culture might sometimes become a bitter pill.

Progressive activism and attempts to edify the common man and propagate the genteel culture at times brought reformers

* *B'nai B'rith Messenger*, Nov. 16, 1917, p. 3. When it became clear that neither Superintendent Albert Shiels nor the president of the Normal School, Ernest Moore, had any influence with the actors, Mrs. Jules Kauffman, president of the Jewish Council of Los Angeles, wrote that the community was divided over the portrayal of Shylock. "Shylock doesn't represent a race but a principle," she said, adding that "fighting Shakespeare would be like fighting the ocean." She reminded her readers that "Jewish women had been treated with honor at the Friday Morning Club," and the morning paper "had made a mistake in saying that the Jewish Women's Council had taken action." The brouhaha involved Friday Morning Club politics as well. A gentile member and losing candidate for the presidency claimed that she would have been more respectful of Jewish wishes. (Vorspan and Gartner, *History of the Jews*, pp. 143–44; the authors put the incident into the context of rising anti-Semitism, but they make no mention of the kind of division within the Jewish community that Kauffman suggested.)

into conflict, or put them on a collision course with the very people they wanted to help. Nevertheless, middle-class reformers tried to soften the process of adjustment and to bridge the gap between officialdom and the private world of minorities by establishing cultural programs through secular and religious organizations. Influenced by national reform figures such as Rauschenbusch and Addams, volunteers established settlements, civic associations, and the Young Men's and Young Women's Christian associations.

Not all volunteers were middle-class English-speaking, white native-born Americans. Immigrants in Los Angeles, as elsewhere, created voluntary associations to protect themselves from unfamiliar surroundings and from alien political and social customs. Foreign-language newspapers, benevolent societies, and religious and secular organizations provided newcomers security in new places and among strange peoples, and protected them from the harsher world of urban America.

Immigrants were also as likely as the native-born to turn to the schools for support. During the period from the late 1880's to the First World War, residents bombarded the Board of Education with petitions for kindergartens, library reading rooms, paved streets, free transportation for their children, language classes, facilities for political, religious, and cultural meetings, playgrounds, and playground supervisors. The list appeared endless, and the schools were ill-equipped to grant all the requests that flooded in from so diverse a clientele. Individuals and private organizations tried to fill the void.

Interest in maintaining and propagating middle-class Protestant values and a genuine concern for the less-fortunate were two of the distinguishing features of Progressivism. In an age before professionalization changed the nature of volunteerism, it was the volunteers' persistence that increased their role in affecting decisions and set education policy on a new course. The development of four services—kindergartens, after-school playgrounds, health care, and penny lunches—provides insight into the moment of change from volunteerism to professionalization.

Women's Clubs and Kindergartens

Caroline and Theodoric Severance reached Los Angeles in 1875, the end of a long journey that had begun on the East Coast. Caroline, considered the founder of women's clubs, and her banker husband had been active reformers in Cleveland and Boston before moving to Southern California to grow oranges. Mrs. Severance, affectionately called "a woman's woman," had founded the New England Woman's Club in 1868, one of the first of its kind in the nation, and in 1878, three years after she and her husband had settled in California, she organized the first women's club in Los Angeles. Perhaps because the Severances saw their role as moral guardians on the frontier or simply because the area lacked the spiritual and cultural institutions to which they had been accustomed, they used their considerable talents to bring some Eastern amenities to the Far Western town. Finding no Unitarian Church, they invited the Quincy (Massachusetts) Unitarian minister John D. Wells to preach in the parlor of their new home on West Adams Boulevard. Finding no kindergarten, Caroline enticed Emma Marwedel, a leader in the kindergarten movement, to come to Los Angeles and open one.[19] The vitality and drive of this couple typified the reforming spirit invading Los Angeles at the close of the century, a spirit that ensured that the city would not remain a frontier much longer. Within a short time the city began to reflect the reform impulse that had taken hold in other urban areas across the nation.

Caroline would have stood out in any city, but because she arrived in Los Angeles at the beginning of its transformation from village to metropolis, her presence looms large. Both she and Theodoric were long-time abolitionists and supporters of Lincoln, and in 1864, when Theodoric was appointed by the president to a Union government post in South Carolina, Caroline and at least one of their children accompanied him. But Caroline had moved away from the Republican party, and in 1906 she switched her allegiance altogether. Rejecting the militarism of Theodore Roosevelt, she embraced William Jennings Bryan. She referred to herself as a socialist on several occasions, a Christian socialist to be sure, but a socialist. "While I am a socialist," she told a reporter, "I think that the Democrats with Bryan as their prophet" stand for the best hope of the country. She was universally addressed as Madame Severance, a reflection of the admiration and respect she had earned for her lifelong work, which she had begun while still in Cleveland as a supporter of women's rights and abolition, and which she continued with the founding of the women's clubs in Boston and Los Angeles. She remained active until her death in 1914.*

Most women's clubs began as literary groups. Members assembled in their homes, served tea and cakes, and discussed the latest novels. Karen Blair has shown that discussions soon moved from literary topics to issues of social concern, and, in this way, the clubs provided an environment that allowed ordinary women to move from their private sphere of home and family into the public sphere. But most of the founding women of the first club were anything but ordinary. Furthermore, most shared Caroline Severance's commitment to society's betterment and, like her, most were activists.

Quite possibly Caroline's interest in kindergartens grew out of her contacts with Elizabeth Peabody, an honorary member of the New England Woman's Club and the first teacher to establish an English-speaking kindergarten in the United States. The kindergarten movement epitomized the work of volunteers in setting school policy. "Children's gardens" began in Germany under the influence of Friedrich Froebel. Dedicated students carried his ideas throughout Europe, and the Germans who emigrated after the 1848 revolution introduced his concepts into the United States. Dr. Henry Barnard, acting as U.S. Education Commissioner, inspired Peabody in her pioneering venture in Boston in 1860.[20]

Peabody met Emma Marwedel in Germany and had been so impressed by the German woman that she encouraged her to

***Los Angeles Record*, May 2, 1906, Severance Collection, box 42, HL. The Severances' strong reforming spirit ran the gamut of 19th-century causes: abolition, temperance, and suffrage, among others. Their wide circle of friends included such heroes of reform as Ralph Waldo Emerson, Theodore Weld, William Lloyd Garrison, and Julia Ward Howe (Blair, *Clubwoman as Feminist*, pp. 31–32; Ruddy, *Mother of Clubs*, p. 42; J. Jensen, "After Slavery," pp. 176–80).

come to the United States. Marwedel lived briefly in New York, then moved to Washington, D.C., where her kindergarten and private school attracted the attention of public officials, including the future president James A. Garfield, whose three children attended Marwedel's establishment. In 1876 Severance arranged for Marwedel to come to Los Angeles and found a suitable house and garden for the new private kindergarten school. She also began a training college for teachers. Among the first three would-be teachers was Severance's young admirer Kate Douglas Wiggin. The kindergarten proved unsuccessful, and two years after it opened, Marwedel moved to the Bay Area. The college continued, but on a sporadic basis until it became part of the Normal School curriculum in the 1890's.[21]

In 1885, undaunted by the failure of the kindergarten, Severance, along with the city's Woman's Club, founded the Free Kindergarten Association of Los Angeles. But the free kindergartens, supported by donations, were quite different from their forerunners: they soon catered specifically to lower-class children. Located in Protestant churches in the poorest sections of the town, they quickly became centers of reform and Americanization. Severance coordinated kindergarten activities through the club's School Committee, and in 1885 welcomed a visit by kindergarten advocates from San Francisco, who she hoped would create "public interest" locally. One, the well-known clergyman Dr. Horatio Stebbins of San Francisco's First Unitarian Church, came prepared with a "report" to impress the audience.[22]

Kindergartens had been recognized as agents of moral reform in Germany before they made their appearance in the United States.[23] In Los Angeles the first kindergartens began as preschools for middle-class children, but it did not take reformers long to seize on them as an effective way to combat the threat of alien culture from immigrant homes. With little outward opposition, they introduced the free schools into areas with large foreign populations. The Los Angeles version was based on San Francisco's Silver Street model, the first tuition-free kindergarten west of the Rockies to teach hygiene and English, along with the regular Froebelian curriculum. Silver Street had been organized in 1878 by Severance's acolyte Kate Douglas Wiggin.[24]

By the mid-1880's, a small assortment of both tuition and tuition-free kindergartens co-existed in the city, and Frank A. Gibson, school board president and husband of Severance's close associate, Mary S. Gibson, recommended that the board consider including tuition-free kindergartens in the curriculum. The board took his advice and in 1886 opened one with apparent success, although at the time Superintendent William Friesner warned that the board lacked funding for any additional undertakings. Familiar with kindergartens—Friesner had visited a tuition kindergarten that his niece attended—he noted that the district lacked both the space to house such facilities and the materials needed to make them successful. But kindergarten advocates like Severance had gained important supporters in city government and on the school board, and in 1889 the city charter granted authority to the board to establish kindergartens. Also that year, city bond sales valued at $200,000 provided the funds to build classrooms, some of which could be used for kindergartens. By 1893 Friesner was able to announce that eighteen of the elementary schools had kindergartens. In the same year the state legislature confirmed that city boards of education could establish kindergartens but ruled that their support must come from private funds.*

In 1913 the legislature went further, decreeing that kindergartens must be established whenever a community demonstrated the need for them by having twenty-five or more parents or guardians petition their local school board. The following year kindergarten expenditures for Los Angeles schools exceeded $165,800, higher than those for manual training and domestic science combined. This sum accounted for over one-third of the funds spent on the Special Departments.[25]

Kindergartens had moved beyond issues of moral reform. Incorporating kindergartens into public schooling, reformers brought together two ideals of American pedagogy, proper fe-

*Hanson, "Kindergarten Movement," p. 79; Freeman, "Board-Superintendent Relationships," pp. 154, 223; Eales, "Los Angeles School System." In 1909 J. D. Fredricks, the district attorney of Los Angeles County, in response to an inquiry by Deputy Superintendent J. B. Monlux, said that the law on school funding appeared ambiguous, and that in his view kindergartens could be supported out of school funds (Board, *Minutes*, 10: 193). Thereupon the board began to make them a regular budget item in the Special Departments category.

male nurturing in early childhood and community responsibility. The private world of the family would be enhanced by the ministrations of a nurturing professional, and the public world would assume greater responsibility as institutions entered the private world at an earlier time. By drawing on these two tenets of American education, Progressives ensured the success of their programs.[26]

In Los Angeles, by 1900, kindergartens had community support, and their acceptance into public education seems remarkably free from conflict. Middle-class parents at Colgrove and Dayton Heights schools petitioned for them; so did immigrant parents at Breed Street in Boyle Heights. A request came from 51st Street for a "colored children's" kindergarten.[27]

If parents did not petition the school board themselves, outside groups might do it for them. For example, when grass-roots support did not materialize at Utah Street School, in the heart of the foreign district, the California Congress of Mothers, a leader in the movement to organize kindergartens statewide and a forerunner of the Parent-Teacher Association, successfully petitioned the board and established a kindergarten there, as it did in other schools with large, foreign student bodies.[28] Middle-class native-born Americans quickly perceived kindergartens as vehicles for assimilation, but their success depended on the acceptance of immigrant parents. Since the compulsory attendance law did not include children of kindergarten age, parents sent their children voluntarily. The rapid acceptance of kindergartens put the board in a difficult position; because of budget constraints, it could not grant all the requests it received. Among those who were turned down were the middle-class parents at Laurel Street School in the Fairfax district, who petitioned for improved facilities as well. The board allowed $300 for repairs and additions but delayed the opening of a kindergarten.[29]

Although the early kindergartens were established for middle-class children and supported by tuition, they quickly became vehicles for assimilation among the poor without losing their appeal among other groups. Reformers had so successfully tailored the schools' activities and included such a wide variety of functions that their appeal cut across lines of class, ethnicity, and race.

The ease with which kindergartens were accepted into public schooling indicates the changes that had taken place by the end of the nineteenth century. As one Los Angeles educator put it in 1910, the struggle between school reformers to define the needs of children had moved from nineteenth-century "factory" uniformity to the Progressive interest in "individuality." The struggle had come to a head during the later years of Superintendent Friesner's tenure, in the 1890's. It was during these years that special classes for slow learners, truants, and manual training (or "sloyd"), along with kindergartens, made their way into public school curriculum.[30]

Settlement Houses and After-Hours Playgrounds

The reformers who succeeded in institutionalizing kindergartens were moved by the wish to instill a healthy dose of American middle-class values, basic childhood training, and cleanliness in immigrants' children, all of which they feared their homes lacked. Likewise, the leaders in the after-hours playground movement hoped to instill middle-class values in their older charges, and they, too, turned to the public schools for assistance.

A nineteenth-century movement emphasizing the positive value of games and play gave rise to after-hours playgrounds. The Froebelian insistence on the beneficial role of play in children's lives, influenced the movement and tied it to the original concepts of kindergartens. But the Progressives also sought to compensate for what they saw as a lack of proper socialization within poverty-ridden families by offering parks and playgrounds for supervised recreation. Many prominent Americans, Theodore Roosevelt foremost among them, preached the virtues of physical activities to ensure healthy bodies; but poor urban youth had no places to exercise. Playgrounds and parks provided space and at the same time might teach habits of cleanliness, and in some cases, discipline and order by purposeful directed play—as opposed to just plain play.

Dance, too, took on new meaning. Dr. Luther H. Gulick, one of the founders of the Playground Association of America and head of physical education for the New York City public schools, saw dancing, particularly folk dancing, as so beneficial to young bodies that he hired a dancer to provide elementary schoolchildren with a proper teacher. Jane Addams favored folk dances as an alternative to the "illicit and soul-destroying pleasures" of dance halls. Some Progressives introduced Southern and Eastern European folk dances in the hope of eliciting spontaneity and gaiety among Anglo-Americans excessively straitened by their Puritan heritage. Others, suspecting the infectiousness of new immigrant customs and fearing that Americans had lost their own play tradition, hoped to revive an English tradition—including maypoles and pageantry—and establish it as American, thereby incorporating immigrants into Anglo-American play culture instead of the reverse.[31]

In Los Angeles, as elsewhere, the movement to include play in the schools caused consternation. Many taxpayers and more than a few teachers and administrators felt children came to school to learn and to work, not to play. Marcus Bettinger, a former teacher, principal, assistant superintendent, and board member, remembered a visit to his school from three neighborhood women who came to complain that the local schoolchildren made too much noise. "Why can't your children . . . stand about the school yard and talk to one another in a genteel way?" they asked. "We hear them three blocks away!" Bettinger went on to remark that many schools were built on "just enough ground to hold the building," and it was considered perfectly proper for a school to prohibit play on its premises.[32]

The organization in Los Angeles most closely associated with the development of school playgrounds was the settlement house. Settlement workers led the brigade of community activists at the turn of the century, and no other group worked with such dedication for urban reform or offered such a variety of amenities to the city's least fortunate. Some of their reforms were experimental, and some later proved inappropriate, but at the time reformers hoped that all of them would uplift the spirits as well as improve the lot of the deprived. As a not negligible bonus, reformers expected their work to help turn immigrants into good Americans. Recent scholarship provides many examples of the importance of women's societies in furthering reforms, and nowhere was this more relevant than in settlement houses.[33] Although men lived in settlements, particularly those administered by religious organizations, most of the residents were women.

By 1911, when Los Angeles's population had reached 319,000, there were six settlements in the foreign district: the Bethlehem Institute, Brownson House, College Settlement, the Los Angeles Municipal Settlement, Neighborhood House, and Stinson Memorial Industrial School. College Settlement and the Los Angeles Municipal Settlement operated under secular auspices; the others had religious affiliations. Collectively, these institutions provided city dwellers with playgrounds, plunge baths, libraries, vocational shops, health care, day nurseries, night schools, and English-language lessons. One of the smaller settlements, Stinson Memorial, founded in 1910 by the Council of Jewish Women, offered activities primarily, but not exclusively, for Jewish children. Located in a neighborhood of Russian Jews, Italians, Japanese, and Russian Molokans, the settlement maintained classes in sewing and needlework for women and provided recreational activities for children, including trolley rides to the beach and the country.[34]

These activities were of very limited scope compared with those of College Settlement, the leader of community action. The Los Angeles Branch of the Association of Collegiate Alumnae had founded this settlement in 1894 and maintained it as a residence in an ethnically diverse neighborhood of Mexicans, Italians, French, Basques, Syrians, and Slovenians. Like Jane Addams and her Hull House associates, College Settlement's director and staff lived on the premises, and they, too, involved themselves not only in their ward but in issues affecting the entire city.

One of College Settlement's most active members was Bessie D. Stoddart. She served as the vice-president of the board for over twenty years and lived at the settlement for a time. Unlike her sister reformer, the affluent and well-connected Caroline

Severance, who saw herself as part of organized womanhood—organized through elite women's clubs—Stoddart represented more nearly middle-class associations. She, along with her sister, Evelyn, who also lived at the settlement from time to time, came up from the ranks of working Progressive women. Bessie had graduated from the Los Angeles Normal School's kindergarten training program in 1899 but chose to devote herself to social service rather than the classroom. In 1897 she solicited the city for a district nurse, and that year the city appointed the first one.[35] Six years later, again under her prodding, the Board of Education hired the first school nurse,[36] and in 1906 she helped found the city's Housing Commission. Stoddart and her co-workers served on many civic bodies, including the probation committees of the Juvenile Court and the Housing and Visiting Nurses commissions. In 1918 Stoddart used her years of civic service to move up in the school administration hierarchy as a member of the Board of Education.

By then she was a familiar figure to the other members. As secretary of the Playground Commission, she had come to the board in 1908 to ask for the use of three school playgrounds during nonschool hours. Playgrounds would replace the streets and alleys where poor children played, she argued, providing a wholesome, supervised environment for the city's less fortunate children. The board granted her request on condition that the Playground Commission pay for any damages incurred and take all responsibility for accidents and the like. During the next year the board managed the three playgrounds; it hired male teachers to supervise two hours after school and on Saturday afternoons.[37]

Stoddart and other Progressives hoped that after-hours playgrounds would help prevent juvenile delinquency. They also wanted acceptable recreation opportunities for Los Angeles immigrant groups. Without playgrounds as alternatives, the working-class community might turn to the new mass culture's less genteel pastimes: supervised playgrounds afforded Progressives more control than did nickelodeons and pool halls. Moreover, children used the playgrounds in any case, and unsupervised playgrounds seemed an open invitation to vandals.

In 1914, in response to requests from residents near Bernardo School, outside the foreign district, Superintendent John H. Francis recommended that a playground supervisor be appointed for weekends and evenings to relieve the "unsatisfactory conditions."[38]

Whether supervised playgrounds curbed delinquency is debatable. Certainly, they did not prevent Americans of all classes from enjoying the mass culture around them. Nevertheless, the schools accepted the challenge, and in his 1914 annual report Superintendent John Francis listed supervised playgrounds as a school program, with a budget of $17,598.[39] For working parents the playgrounds also represented a continuation of child-care services. In theory mothers could accept full-time jobs and feel that their children were reasonably safe from the baser aspects of urban life. The following petition from the Molokan Russian colony grants us some insight into the level of acceptance that the playgrounds had in immigrant communities. At times the Molokans vehemently resisted school services, but in the early 1920's, as the elders perceived their hold on their children weakening, they turned to the city for help to keep their older children out of mischief:

> We think that you Americans can understand us and understand how hard it is for us in some ways to adjust ourselves and our children in the life of nowadays, to keep the good that we have and to help increase both. Our children got into mischief and trouble on the street because they have no place to play. We beg you to have playgrounds open for our children.[40]

Both the playground movement and the kindergarten movement illustrate how self-interest and reform worked together. In expanding middle-class values of social and moral responsibility into Los Angeles schools, authorities went on the attack against the new mass culture, but that process also opened up positions for kindergarten teachers and helped people like Stoddart to advance their political careers. At the same time both movements demonstrate the reformers' very real and keen interest in improving the lives of urban children. The board's willingness first to accept and later to incorporate services indicates its susceptibility to community pressure and its interest in expanding its position as provider of public services and in becoming an arbiter of middle-class values for the city. The combination of self-interest and reform brought unlikely groups together for specific projects. In their own way and for their own reasons, middle-class reformers and Molokan immigrants expanded the city's involvement in playgrounds.

Health Care

The school health program was quite a different story, the service that provoked the most conflict during the Progressive period. Creating a health service caused controversy among the reformers themselves and between them and school officials and parents. It was one thing to provide supervised playgrounds, and another to dictate how a family cared for its children's health. Many immigrants, in particular, dealt with illness in their own way, using such time-honored modes as faith healing. To some the medical profession represented the fearsome authority that had impelled them to leave their homeland. As late as 1916 the Molokans still resisted hospitalization and opposed preventive medicine and surgical procedures. When the parents of a child with tonsillitis complied with the school nurse's suggestion that the child be operated on, the family faced ostracism from the Molokan community.[41]

Of course, immigrants were not the only element that resented interference by medical personnel. In the same year some Christian Scientists wrote to the board asking for clarification on what constituted an epidemic. They felt the decision on whether to keep their children home from school or to vaccinate them against smallpox belonged to the parents and not to the City Health Department. They wanted reassurances from the board that their children would not be vaccinated without their approval.[42]

The School Health Committee accepted greater responsibilities not because of any grass-roots movement, but because administrators and teachers felt that children needed at least minimal care. As they saw it, medical science had made great strides since the turn of the century, and if families could not provide the kind of care that was now available, someone else should do it. The push for greater services thus came from school personnel and health-care professionals as well as from reformers. In 1904, after 500 copies of a 1903 article from the *California State Journal of Medicine* entitled "The Eyesight of School Children" were distributed to the schools, a local oculist, R. A. Harris, offered free eye examinations to poor children with defective vision. Dr. Harris caused some consternation at the board by representing himself as "refractionist to the public schools." The good doctor's self-interest was a little too apparent, and board members immediately sent him a communication advising him not to consider himself in such terms. The next month's board minutes listed eleven oculists who had volunteered their services and, in some instances, offered to provide eyeglasses at a reduced cost. In cases of extreme hardship the board provided carfare to the doctor's office.[43]

The school district did not have an actual health department until 1912. Before that the Health Committee, made up of board members, worked with the city's Health Department and accepted help from volunteers. Bessie Stoddart had influenced the board to accept the first school nurse in 1903, and in the fall of 1907 the board hired physicians and nurses and provided for a yearly physical examination for pupils, to be carried out under the supervision of the science director of the two existing high schools, Los Angeles and Polytechnic. The committee expected to reduce defective eyesight, hearing loss, enlarged adenoids and tonsils, poor teeth, and irregular heart beats but explicitly stated that it meant only to identify problems, not treat them. Parents unable to pay for treatment could make arrangements to take their children to a free clinic, administered by a private organization, or to a city agency.[44]

The board received requests to further the schools' role in the health-care field. In 1910 the Parent-Teacher Association asked it to help provide care for indigent children by donating a portable building, to be placed on the grounds of Children's Hospital and administered by the association with hospital personnel attending to the care.[45] But the more involved the schools became, the more the controversy surrounding that involvement grew. Objections came from many sources. In 1910 petitioners protested the teaching of "sex hygiene" classes, and the board acknowledged that parents had the right to keep their children out of the classes.[46]

The 1912 formation of a professional school Health Department came about after an investigation of a questionable physical examination at Hollywood High. The subject's mother objected to the school's treatment of her daughter, Florence Campbell. The board concluded that neither the Health Committee nor the Department of Health, Development, and Physical Training had authorized a "physical sex" examination for Miss Campbell, and as far as it was concerned, none had been given.[47]

Even so, the schools expanded their role, staffing the new Health Department with eleven physicians and seven nurses. The board set new guidelines for physical examinations, with the caveat that the department's "powers and responsibilities [would] be recommendations only."[48] Parents would receive notices of examinations two weeks beforehand. In that way any objections they had could be voiced. Sanitary conditions, such as bringing urinals up to city standards, also came under the department's jurisdiction. The new rules tried to eliminate any conflict of interest; physicians employed by the schools were prohibited from referring students to specific doctors for further consultation.

By anyone's account the Health Department earned its keep. A partial list for the 1913–14 school year suggests the extent of the services: 41,891 examinations, turning up 5,461 cases of abnormal tonsils, with 1,219 tonsillectomies; 47 cases of tuberculosis, with 40 treated; 612 cases of malnutrition, with 252 treated, and 498 cases of anemia, with 294 treated.* The nursing staff made 4,110 follow-up home visits, or an average of 587 for each of the seven nurses between September and June. And the

*The school reports do not say why some diagnosed cases were not treated. Since the schools' responsibility was confined to indigent children, the unrecorded treatments may have been handled elsewhere. Resistance to medical care may also explain some of the cases.

dental clinic, administered by the Parent-Teacher Association, proudly reported that its staff had filled 3,010 teeth and had extracted 805.[49]

Even though the schools enlarged their health-care program, the City Health Department continued to augment its own school services. Chief Nurse Margaret Sirch, for example, asked the board to allow the city to use rooms at Castelar Street School for an infant welfare station during the summer months and to offer summer baths at Hewett Street.[50] She also requested that the board place City Health Department bulletins in "foreign district" schools to inform parents of available services.[51]

Not all such requests were easily granted, and at times they caused conflict between the city and the schools. For instance, in 1916, when the Civil Service Commission requested that the schools' female physicians examine all female candidates for school positions, it was informed that the schools simply could not comply. It was not that there were no female physicians; they in fact represented 5 percent of the medical profession and dominated public-health work in this period,[52] and the board undoubtedly still employed more female physicians than males, as they had two years earlier. The problem was a simple matter of arithmetic: female teachers far outnumbered the males. Out of a combined teacher-administrator population of 2,380, 2,017 were women. In 1914 the board employed six female physicians full time and five male physicians part time; the only full-time male was the supervisor of the Health Department. Whether the board actively recruited female physicians is not known, but, if it did, large salaries were not a consideration. Each full-time physician earned $2,100 a year. Salary scales differed among the part-time males. One half-time male earned $900 a year, and the other four part-timers earned $1,200. The supervisor received $2,700. It is not clear whether the part-time male physicians were specialists and commanded higher salaries, or whether male physicians simply refused to work at the full-time rate. As for the seven nurses, they received only $1,100 a year for their long hours of work.[53]

Schools were accepting more responsibilities for health care and relied more on professionals and less on volunteers. Psychological testing to determine "mental deficients" came in 1914, with arrangements for the separation and hospitalization of "mental deficients" who became seriously ill. Schools provided "open-air" classrooms, ventilated by large, screened windows, for tubercular children; accommodated physically handicapped and anemic children with separate facilities; and provided extra nurses for day nurseries. The department and the Board of Education accepted the responsibility for the health care of all the children in their charge, from tiny tots to high school seniors, including even bathing, if necessary. A 1917 publication touting the department's achievements featured a photograph of a child sitting in a grimy, dirt-ringed bathtub. The caption reads, "His reward will be a swim. Tub baths are a necessity in some cases."[54]

The motives of the Health Department staff were similar to those of the school reformers who urged and developed playgrounds and kindergartens. They shared a Progressive belief in the power of the institution to do good. They wanted healthy children attending school and saw their mission as combating the spread of disease. Conflicts developed when certain members of the medical profession thought they might increase their practices by identifying themselves as an official school doctor, when city commissions made recommendations that the schools could not or were unwilling to implement, or when parents resisted treatment for their children. By their efforts, Progressives effected a public policy designed to keep children healthy, to treat those with infirmities, and perhaps most important, to retain them in the public schools.

Penny Lunches

Only people with the coolest hearts feel no uneasiness when they hear of children suffering from hunger. It is little wonder, then, that feeding hungry children became an overriding concern of socially minded citizens in many cities during the Progressive Era. Settlement houses had provided soup kitchens, along with their child-care facilities, and to many it seemed a natural step to bring food to needy students in the schools. Teachers complained that many children went all day without nourishment, and that it was difficult to teach undernourished children. Moreover, by the 1880's nutritional research in academia had supplied new information on the importance of good eating habits. In 1889 a group of college-trained women in Boston opened the New England Kitchen to provide what they considered wholesome lunches to poor workingmen; then in 1893, at the instigation of the kitchen's supervisor, Ellen Swallow Richards, the Boston School Committee ordered the schools to sell only food approved by that institution. Private organizations began serving lunches in schools in Cleveland in 1893, in Philadelphia in 1894, in Chicago in 1902, and in Saint Louis and Rochester, New York, in 1903.[55]

The menus were based on "scientific" data circulated by supporters of the New England Kitchen and Richards's newly organized American Home Economic Association. Much of their information proved incorrect, often being based as much on biases against ethnic foods as anything else. And to a later age their methods seem wrongheaded, if not downright unhealthy. For instance, early nutritionists found little value in fruits and vegetables because they contained too much water and too many carbohydrates and not enough protein; they were mostly good for adding color to otherwise dull plates. In any case the recommended cooking process ensured that vegetables would lose their nutritional value. Boiling was the preferred method. The recommended boiling time for string beans was one to three hours, for asparagus forty-five minutes, for celery a half hour, and for cucumbers twenty minutes; beets got the full treatment at twelve hours. White bread was preferred to whole wheat, and the dieticians discarded potato skins altogether. Richards and other nutritionists had little success in persuading immigrants to follow their lead, and it is possible that the introduction of lunches in public schools, including Los Angeles, grew out of a hope that by teaching children good dietetic habits, children would reform their parents.[56]

In Los Angeles the Civic Association was the main mover behind the adoption of the school lunch program, which got its start (at Custer Avenue School) in 1906, when one of the association's leading members, Joseph Scott, served on the school board. The close connection between the two groups ensured the program's success, and in the next four years lunch programs were established in Ann, Castelar, and Macy. Some expenses, such as pay for women helpers, were borne by the association and the board. A self-sustaining dimension was realized in the penny-lunch program, instituted first at Ann Street School in 1909.[57]

The penny lunches provided a hot midday meal to needy children at the cost of one cent, though if a child could not afford the penny he or she received a lunch anyway. Years later a former teacher, Etta Flagg, contended that though Superintendent Francis willingly agreed to take over the program in 1914, he had not favored it at the start. By then seven schools had hot lunch services, costing about $80 per month, with the schools supplying $20 and the Civic Association making up the difference.[58]

Superintendent Francis, in his 1914 annual report, written in part to justify his position and to counter charges made by three of the seven board members who threatened his recall, proudly announced that the schools expected to have nine lunch centers in operation by the end of 1915. Flagg's interpretation may not be entirely correct for Francis epitomized Progressive zeal. He may have moved cautiously in this area not because he did not favor the lunches but because, as the following chapter reveals, he had embraced so many other new programs that he may have feared that he was moving too far ahead of the board and exhausting its patience.

With or without Francis's enthusiastic support, the lunch program continued to grow and soon offered a noon meal to most poor children who lived in the foreign district. As a side dish, the program offered a modicum of Americanization. Lunches consisted of a bowl or two of meat or vegetable soup with a half to one loaf of French bread. Each principal decided who needed free food, and in some cases children were asked to earn their lunches. Often the meals were prepared by girls in the school's Domestic Science Department, who could count the job as part of their schoolwork and at the same time earn their lunches. In this way some Progressives construed school lunches as providing practical as well as humane functions. The programs offered training in American-style kitchens for poor girls when they left school. At some schools the lunchrooms were set up with white tablecloths, and children were expected to learn proper manners along with good eating habits. Dr. Irving Bancroft, supervisor of the Health Department, singled out Mexican children as an example of a group in need of good nutrition. He considered them "very prone" to "a severe form of tuberculosis, and this usually attacks the child with poor nutrition."[59]

In late 1916 the board's Law and Rules Committee reported that prices were being raised to five cents or ten cents a dish and suggested that the board adopt a general policy concerning the lunches. For one thing, the service had become so popular that schools located in other sections of the city wanted to participate and had requested assistance. For another, the board had expressed a wish to keep vendors from coming to the school grounds. Without a policy the board had no control over who sold food or its quality.[60]

There is no indication that either the Civic Association or the board ever asked parents what they thought constituted a proper lunch for their children. Molokans and Orthodox Jews, for instance, kept strict dietary laws based on the Old Testament, but there is no evidence to show that the organizers of the penny lunches were particularly concerned about such matters. Indeed, given the nutritionists' recommendations on boiling vegetables, Mexican families may well have preferred the local vendor just outside the schoolyard.

Vendors lent considerable color to the already colorful foreign district. In a reminiscence, Harry Maidenberg reminded his classmates from Amelia Street School of Nicholas Martinez, featured in an 1895 photograph with a tub of ice cream on his head: "[that] old timer, . . . yelling 'Hot tamal-ee-ee,' and in the summer the same old man with 'Ic-ee-ee Cre-ee-am,' you could hear him for blocks." Maidenberg also fondly remembered "the Hot Waffle Seller in his canopy buggy, selling his waffles as he sang arias from Grand Operas. He was an inspiration to the youth of that day who wondered what Grand Opera was."[61]

No one has accused the penny lunches of adding color to Los

Angeles, but they were successful nonetheless. They offered an adequate meal at reasonable prices, along with a morsel of Americanization, and gradually convenience and economics persuaded the communities to accept them.

School Services and Immigrant Communities

The penny-lunch program, the kindergarten and playground movements, and the health services all began through the efforts of volunteers. As the programs became more successful and grew too large for volunteers to handle on their own, the board helped out financially, set guidelines, and brought in professionals to administer them. Some of the programs employed neighborhood residents. Matrons from the communities, for example, served lunches and assisted in the nursery day-care centers. In this way schools not only educated school-age children but played a greater role in the community.

Not all the poor responded favorably to the new services. Many saw them as attempts to drive a wedge between themselves and their children. Immigrants were particularly cautious. Leonard Covello, an Italian immigrant in New York, became an educator, author, and advocate for ethnic diversity in public schools. He described the reservations parents had about sending their young children to schools where they learned ideas that their parents did not understand.[62] Although many immigrants resented the school's indoctrination, attendance records attest, and recent ethnic studies confirm, that most sent their children to school.[63] But many also took steps to remedy the matter, as Molokans in Los Angeles did. So far as they were concerned, the schools were usurping their authority over their children. In an attempt to retain their traditions, they and others like them tried to turn the situation around by using the schools for their own ends.

The Molokans exemplify a cultural group caught in the web of social change. A pietistic Protestant sect, they had emigrated from the Transcaucasus region of Russia in 1905, and by 1910 almost 5,000 lived in Los Angeles's foreign district. Their departure from Russia coincided with the Russo-Japanese War, a time when they faced harassment and conscription by the Czar's officials. To an extent, their immigration resembled that of Eastern European Jews; both fled persecution, and both came to the United States in family groups with intentions of staying. Unlike the Jews, however, the Molokans who settled in Los Angeles placed no apparent value on formal learning. Except for a limited reading of the Bible, their traditions were oral. In many ways, their traditions were similar to the Quakers: they were pacifists; they had no clerical hierarchy; they elected elders from the community; and since they built no churches, their meeting houses, or *sobranies*, resembled Quaker meeting houses. The Molokans' communal life centered around their sobranies. They did not reach out to the general community except when necessary. They had no foreign language press, as most immigrants had, and only a small fraction of them were literate.[64]

Pauline Young's 1929 study, subsequently published as *The Pilgrims of Russian-Town*, suggests that the Molokans picked Los Angeles as a terminus because the climate reminded them of their homeland. They congregated in the foreign district, on the west side of the Los Angeles River, near the lumber yards and industrial plants where they worked. Most of the men sought jobs as unskilled laborers, and if women worked outside their homes, they worked as domestics. They lived in terribly crowded conditions; many families shared one house. Families pooled their incomes, however, and within a few years many moved across the river to the "flats," adjacent to Boyle Heights. Married children lived with the man's family, and the new daughter was expected to contribute to the family's income.

The Molokans' foreignness had a considerable impact on their neighborhood. A local reformer described them as "strange . . . Russian peasants, . . . industrious, dignified, preoccupied with their own affairs."[65] Their unusual attire attracted attention in a district full of unusual dress. In public the men wore suits over their Russian shirts. Women and girls wore dresses with very full, long skirts and draped shawls over their heads; married women wore skullcaps under their shawls. Most of the men were bearded.

By the time the Molokans arrived, school attendance was

compulsory. As with other groups, some families tried to resist compulsory education, but both the fear of the truant officer and a desire for English proficiency compelled most to register their children at Utah Street School. The four-room schoolhouse in "the flats" had been built in 1904, about a year before the migration began. The resourcefulness of Principal Alice Cushing won the hearts of many Molokans, who in later years referred to her as "little mother."[66] One of the teachers, Lillian Sokoloff, noted the impact the Molokans had as the small school nearly burst its seams. By 1918 or so, Utah Street had over a thousand students, 40 percent of whom were Molokans.[67]

Yet even dedicated school people like Cushing might threaten the community's traditions. One of the first to be challenged was the wearing of shawls. According to Molokan custom, shawls defined femininity, modesty, and even virginity. But school people and the Health Department took a dim view of them: the shawls contributed to diseases and lice, and the girls must remove them during school.[68] What the girls did when they left Utah Street was a different matter. As with other immigrants, these Molokan traditions ebbed as the younger generations assimilated.

Schools played no role in the Molokan culture. Moreover, they often interfered with the family's economic plans. Compulsory education laws made it difficult to keep older female children home to mind younger siblings while the women worked outside. Boys attending school were not working to help support the family. The studies of Young and Sokoloff reaffirm the familiar story of immigrants caught in the web of assimilation and social change.

The threat of assimilation aroused fear in the colony, and in 1908, at a meeting of elders and parents of school-age children, the Molokans decided to write the Board of Education to request that the Utah Street School open a room every afternoon for Russian-language instruction. The colony had engaged a teacher. The board agreed, and the sessions appeared successful; after eight months, the Molokans requested the use of another room at Utah. Apparently pleased with the arrangements, the elders wrote to the board three years later, thanking it for the use of the facilities.[69] Whether or not the Russian lessons retarded the children's assimilation is unclear. Young wrote of the conflicts she found within the community in 1929 as the Molokans became more and more Americanized with the passing generations.

The Molokans' request for facilities to teach their language and culture appears to be one of the earliest in this domain, but it was by no means the only one of its kind. German-speaking groups had regularly asked for rooms in the late nineteenth century. During the prewar period many ethnic groups petitioned the board for the use of schoolrooms. The Dante Alighieri Society asked to use rooms at several schools for teaching Italian language and culture.[70] The Alliance Française wanted rooms to teach French.[71] Rabbis asked for rooms to teach Hebrew and Yiddish.[72] The Jewish Radical Club wanted rooms at Custer and Cornwell schools to teach Jewish culture.[73] Armenians held evening classes at First Street School, and the Croatians requested rooms at Castelar.[74] The board acceded to most such requests but occasionally said no. A Swedish group that asked to hold a meeting at Grant Avenue School was turned down because the board felt the affair would have too much of a religious overtone. The schools could not be used for religious purposes.[75]

Some groups joined forces: French, Germans, and Italians petitioned for a school where their children would be taught in their own languages, and for a short time the district operated the Cosmopolitan School, which combined foreign-language teaching with English instruction.[76] The self-interest of these groups and this particular school raised questions beyond the simple matter of allowing native languages and culture to be taught in after-hour classes. Teaching subject matter through foreign languages was seen by many as divisive and as a self-serving attempt by certain ethnic groups to further their languages over English. The controversy surrounding the Cosmopolitan School also sharpened some already sharp pedagogical disagreements, for not everyone agreed on the merits of teaching foreign languages to young children.[77]

The fact that immigrants petitioned the board reflected the skill with which newcomers asserted themselves. Hoping to reinforce their native cultures and slow assimilation, immigrants asked the school to provide extra services in the form of school rooms. But in addition, and more significant, in petitioning the board the immigrants showed how efficiently they had learned to manipulate the process for their own purposes. In most instances the board furnished the space, but its interest lay in Americanization. As a 1916 report of the board's Advisory Committee put it, even though Los Angeles had a smaller percentage of foreigners than many Eastern cities, 20 percent of its population had immigrated from non-English-speaking countries. The authors stated that it behooved the city to teach these people English.[78]

Private organizations approached the board with their own policies. Sometimes volunteers requested facilities on behalf of a specific group, as the YMCA did in 1914, seeking space at Boyd School to teach English to Japanese immigrants. Two years later the YMCA came back to the board again, this time asking for accommodations for some Armenians who had been using a private establishment for their evening classes.[79] More typically an organization would ask the board's permission to establish an evening class within a school. The Friday Morning Club, the largest women's club in Los Angeles, with a membership of several thousand, requested teachers to teach foreigners; the Federation of Women's Clubs requested night and home teachers; the YMCA wanted to hold classes at Macy Street School; and the Daughters of the American Revolution wanted classrooms at Utah.[80] Communities also came to the board on their own. Black Americans wanted a night school at Rosemont for those who worked during the day and could not attend regular classes.[81]

Thanks to these many requests, school officials were alerted to the need for greater emphasis on classes for foreigners, with the result that Los Angeles was the first city to have its evening work accepted in the courts in lieu of an examination for citizen papers.[82]

The Professionalizing of the Task of Assimilation

No longer content with local attempts, by late 1916 the state stepped up the campaign for Americanization. In November newly appointed Superintendent Albert Shiels told the board that the State Commission of Immigration and Housing asked the schools to publicize new classes for teaching English to foreigners. Fueled by fears of war, the campaign to bring non-English-speaking adults into the schools began in earnest. Shiels included in the list to dispense this information fifteen foreign-language newspapers, twenty-one foreign societies, and several private and public agencies.[83] With the growing numbers of foreign-born settling in Los Angeles, and the increasing resentment toward those who did not assimilate, the role of teaching English to foreigners shifted from volunteers to professionals. This trend became stronger after Mary Simons Gibson introduced the California Home Teacher Act of 1915. In March 1917 Shiels appointed Ruby Baughman supervisor for immigrant education and began to reorganize the evening schools along the lines he had outlined the year before.[84] Shiels noted that "excellent philanthropic motives" had initiated legislation to teach foreigners, but professionals really knew what suited students best: "The problem is better understood by teachers."[85]

The schools' importance in the community grew as they began to take over the functions of private or civic organizations. Rarely did the schools themselves initiate the services; but once a service proved successful, only an institution like the public schools had the money and influence to keep the program running. Francis recognized this and wanted the schools to become indispensable centers in their neighborhoods. "During stringent times," he wrote, "their people came to them for help securing employment, for food and clothing, for advice on personal affairs and when in trouble with the officers of the law."[86] This movement was not confined to Los Angeles by any means but part of a national trend in the aggressive expansion of the role of schools. In 1920 John Daniels, a sociologist, noted that nine out of ten immigrants felt the most important American institution effective "in making the immigrant part and parcel of American life" was the public schools.[87]

The public schools were winning the battle. They had become the place where immigrants sought advice in personal and financial matters and help with legal difficulties. But the price was high. Often there was a loss of parental influence as teachers and administrators replaced traditional voices. Schools dictated dress and health codes and lunch menus, and tried to set patterns of play. Schools borrowed settlement-house ideas and incorporated them into public policy.

As professionals took over from volunteers, female reformers created jobs for other women and for themselves. Kindergartens opened a new category for women teachers; the Health Department made positions for nurses and female doctors; penny lunches hired neighborhood women; and Bessie Stoddart sat on the school board. But the jobs the women created were extensions of their volunteerism, extensions of their domestic sphere, jobs that rarely threatened men and were not meant to challenge the social order.

Professionalism reshaped Americanization programs. The schools, with their burgeoning pool of trained staff, could better administer programs grown too massive for the volunteers. Professionals, often motivated by the same forces that had motivated volunteers—self-interest, a fierce defense of their middle-class values, and political power—worked with them to make the transition from immigrant to citizen easier on all concerned.

Photograph sources: *1, 2, and 4,* the Department of Special Collections, University Research Library, UCLA, Collection 99, Los Angeles Views; *3,* The Huntington Library, San Marino, California, Ephemera Collection, Harry F. Maidenberg, ed., "Do You Remember" (pamphlet); *5,* The Huntington Library, San Marino, California, Margaret Collier Graham Collection, box 37(2); *6,* the Department of Special Collections, University Research Library, UCLA, Collection 200, California Ephemera; *7–14,* the Security Pacific Collection, Los Angeles Public Library.

1. The students of Spring Street School, ca. 1855. Louise Hayes, the teacher in charge of the girls' department, stands in the back. William Wallace, in charge of the boys' department, is not shown.

2. "The Round House," where Miss Marwedell, assisted by Kate Smith Douglas Wiggin, is said to have conducted kindergarten classes in the mid-1870's. A sign on the far right fence reads "School of the Kindergarten." Erected in 1848, the building was located on Main, between Third and Fourth streets.

3. Nicholas Martinez, the original street ice cream vendor in Los Angeles, 1895.

4. Los Angeles High School class of 1897 going to the Fiesta. The 1890's introduced two annual outdoor festivals to Southern California: the Pasadena Tournament of Roses (1890) and the Fiesta de Los Angeles (1894). They combined the growing national interest in pageantry with the Southland's love of floral display. The naming of the Los Angeles pageant "fiesta" represented an attempt by a small number of Angelenos to revive the region's Spanish heritage.

5. Mary Simon Gibson, a Progressive Los Angeles club woman and reformer, 1890. Appointed to the California Commission of Immigration and Housing by Governor Hiram Johnson in 1913, Gibson lobbied for passage of the California Home Teacher Act of 1915.

6. Newspaper coverage of a welcome-home rally at the railroad station for Superintendent John H. Francis. *Los Angeles Herald*, Oct. 25, 1914.

7. Students in a manual art class at Ann Street School, ca. 1910. Before the 1917 Smith-Hughes Act institutionalized vocational education, Ann Street School was holding manual art classes for upper grade boys and girls.

8. Tenth Street School playground, 1926.

9. Los Angeles schoolchildren line up for dental inspection, ca. the late 1920's or early 1930's.

10. Students being tested for deafness, ca. the late 1920's or early 1930's. The blackboard at right indicates that sloyd is scheduled for Friday's class.

11. Children studying calligraphy at the Chinese Methodist Mission, ca. the late 1920's. The school was located at 522-1/2 North Los Angeles Street.

12. Jefferson High School girls getting ready for ceremonies for the 1932 Olympic Games, being held in Los Angeles.

13. Students at Washington Street School, ca. 1930's. Children were urged to open savings accounts as a means of building character. The money was collected at school for deposit in local banks, which had established school savings sections.

14. Children in front of the main branch of the Los Angeles Public Library, displaying samples from the library's collection of foreign language books and books in translation, 1928.

3

John H. Francis, Albert Shiels, Mary S. Gibson: The Tensions of Reform

> A remarkable series of changes are now going on in American Education. . . . Science, industry and intercommunication brought a pressure for knowledge hitherto unneeded, and at the same time the very same forces brought our people the wealth to provide it. [Education] is as different today as an up-to-date Cadillac is different from a two-seated surrey.
>
> —*Ernest Carroll Moore, 1928*

The transition to professionalism and greater efficiency in public schooling was not so smooth as Dr. Moore would have had his readers believe. Although a consensus of city leaders agreed that political reform, particularly in the schools, was necessary to rid the system of corrupt practices, how it was to be achieved was something else.

The 1914 battle over the superintendency exemplifies the politics of reform as reformers inside and outside education vied for political and professional power. The struggle between Superintendent John H. Francis and a minority of school board members over Francis's reappointment developed into a full-blown war, pitting General Harrison Gray Otis and the *Los Angeles Times* against board member Joseph Scott. The outcome was Francis's resignation and the hiring of Albert Shiels. Francis had taken authority away from board members when he established junior high schools, initiated differentiated curriculum, and promoted and retained teachers who supported his policies. Shiels, a more cautious administrator than Francis, adroitly managed the board during the turbulent years of the First World War. Shiels avoided many of the pitfalls that plagued his predecessor, and with the aid of Mary Simons Gibson, a member of the California Commission of Immigration and Housing, greatly expanded the school's role in the community.

Gibson, with support from Shiels, overcame the objections of many educators and moved schooling out of the schoolhouse directly into immigrants' homes and workplaces. Under the auspices of the California Home Teacher Act, Americanization reached into the heart of immigrant communities. There, its originators hoped, it would give immigrant women the tools for assimilation.

Gibson and her co-workers exemplify the way California women used their recently won suffrage to gain new political power. Gibson and others served on state commissions, wrote legislation and lobbied for its passage, and helped implement the new laws. Like their male counterparts, they consulted professional groups to provide added political status. And they turned volunteer positions into positions that could be administered only by professionals.[1]

The Progressives at Battle

By the time John Haywood Francis became superintendent of the Los Angeles system in 1910, the school board had been centralized, and the position of superintendent had become one of considerable power. As in many urban school systems superintendents had taken on many of the functions previously held by board members. Modeled after business boards, boards of education had become more corporate. They established policy but allowed the day-to-day administration to be carried out by specialists—the superintendent and his staff.

In many ways Francis typified the early Progressive superintendents of urban schools. Educated in his native Ohio, he came to California and received a Master of Arts degree in 1892. He taught commercial law, economics, and accounting in the Sacramento Delta before his arrival in Los Angeles in 1896. From teaching commercial education, he moved up the educational ladder to become principal of the city's newly built second high school, Polytechnic, and then superintendent.[2] In the nineteenth century few of Los Angeles's superintendents had been educators: the schools had been administered, as James M. Guinn, a former superintendent, remarked, by "merchants, lawyers, doctors, preachers, anything but teachers."[3] By the twentieth century professional educators had a firm hold on the post.*

The period prior to Francis's appointment had been one of unprecedented expansion and reform. Compulsory school laws and inclusive social services had worked to increase the size and functions of schools. And education in general had grown in influence and importance, thanks in large part to the Progressives' calls for the restructuring of public schooling. By the twentieth century most educators had moved away from the notions of Horace Mann's common school, where children, no matter what social class, would be offered the same curriculum. The new theory held that schools could not ignore differences; even in a democracy not all children were equal. In 1910 Assistant Superintendent Marcus Bettinger claimed that, by "releasing the pupils from the tyranny . . . of examinations" and creating "special classes for taking care of different types of pupils," the Los Angeles system had been transformed from a "factory notion of uniformity to the humane notion of individuality."[4] Francis had every intention of carrying on in the same fashion. Both of his immediate predecessors, James Foshay and Ernest Carroll Moore, had supported expansion and reform, and Francis, aggressive and talented, continued and, indeed, exceeded their programs. In his 1914 report he ticked off the accomplishments: penny-lunch programs, kindergartens, school

*One professional educator of the nineteenth century was Superintendent Chloe B. Jones (1880–81). Jones had served as principal of the high school before her appointment as superintendent. She was relieved of her administrative responsibilities after one year and sent back to the classroom, apparently because she had begun to superintend in too modern a manner, changing curriculum, choosing textbooks, and assigning teachers. These privileges belonged to the board. After Jones was dismissed, the board appointed Guinn superintendent. (Freeman, "Board-Superintendent Relationships," pp. 198–202.) Severance had supported Jones, and she wrote from Massachusetts to her friend Margaret Graham of her "indignation" upon hearing of Jones's "removal." (Caroline Severance to M. C. Graham, Sept. 27, 1881, Graham Collection, box 24, HL.)

playgrounds, a health department, and the development of an intermediate school. A combination of his abrasive manner and the intermediate school precipitated his difficulties with the board in 1916.

Intermediate schools (or junior high schools as they came to be called[5]), along with vocational education, helped to shape the modern comprehensive high school. Wedged between the elementary and the secondary schools, they offered a differentiated curriculum, what Bettinger called that "humane notion of individuality." Not everyone was so admiring, and a particular problem had to do with timing. Many educators believed in differentiated curriculum but tended to think that the early adolescent years was the time to expose children to broader courses, not a time to teach them specific occupational skills. The psychologist G. Stanley Hall, founder of the child-study movement, had developed new theories on the adolescent years, and his writings, beginning in 1904, had considerable influence in stimulating the junior-high movement.[6]

A compelling argument for vocational training arose from the fact that even though compulsory education mandated that children stay in school longer, many working-class families chose to disobey the law. Educators thought that by teaching work skills at an early age they would persuade parents who saw no need for further education to keep their children in schools.

Since 1905 committees of manufacturers and educators had stressed the importance of industrial education. Dividing children into groups according to skills not only created greater school efficiency, they argued; it also bolstered national industrial output, as witness the success of industrial schools in Germany. Some saw the junior-high movement as a key factor in the development of human capital. Instead of waiting until the ninth grade to match students and their educational programs to the labor market, some asked, why not begin in the seventh? Yet many educators had a nagging concern that too much differentiation would lead to a class-based educational system, a system that seemed the very antithesis of democratic goals.[7]

The National Education Association silenced much of the debate when it published *Cardinal Principles of Secondary Edu-*

cation in 1918. The NEA recommended incorporating junior highs into the public school system but suggested that those years should be spent experimenting with various vocational courses, leaving final decisions until high school. A year before the publication of *Cardinal Principles*, Congress saw fit to pass the first major federal education bill, the Smith-Hughes Act. Joel Spring notes that the act not only expanded vocational education but defined "a national interest in education" justifying "federal intervention."[8] Faced with growing numbers of students in urban areas, junior high schools equipped with vocational shops and differentiated curricula proliferated.

Superintendent Moore introduced the idea of intermediate schools in Los Angeles. In his 1907–8 annual report, he called attention to the needs of some students to begin studying Latin and the Romance languages along with mechanical drawing, woodworking, and domestic science in the seventh and eighth grades.[9] Moore's call for an intermediate school went unanswered because of more pressing matters, notably the overcrowding of school facilities as the city's population boom continued. In February 1907 the board reported that sixty school rooms had fifty or more students, thirty-three temporary buildings needed replacing, and the two high schools were so terribly overcrowded that a third must be built.[10] Innovation had to wait, and Moore must have seen that the intermediate school lay in the future.

Unlike Moore, who had taught at the University of California before accepting the Los Angeles superintendency, Francis had come up through the ranks of the city's schools. Having taught at and been principal of Polytechnic High, he was aware of the interest in a comprehensive secondary school offering a varied curriculum. The first intermediate school in California had opened in Berkeley in 1910, the year Francis took up the Los Angeles post. The originator of the Berkeley school, Frank K. Bunker, had been an assistant superintendent in Los Angeles before his appointment in Berkeley and was considered an able leader who knew, as one of his co-workers wrote, "that he cannot lead unless the people will follow."[11] There was no indication that Francis was moving too fast when, in 1911, he opened Berendo Junior High, 14th Street Intermediate, 30th Street Intermediate, and Twenty-First Avenue Intermediate. In the next three years he opened four more junior highs.[12] Whatever misgivings some had about the intermediate schools, they made little public mention of them until Francis came up for renewal in 1914.

At that point it became clear that not everyone welcomed the new schools; for one thing, they were expensive. The city's taxpayers were already paying for increased social services, including penny lunches and playgrounds, as well as for earlier academic innovations like the evening schools that provided English classes for immigrants. Francis supported a system of Americanization that focused on certain designated "neighborhood" elementary schools—schools with populations of 50 percent foreign-born children or children of the foreign-born that also served as social welfare centers, offering the full array of social services that had gained board approval. In 1913, as we have seen, at the behest of French, German, and Italian ethnic groups he had also organized the Cosmopolitan School, which offered foreign languages in the fourth, fifth, and sixth grades and taught some subjects in foreign languages. For a short time the idea of teaching foreign languages at an early age caught on, and in 1914 800 elementary students studied foreign languages in five other schools.[13]

In 1911 voters had approved a bond issue of $1,160,000—by an overwhelming majority of 4,956 to 796—to pay for developing four intermediate schools along with other educational improvements.[14] Now in 1914, with eight intermediates in operation, would the voters be asked to pay for more? Moreover, some critics discerned that intermediate schools took children from the seventh and eighth grades and put them in separate facilities, robbing the elementary schools of their most mature students. Others did not like the differentiated curriculum, which allowed girls to take courses in domestic science and boys to spend their hours in shops, wasting time on unessential studies that might be better spent on "rudimentary subjects." Parents complained because their children needed to travel greater distances to school. But most importantly, critics said that intermediate schools took the best, most qualified teachers out of the elementary schools.[15]

This complaint went to the heart of the charges against Francis: that he was changing teacher promotion policy without the board's say-so. When Francis took steps in this direction, he drew the ire of both teachers and board members. The board felt he had overstepped the bounds of superintendent; better educated teachers saw his move as a threat to their professionalization and to the merit system. In 1912, without consulting board members in advance, Francis pushed a new teacher promotion policy through the board. His plan, known as Schedule B, allowed the superintendent to promote teachers regardless of examination scores and, as his detractors contended, to raise his friends to positions above those of supposedly more qualified teachers.[16]

Francis had succeeded in getting Schedule B approved only because two of his critics had been absent from the meeting. His success was short-lived.[17] At the first possible meeting of the full board, over the protests of the superintendent, the board adopted a resolution "abrogating Schedule B" because "the Superintendent has shown an autocratic and disloyal attitude towards the wishes of his superior officers, to-wit: the Board of Education."[18] But Francis's alleged aggressive behavior continued. He was accused of appointing principals without high school certificates to the intermediate schools. Many intermediate teachers had high school credentials, and appointing principals with less certification than their teaching staff was seen as contrary to the goals of professionalization. After all, requirements had been upgraded to fit the new nonpartisan approach to education. It would be foolhardy for a superintendent to interfere. Professionalization went hand in hand with total acceptance of the new requirements.* Francis acquiesced in higher authority and

*Freeman, "Board-Superintendent Relationships," pp. 353–57. Based on the 1908 recommendations of the board's Rules Committee, the new requirements for elementary teachers were graduation from a four-year high school, a two-year course in an accredited normal school, a passing grade in a competitive examination, and either a year's teaching experience or a special recommendation from the president and faculty of the normal school. A high school certificate required two or three years' work at a university. Special teachers

thought the issue was over. He was wrong; it resurfaced in 1914 as part of the accusations against him.

To the surprise of many Angelenos, when the board met in April 1914, three members voted against renewing Francis's contract. More than that, the three—Joseph Scott, who had presided over the board from 1907 until 1912; his successor, James M. Guinn, who like Scott had been on the board since its reorganization in 1904; and Mrs. R. L. Craig, who joined in 1912—had come ready to nominate another candidate.[19] They had in mind Assistant Superintendent Susan M. Dorsey.[20]

Immediately before the April meeting, a series of seemingly unsolicited letters praising Francis's accomplishments had flowed to the board.[21] As soon as Francis learned his position was in jeopardy, he moved to counter with the recommendation that "a thorough and exhaustive investigation and survey" be conducted, and that it include "the physical, mental, moral, and other educational features of the work being done here." He called for experts to conduct the investigation and asked that it begin the following September.[22] Over the objections of the minority, Francis was reappointed for four years, but no action was taken on his suggestion for an investigation.*

At a special meeting on June 30, three members filed formal charges against Francis. Their list of accusations was long: failing to handle "Pernicious Political Activities in the School De-

had to complete training courses in their subject and take a professional examination. In addition, a high school teacher had to show maturity, and all teachers, at whatever level, had to be in excellent health. The item calling for high school teachers to show maturity could be turned around and used against young female teachers, who were often labeled "girl teachers."

*Francis's request for an expert to investigate and prepare a school survey was not unusual for the period. Moreover, he expected no surprises here. Professors from leading universities, including Ellwood Cubberley of Stanford, had visited the newly reorganized intermediate schools and had expressed their admiration. (Board, *Annual Report, 1914*, p. 177; Eales, "Los Angeles School System," p. 144). David Tyack has remarked that one of the things that differentiated the Progressives was their reliance on "experts"—the consultants who were brought into city schools to investigate and rank them according to efficiency and innovation. Around the country 67 surveys completed by outside experts were published between 1910 and 1919, and they proved so convincing that in the next eight years 114 more were published. (*One Best System*, p. 191). One imagines that no respectable school board could hold its collective head high if it had not commissioned a survey.

partment," which referred to instances where he either called for or at least did nothing to prevent teachers' openly backing certain board members for reelection when the board had prided itself on being nonpartisan; showing a "Lack of Appreciation of the Teachers' View Points" and changing the merit system; promoting friends to positions and, therefore, ignoring competitive examination results; causing "Deterioration of the Elementary Schools through Extensive Attention to the Intermediate Schools"; defending an assistant superintendent "Offensively Addicted to the Use of Smoking and Intoxicating Liquors"; exerting a general but unspecified demoralizing influence; and last, demonstrating a clear "Temperamental Unfitness."[23] The committee thought the charges serious enough to capitalize almost every word of its report.

Guinn, well known as a chronicler and lecturer, had served as superintendent in 1881 and again in 1883. He had studied at Antioch College under Horace Mann and continued to believe in Mann's common school ideal. Guinn felt the accusations had not specifically criticized Francis's most offensive act—the corruption of that ideal—and filed a separate charge at him for developing the intermediate schools. These schools were costly, said Guinn; the teachers were being overpaid, and that was disrupting general salary schedules.[24] And in fact only two weeks before, intermediate teachers had held a meeting to complain about their salaries, arguing that they held the same certification as high school teachers and worked longer hours.[25] Guinn summed up his opposition to intermediate schools and any attempt to raise the teachers' salaries. "Intermediate teachers get $24 a month more than do elementary teachers, who do just as much work." Their salaries might be legal "but [were] not morally defensible."[26] Guinn went even further in his mistrust of intermediate schools and of Francis. "The elementary schools have no course of study: it is all fads," he said. "Francis doesn't know elementary school work and he won't learn. They teach German and French and other languages when they need more spelling and arithmetic."[27] Craig joined Guinn in contending that the intermediate schools caused the neglect of the elementaries.[28]

Francis hired a lawyer and called a special board meeting for July 20 to present his case. He denied all the charges at great length but spent most of his energies defending his position on the promotion of teachers. It was not true, as the minority board members claimed, that he had appointed some principals without the board's approval. The three men particularly in question had high school certificates and were highly qualified as well, having served as principals of large grammar schools for between fourteen and eighteen years. In other instances principals had been retained from the grammar schools when they were converted to intermediates. Francis went out of his way to show Scott as having full knowledge of and implicitly approving his actions. And sometimes he went so far as to suggest that Scott did not always conduct himself in the best interests of the people of Los Angeles. He had tried to intimidate Ernestina Lopez, one of the teachers at Polytechnic Evening High School, with "loud and unkindly language" in front of others. "Later he pursued her with correspondence of such a nature as to cause her to fear for her position."[29] The incident illustrated the tension between board members, the Superintendent's Office, and classroom teachers.

On July 21 the controversy took on a different tone, and anti-Catholic rhetoric made front page news in the *Los Angeles Examiner*. The *Examiner* published a series of letters from prominent educators—Nora Sterry, principal of Macy Street; Ethelda Drake, principal of Ann Street; and Hattie Bancroft, assistant superintendent of Home Economics—to the effect that Scott had interfered in their school programs. Scott had written letters, some of which the *Examiner* published, asking whether meat or meat soup was served on Fridays. He had asked Mary Workman, a well-known Catholic who worked at Brownson settlement, a Catholic institution, to investigate the situation at Macy Street. Workman, in turn, had informed Sterry of the request. The educators felt that Scott had overstepped his position. Bancroft wrote to Francis, in a letter also published in the paper, that she resented Scott's "usurpation of the duties of your office and of those directly under you." She continued, "instances as this make very evident the cause of the so-called discord in present school affairs."

The following day Scott had his turn. He told the *Examiner* that Francis had used the letters, published the previous day, to cover up the real issues of his own high-handedness. He accused Francis of "religious bigotry," and, he continued, "neither myself, nor my religion are of issue in this case, and no one knows it better than John H. Francis." *

The tensions created by the politics of reform revealed a mixture of motives. Francis's detractors had what they considered legitimate grievances against the superintendent. He had tilted the balance of acceptable school governance away from the board and toward his office; and when board members voiced opposition to his actions, he enlisted the support of teachers and students, thereby tainting the process with politics and extreme partisanship.

Francis's aggressive action worked for the moment. The majority of the board voted to dismiss all charges and rescind a call for an investigation. Nevertheless, the minority members continued their fight against him in one way or another and hoped the 1915 election would add to their numbers. Meanwhile Francis and his supporters continued the type of political maneuvering that Scott and the nonpartisan board had pledged to end. In May 1915 pro-Francis candidates for the board arranged a number of campaign meetings, a fact that the *Times* dutifully reported: "Pro Francis candidates . . . are making their fight on a platform which pledges support for Francis's policies."[30] Three days later the *Times* told readers: "A determined effort, not

*J. Randolph Haynes Collection, box 134, UCLA. In another instance, an unidentified but blatantly anti-Catholic paper printed some of the same letters along with a few others in its "Gopher Column." The Gopher saw itself "fighting Priestcraft in the State of California." In a letter to Miss Stephenia E. Hill of Hostetter Street School, Scott asked whether the Friday penny lunches included meat and whether Catholic children had alternative meals. He explained that Catholics "abstain from meat on Fridays in memory of the death of Him whom they are to regard as Savior and Redeemer of the world." In another letter, also previously printed in the *Examiner*, Scott spoke out against what he saw as anti-Catholic rhetoric by an evening lecturer at the San Pedro High School auditorium (n.d., California Ephemeral Collection 200, box 30, UCLA).

at all times honest, is being made to discredit the pro-Francis candidates. [Their opponents] have resorted to reprehensible tactics."[31] The paper continued to hammer home the message, insisting that "the 'non-factional' or 'non-political' or Joescott ticket for the school board should be defeated at all costs."[32]

The reform battles had left most Angelenos in the dark. More than anything, the controversy had confused voters. One befuddled citizen simply asked for someone to explain whether Francis mismanaged the schools. Was he extravagant? Was the trouble over the vocational, or evening, or intermediate schools? What was his crime?[33]

Francis's supporters began to rally. One educator, whom the *Times* interviewed and who asked to remain anonymous, suggested that the entire matter be referred to the State Commission of Education. The three commissioners were "experts in every line involved in the controversy" and would make suitable referees. On the same page the paper reported that the heads of three student bodies in the city's largest high schools had laid plans for "a monster student demonstration" to support the superintendent, and that following the student rally, teachers would then demonstrate in support of Francis.[34]

The infighting among reformers led to an unusual alliance based on the self-interest of the various parties and underlies some of the complexities of school reform. Francis seems to have had the unflinching support of General Otis and the *Times*. Otis, who vehemently opposed most Progressive programs, somehow found it in his heart to support one of the city's most Progressive leaders. One might argue that some of Francis's policies placed him in a class with the prereform educators, who controlled the mechanisms of teacher promotion and relied on seniority rather than on examination. This incident illustrates the complexities of professionalization. Yet in other areas, Francis stands at the apex of Progressivism.[35]

Otis's support may have to do more with his dislike of Board President Joseph Scott than anything else. For several years the publisher had been Scott's unabashed enemy. According to an interview the eighty-three-year-old Scott gave in 1950, the trouble grew out of a controversy between the onetime allies

Superintendent Moore and Otis. In 1907 the National Education Association arranged to meet in Los Angeles, for the second time in ten years,[36] and the city wanted to show its hospitality. Moore acted as local-arrangements coordinator and asked Otis to give the welcoming address. On the occasion of the NEA's first Los Angeles meeting, in 1899, a group of dissatisfied teachers, who felt the association was dominated by administrators, had founded the National Teachers Federation. The new organization accepted only classroom teachers as members.[37] This action was presumably still fresh in Otis's mind when he wrote his speech.

As Scott recalled, the 1907 arrangements committee read Otis's speech and found it inappropriate. Moore had the responsibility to point this out to Otis. Otis, well known for his open-shop sentiments, had apparently prepared a speech that read like an anti-union tract. Moore, aware of potential teacher militancy, explained to Otis that many of the teachers were from working-class backgrounds and would find an anti-union speech offensive. Otis refused to change a word, and Moore was forced to find another speaker.* After that, Otis tried to make life miserable for both the board members and Moore. Scott, a board member since 1904, stood steadfastly behind Moore. Nevertheless, Moore, who was reelected as superintendent in 1910, resigned that year to return to academic pursuits as professor of education at Yale and then at Harvard. When he returned

*Moore presented a different view of this incident, focusing not on Otis as a speaker at the 1907 convention, but rather on his contribution to a guidebook that city leaders had been asked to prepare for the NEA meeting. In his function as a member of the committee charged with the final decision on publication, Moore insisted that the guidebook not be published because Otis's anti-union article would prove offensive to the teachers. Moore later noted that he was on Otis's "blacklist." The *Times* editor is reported to have treated Moore "as if he was dead." Moore termed Otis an "unscrupulous enemy" after the *Times* accused Moore of pandering to the wishes of non-Christians by taking Christ's name out of closing school exercises held the day before Christmas vacation. Moore called the accusation untrue, but reminded the community that the Constitution clearly separates church and state, and that Jewish parents look to him "to protect their children" just as others do to protect theirs from "any favor of denominationalism or irreligious teaching" (*Los Angeles Herald*, Dec. 18, 1907, John Randolph and Dora Haynes Collection, box 134, UCLA).

to Los Angeles in 1917, it was as head of the Normal School, and he guided that institution through its transformation into the University of California, Southern Branch, and served as its first president.[38]

The Otis-Scott battle continued and became more and more public. In 1910 Los Angeles had been shocked by the dynamiting of the *Times* publishing plant, where twenty-one men died, and the subsequent arrest of pro-labor activists. The case stimulated national attention, and the American Federation of Labor's chief, Samuel Gompers, personally asked the famous lawyer Clarence Darrow to take the case. As soon as Darrow arrived in Los Angeles, he hired Scott to assist him, thinking that Scott's reputation—a Republican in such good standing that, at an event welcoming touring President William Howard Taft in 1909, he was a principal speaker—would help the defense. Scott joined the defense team of the accused McNamara brothers, much to the consternation of Otis.[39] James B. McNamara's confession destroyed the case for the defense and left many in Los Angeles and around the nation stunned. After the trial the *Times* used every opportunity to lambaste Scott. During the heated school battles, for instance, articles began with leads such as, "Does Scott Own the Schools?"; and an editorial denounced "one-man rule of any public institution."[40] Scott saved the papers and successfully used them in a civil libel case against the Times Mirror Company in 1915. The case was upheld by the California Supreme Court in 1918.[41]

Scott, Guinn, and Craig chose not to run for reelection in the spring of 1915, and the campaign brought in new members to the board. The most notable addition was Walter Bordwell, who came on as "an avowed neutral," with the largest number of votes of any candidate, and replaced Guinn as board president.[42] Bordwell had served as judge during the McNamara trial, and from his large margin in the 1915 election, it appeared that many Los Angeles citizens approved of his handling of the case and thought he would manage the school board perplexities with similar judicial style.[43]

It was not immediately clear which way the board was headed. Charges continued to be lodged against the schools' management, intimating that Francis was still in trouble, but Francis ably fended off each new wave of distrust. In the winter of 1916, at the superintendent's suggestion, the board decided to hire an expert to make a survey of the schools. Bordwell asked university presidents Nicholas Murray Butler of Columbia and Harry Pratt Judson of Chicago to recommend "disinterested" experts. Butler and Judson recommended Albert Shiels and Walter Jessup.[44] Both arrived a few months later and set to work. Archetypes of administrative progressives, Shiels was head of the New York City school district's Department of Reference and Research, and Jessup was the dean of education (and future president) of the State University of Iowa. Both had good publishing records.[45]

Their survey, the *Report of the Advisory Committee to the Board of Education of the City of Los Angeles,* found no evidence of any wrongdoing or mismanagement on Francis's part and, in fact, praised his Americanization programs. But Francis did not wait for this vindication; he resigned in early May before the survey had been completed. Tired of the controversy, he returned to Ohio to become the superintendent of schools in Columbus that September.*

One of his last acts as superintendent was to protect the positions of some of his loyalest faculty, particularly Assistant Superintendent Grace Fuller. Fearing that the new board wanted to rid the district of any remnant of the controversy, Francis decided to renew teaching contracts earlier than usual. On June 1, 1916, the board met to review the contracts of Fuller and forty-one teachers. An overflow crowd of clubwomen, teachers, and representatives of parent-teacher organizations greeted members when they arrived at the meeting. Within minutes it was clear that the board would not be intimidated. No amount of pleading, no student petitions, would save Fuller's position. She was dismissed, along with sixteen of the teachers. Bordwell had not been swayed, and his comments make his motives

*Polytechnic High was renamed John H. Francis Polytechnic High School in 1934, at the time of Francis's death. A bust of the former superintendent adorns the entrance to the school, now located in the San Fernando Valley.

clear. In the best interests of the schools, he said, those teachers who "actively participated in offensive agitation" were "in direct violation to the known wishes of the board of education" and would not be retained. Teachers must be nonpolitical and nonpartisan.[46]

The man who replaced Francis, Albert Shiels, who came to investigate and stayed to superintend, was at least as interested in offering the children of Los Angeles a varied curriculum as Francis, although Shiels was careful to cloak his plans in terms of fiscal prudence and to pay close attention to his job's restrictions.[47] He may have talked economy, but in his brief three-year tenure he expanded both services and curriculum. Remembered for his organizational skills, Shiels left his mark on the city schools for his expansion of the Department of Vocational Education and creation of a Department of Research and Development with special emphasis on intelligence testing. Teachers may have been the losers. They were given a strong message not to take part in political campaigns and never to cross the Board of Education.

Shiels and the War Effort

One of Shiels's first acts as superintendent was to initiate a series of pamphlets advertising school services. The first, *Health Supervision in Los Angeles City Schools*, published in June 1917, was written by the director of the Health Department, and Shiels wrote the introduction. It regaled the reader with marvelous photographs and copies of school health forms, with an accompanying text that explained all the intricacies of the Health Department. The pamphlets continued through the 1940's and followed the same pattern, with each either featuring one department or publicizing special activities, in the manner of the 1918 *Los Angeles City Schools and the War*, the tenth in the series.

Shiels, like Francis, had an interest in the problem of assimilation. As a principal in New York, he had sought to expand his school's evening classes and Americanization programs. Shortly before he left his job as the city's director of Reference and Research, he edited a pamphlet, *The School and the Immigrant*, and wrote two of the six articles. The pamphlet covered such topics as occupations for foreign workers, the development of social and recreational activities, civics, methods for teaching English, and naturalization.[48]

Also like his predecessor, Shiels expanded curriculum in the elementary schools. By 1916, for instance, Utah Street School, in the heart of the Molokan district, had grown from four teachers in 1904 to twenty-four, including a playground teacher, and offered classes in textiles, sewing, gardening, cooking, manual training (sloyd), drawing, and weaving, along with regular academic subjects. Ann Street, the site of one of the first penny-lunch programs, offered the same diversified curriculum and, in addition, had classes in laundry and manual arts.[49]

Shiels confronted unprecedented educational problems in directing the schools through the war years. The United States had cut off diplomatic relations with Germany only four months after he took over, and by April 1917, when President Wilson declared war on the Central Powers, war was on everyone's mind. The city had hosted a Preparedness Parade the year before in which 69,000 enthusiastic marchers participated, with many thousands of other enthusiasts watching. The *Times* reported that a "spirit of Americanism echoed in the sturdy tramp of marching thousands." Los Angeles escaped the disturbances that plagued San Francisco's Preparedness Parade. That unfortunate event saw the death of ten marchers and resulted in the arrest and tumultuous trial of the socialist labor agitator Thomas Mooney. By comparison, Los Angeles stood forth as the very model of patriotism and tranquility. The main concern there was strengthening the military installations. Alarmists had warned that an unfortified harbor spelled disaster for the area, and their campaign succeeded in bringing a reorganized and strengthened National Guard Company and the long awaited completion of Fort MacArthur at San Pedro.[50]

Not all the military activity centered on the harbor. Affairs south of the border were a particular preoccupation after President Wilson released the Zimmermann telegram on March 1,

1917. The infamous telegram, from the German foreign secretary to the German minister in Mexico, suggested that in the event of war with the United States, Mexico might consider alliance with Germany. In return, a victorious Germany would restore territories Mexico had lost in war with the United States—including California.[51] Legitimate fears and a dose of xenophobia combined to produce a tightening of patrols along the Mexican border and the beefing up of the California Engineers unit of the National Guard.

Not surprisingly, the first ethnic group to feel the negative repercussions of the war was the city's German community. Xenophobia struck Los Angeles no less forcibly than other sections of the country, and anti-German feelings ran strong. The German community had long played an active part in the city and in its schools. Germans had established a Turnverein society by 1870 that reflected the religious diversity of the German community. Many of the founders were Jews. According to Harris Newmark, the pioneer city chronicler, after a humble beginning the Turnverein-Germania erected its own building on Spring Street and founded a German school. Based on models elsewhere, the society offered a complete athletic program.[52]

Turnverein Hall soon attained such eminence that civic and theatrical groups rented it for performances. In January 1878 the city feasted on theatricals by a visiting troupe of actors led by the flamboyant John W. "Captain Jack" Crawford.[53] A few years later the city school system used it for high school commencement exercises. The German school first met in the Round House, a popular, circular-shaped meeting house, but in 1883 its patrons petitioned the board for the use of a room to conduct a late-afternoon "German School." German Americans also helped organize the short-lived Cosmopolitan School. They exerted considerable influence on the schools in part because of the sheer size of their population. In 1908 German children constituted the largest ethnic group in the schools; out of a total school enrollment of 33,422, 2,431 students were German-born or children of Germans, including 406 students who were classified as Hebrew Germans.[54]

Yet the German community, integrated and respected as it

was, could not escape the anti-German feelings the war had created. The Turnverein-Germania leased its building to the city in 1919. In the mid-1920's, when anti-German hysteria had subsided, the society built a new structure on West Washington Street, closer to the members' settlements in the newer, western sections of the city.

The war turned many Americans against all things German. German-language classes were canceled in January 1918; an exception was made for high school seniors who expected to conclude their course of study by June. German music also became suspect and was officially suppressed.[55] The board was flooded with requests to replace the word kindergarten with something more American sounding, but in the absence of an agreeable alternative, "kindergarten" endured. Petitioners asked that pro-German references in textbooks be removed. In December 1918 the board called for a full examination of all textbooks by the State Commission of Education. Teachers accused of pro-German sympathies, or at least not being anti-German enough, had to prove their allegiance or face dismissal. Some German American teachers changed their names: Myrtle Domerhaussen, an elementary teacher, became Myrtle Domer. At the same time Superintendent Shiels tried to reassure the members of the German American community that the school system's hostility was directed at Germany, not at them.[56]

Supporting the war effort became a high priority for all American educators. Arthur Dean, professor of vocational education at Columbia's Teachers College, rushed his book, *Our Schools in War-Time and After*, into print in 1918. John Dewey, in the first of a series of pamphlets prepared for the government describing how Americans at home might help the war effort, proposed that students and teachers aid the war effort by serving on the nation's farms. Dewey's 1917 work bore the subtitle, "A Message on How Schoolchildren Can Aid the Nation," and outlined a program designed to avoid any suggestion of European militarism. A pacifist before the United States entered the war, Dewey tried to reconcile his old beliefs with his current ones. Children should not "monkey with" rifles, he said. But there was work for them that was "important, valuable and educational."[57]

Like Dewey, Shiels had had little taste for a military adventure before the war. But he too supported the war effort after America's intervention. He provided for the students and teachers to help local groups roll bandages, pick crops when laborers left the fields for war duty, and other activities, and arranged leaves for teachers who enlisted in the military. He had not had much taste for military education, either, after Congress passed the National Defense Act in 1915, setting up funds for an elaborate Junior Reserve Officer's Training Corps program. Not long after, in September 1916, the Los Angeles Chamber of Commerce recommended establishing the program in high schools. Shiels, who had only just taken up his post, responded by saying that this was a matter for board members and parents to decide. "I have no interest in the so-called military spirit and do not favor it," he told the *Times*. "If military training is introduced into the high schools merely to fit the young men for efficiently defending their country and for no other purpose, its results would be beneficial."[58] The board was torn, but the new president, Bordwell, favored the idea, thus settling the issue. By 1918, some 3,000 boys were enrolled in the JROTC. Though all the funding came from the federal government, including the salaries of the military officer–instructors, the Military Department remained under school supervision.[59]

Shiels appointed a school general committee to oversee all other committees until the hostilities ended. He initiated special programs and channeled existing programs into war-related lessons. English classes became courses in patriotism; oral and written themes extolled American greatness more than ever. Under his auspices the Manual Training departments conducted a survey in late June and listed names of students in the various technical fields. The survey enumerated those pupils ready to serve their nation as, for example, telephone operators and electricians.

As war fever intensified, government officials, in an attempt to keep an eye on the foreign population, began registering aliens. Los Angeles county alone registered 4,000 in 1917.[60] The city's foreign-born population had remained fairly constant since the turn of the century, hovering between 18 and 19 percent. However, the percentage of foreign-born children or children of the foreign-born in the schools was considerably higher. In 1920 they accounted for 20,728 of the 50,445 students—or a full 41 percent of the total school population.[61]

Since this part of the student body was growing rapidly—in 1908 the figure had been slightly under a third[62]—it is hardly surprising to find that both Shiels and the board were willing to invest heavily in immigrant education. They simply saw a need that had to be filled.*

The war did not stop the school reformers' initiatives. The war years saw more and more programs installed, not only in the evening schools but also in the day schools. Prewar programs were expanded, and new ones were introduced. Neighborhood schools, for example, offered more rooms than ever to teach English to foreign children. The city's women's clubs, with help from school officials, also actively engaged in Americanization activities. They arranged for teachers to instruct mothers in English in their homes, and they organized elaborate bazaars and pageants to honor and recognize the immigrant heritage.[63]

Yet none of this was without conflict, with the result that educators found themselves deeply involved in issues that influenced and changed their policy on immigrant education. Efforts to reinforce Anglo-American culture and language took hold in Los Angeles, and school people acted accordingly. That reflected the changes taking place throughout the nation. The war created a new dilemma for many Progressives and forced them to redefine their ideas of Americanization, a program with little theoretical base. Within a few years many would join with other Americans in campaigning for stricter immigration laws. But in the years surrounding the war, Progressives still thought that democracy would prevail, and they placed much of their hope in the public schools. Schools became the bulwark of Americanization efforts.

*Indeed even before Shiels entered the scene, Los Angeles had a reputation throughout the state as a model for immigrant education. A 1915 pamphlet published by the California Commission of Immigration and Housing proclaimed: "Los Angeles pays more attention to the education of the immigrant than other California cities" (CCIH pamphlet 1, p. 1, in John Mury Collection, Bancroft Library, University of California, Berkeley).

The California Home Teacher Act of 1915

In 1915, four years after California women won the right to vote, the California legislature passed the Home Teacher Act. The first of its kind in the nation, the act was designed to Americanize immigrant women, mothers who normally did not seek English or naturalization classes elsewhere. It stipulated that certified teachers only, trained in special courses, were to teach these women, and that each of these teachers was to be assigned to a regular elementary school and be directly responsible to the school's principal.

The Home Teacher Act provides a splendid opportunity to study the politics of reform on several levels. On one level it illustrates the new political power of recently enfranchised women and their strategies to continue their social reforms. It also suggests that women successfully campaigned for reform where they had traditional ties and alliances. On another level the act shows how special interest groups used the schools to promote particular programs and demonstrates the pressures the schools were under to accommodate powerful organizations like the General Federation of Women's Clubs. And on still another level it gives glimpses of the struggles of female teachers to upgrade their status and to strengthen their position within the profession. In this case professionalization meant that a group of elementary teachers seized the opportunity to improve their positions and create a specialized department within the school bureaucracy.

The need to continue Americanization programs was apparent to most educators in the years immediately before the war, and it comes as no surprise that Shiels passed on his concerns to the board. "Very great progress has been made in the education of our immigrant populations," he wrote in March 1917, "so that they may not be a menace to the city of Los Angeles."[64] Shiels sought to assure board members that intensive mechanisms to Americanize immigrants were in place. Conscious of the growing ethnic diversity in the schools, Shiels and his native-born, white board feared the impact of unassimilated immigrants on the city's cultural homogeneity. The war had heightened fears they and many Americans of similar background had, dark views that too much diversity would result in a balkanized society. Shiels contended that he had the situation well in hand, and that more intensive measures to assimilate immigrants had begun.

The initiation of various social services in the schools by previous boards had been applauded by many Angelenos. At times there was an almost downright euphoria about what was possible, as when a 1912 *Examiner* headlined an article on a PTA program for free orthodontia in the schools in this fashion: SCHOOLS HERE WILL BEAUTIFY UGLY CHILDREN.[65] Rearranging "ill-proportioned faces" sounds extreme, but such things as tub baths and model cottages seem quite in keeping with the spirit and purpose of the Home Teacher Act. And if immigrant women could not attend the evening school, a volunteer would arrange a time and place to suit their convenience.

The continued efforts of educators and reformers to provide care for the immigrants took the form of benevolent paternalism. Their paternalism was shaped in part by their hope to control immigrants, to set standards for them, to uplift and turn them into acceptable Americans. But in the best sense, true Progressives that they were, they were guided by the optimistic belief that a better life was within everyone's reach and saw themselves, the right-thinking and morally sound, as the medium to make it all possible. Reverend Dana Bartlett of the Bethlehem Church and Settlement, the quintessence of a civic-minded reformer, for example, had devoted most of his time to working with the city's poor, and he perhaps expressed better than anyone the reformers' uplifting views. He and the PTA shared goals of beautification—he wished to beautify the city and the PTA wished to "beautify ugly children."

In his 1909 book, *The Better City*, Bartlett wrote: "Ugliness has no commercial or ethical value. The crowded tenement, the rookery, a city's ill-kept streets and yards are not incentives to higher living."[66] By helping the poor to overcome their misfortunes, Progressives like Bartlett hoped to help everyone. Bartlett never raised the issue of paternalism because of an unswerving faith that the solution to society's ills lay precisely in that method of help. "It is a question of how much philanthropy helps solve the problems of the world," he wrote, and "as long as there are forces at work producing conditions which make for poverty and dependency, no one will deny that it is a splendid charity."[67] Bartlett, along with many civic leaders in Los Angeles, anticipated an acceleration in the size of the immigrant population that would force reformers to invest ever-more energy in education.

And indeed the city was thriving. Its population grew from 102,479 in 1900 to 576,673 in 1920. The growth in area was equally spectacular; in 1900 the city had an area of 43.26 square miles; in 1920 it had 363.92. By then it was the nation's tenth-most-populous city (soon, in 1930, to rank fourth). Its harbor handled more tonnage than San Francisco's, and it was now not only the largest city on the Pacific Slope but in many ways the most modern city in the nation.[68] As early as 1910 the automobile had come into general use in the city, and its easy acceptance soon made it symbolic of Southern California. In 1915 the *Times* ran an article entitled "Old Horseman Dead," telling of an old man watching a city street all afternoon to see a horse go by. After five hours and no horses, the forlorn man turned on the gas. The horse business was dead, and so was he.[69] Los Angeles had become a major city, and California a major state; its citizens looked to the future, not to the past.

The phenomenal growth called for more planning. Reorganization and bureaucratization characterized the period. In 1913 California's Republican governor, Hiram Johnson, had formed several state commissions, one of them, Immigration and Housing, designed to study potential growth. Johnson predicted that the opening of the Panama Canal in 1915 would heighten foreign migration into the state from Europe, and he wanted his government prepared. Not everyone reacted favorably to the new governor, his Progressive views, or the commissions. Otis and his son-in-law, Harry Chandler, disliked Johnson, and the feeling was mutual. Johnson once described Otis as "vile, infamous, degraded, and putrescent."[70] The *Times* complained that California was overburdened with commissions. Johnson had enlarged existing ones and created new ones at such a rate that by late 1914 the state had spent over $3,500,000 on them.[71]

But Johnson had great support, especially among women. He came to office on a Progressive Republican ticket that owed much of its success to their hard campaigning throughout the state. His victory was theirs, ushering in a new political period in which women gained the vote and with it, full citizenship. Johnson repaid some debts by appointing thirteen women to various state commissions.[72]

Johnson devised the Commission of Immigration and Housing to study all problems associated with immigration. The 1913 Wheatland labor riots in the hop fields of Yuba County, near Marysville, impelled the commission to investigate both labor and living conditions of the state's workers. Its tasks included determining the number and distribution of immigrants; looking into their industrial opportunities and informing potential employers of their availability; investigating housing conditions; finding ways to assimilate immigrants; and setting up a bureau of complaints to hear immigrant grievances. The commission had three offices: the main one in San Francisco, with two branches in Sacramento and Los Angeles.[73]

Two people closely associated with the commission had connections with Los Angeles schools, civic organizations, and immigrants—the reverend Dana Bartlett and Mary Simons Gibson. Bartlett, well-known for church and settlement work and for his involvement in the 1913 Pacific Coast Immigrant Congress in San Francisco, served on the committee that tailored the commission for the governor. Gibson then served on the commission itself.[74]

Gibson, a native of the Santa Clara Valley, moved to Los Angeles in 1878, where she taught in the fledgling schools as one of eighteen teachers. She married businessman and president-to-be of the Board of Education, Frank Gibson, in 1881, and began the civic work that built her reputation as a Progressive reformer. She had toiled tirelessly for women's suffrage, and she was an ardent supporter of Johnson. He could hardly have picked a more qualified and dedicated person. In a few years

Katherine Philips Edson, another Johnson appointee, would consider Gibson "the most important woman in Southern California and I think in the state."[75]

Before suffrage Gibson epitomized women's reliance on their own institutions to change public policy; she continued the tradition after California women gained the vote. Her work on the Immigration and Housing Commission, characterized by that reliance, had wide-reaching effects on immigrants and educators. As a major author of the commission's first report, issued in 1915, Gibson, along with Amanda Mathews Chase, set up the machinery to bring teachers into immigrant homes on a regular basis.

The assimilation of immigrant mothers seemed an urgent problem to Gibson and her fellow reformers because they saw foreign women losing control of their English-speaking children. The 1915 report stated: "With the woman in her poor home there are few points of contact with educational opportunities. The Americanization of the children in public schools often adds to her difficulties. The children take command of the home and become ashamed of the mothers. By statistics it was found that this is adding to delinquency and filling juvenile courts." The authors assured the readers that the quickest way to alleviate the problem would be "to educate the women in our language, our laws, and our standard of living." The commission proposed legislation to train special teachers in Americanization.[76]

As an architect of the Home Teacher Act, Gibson was surprised and chagrined when certain educators and church groups opposed it. These nay-sayers raised questions about the potential for conflict in Americanization programs, particularly those intended for adults. Critics claimed that the act was paternalistic and an invasion of the home. Moreover, they regarded it as an attempt to defraud the children for whom school monies had been raised in the first place.

Undaunted, Gibson went on the attack. She called on associates in the California Federation of Women's Clubs and the Women's Legislative Council of California, the legislative arm of the women's movement, to support the bill. Clubwomen prepared a program to convert the opposition that included lobbying, fund-raisers, and publicity, complete with tools such as visual aids—all methods used during the suffrage struggles.[77]

Gibson sought to appeal to the widest audience. First she focused on the family. Rather than viewing the immigrant mother as the family anchor, she argued that immigrant families suffered in the United States because the women had lost the respect of their Americanized children and husbands. The women maintained their foreign customs and behavior long after the rest of the family had assimilated. As a result they had become a source of shame to their acculturated families. In districts where evening schools offered classes in English and in citizenship, adult children and workingmen attended, but their mothers or wives did not. The disproportionately high numbers of children of immigrants in juvenile court stood as testimony to the breakdown of the family. The Home Teacher Act would bring schooling directly to mothers, and thereby save the family. Success depended on foreign women molding their children into model American citizens; under the rubric of "republican motherhood," foreign mothers would regain their rightful place within their families.[78]

Second, Gibson appealed to patriotism. Radicals had made deep inroads into immigrant communities, she noted, pointing to the involvement of the Industrial Workers of the World in the 1913 Wheatland riots to underline the urgency of her plea. Lessons in the English language and in American customs, laws, values, and culture, such as the Home Teacher Act provided would be an antidote to radicalism.[79] (She might have offered an equally important reason for teaching women English. Under federal naturalization laws foreign wives automatically became citizens with their husbands. Husbands needed to learn English and comply with the law's requirements, but not wives. California's new suffrage law made it possible for non-English-speaking, non-Americanized wives to vote.)

Gibson's third approach, her trump card, was to appeal to educators on the grounds that the Home Teacher Act would improve the status of the teaching profession. Many Americans still thought of elementary instructors as "girl teachers" and questioned whether they had the training to prepare the future generation in the important task of citizenship.[80] Even less trained were the people who taught the English-language classes. Up to this point most of the work had been handled by volunteers from various organizations, few of whom were licensed teachers. Because each group worked autonomously, there was no overall direction or any guidelines to follow.[81]

In creating the Home Teacher Act, Gibson hoped to carve out a small but secure niche for female administrators. It was a goal that moved beyond the concept of female teachers as nurturers toward treating them as professionals. Professionalization had earlier swept through the ranks of education, raising the status of male administrators. Boards of education, modeled on corporations, initiated policy, and their hand-picked superintendents implemented policy. Superintendents, almost exclusively men, held advanced degrees from the new schools of education. Classroom teachers, too, had to meet higher standards, particularly in the elementary schools; but because these positions had become associated with women, the higher standards did not mean higher status. Almost the entire corps of elementary teachers in 1915 was female, yet barely a handful of women rose to administration echelons or became principals above the elementary-school level.[82]

Moreover, teachers were expected to conform to the dictates of an impartial school board that had little knowledge of their teaching, but nevertheless maintained direct control over them and their students. Women teachers had fought for respect in the profession by joining the NEA in 1866, the first year that they were admitted, but the organization treated them as second-class citizens. They attended meetings but were required to sit in the galleries and could not participate. Finally, as we have seen, in a move to find a voice within the profession, female teachers joined together in 1899 to form a society open only to classroom teachers, the National Teachers Federation.[83]

Although Gibson's proposed bill passed with only two dissenting votes and Governor Johnson signed it into law, she failed to obtain the support of the state's educators. They stuck to their guns, insisting that public schools were for children. Moreover, they opposed hiring home teachers because they refused to go against the conventional wisdom that argued, "Americanize the children and the children will Americanize the home." What made matters even more difficult for Gibson, the act provided no money to bring in teachers on a trial basis. Yet always the consummate politician, she found a way to implement her policy: she enlisted the Daughters of the American Revolution, a group famous for its patriotism, to sponsor the initial program.[84]

Gibson asked Amanda Mathews Chase to volunteer as a home teacher for one year, with her salary to be paid by the DAR,[85] and she asked a school district friendly to the idea of adult education, structured for immigrant women, to work with Chase. Los Angeles became the demonstration site.[86]

Amanda Chase seemed well suited to introduce the new program. Chase exemplified the idea of the "new woman" as a professional. She had graduated from Los Angeles High School in 1886, held a university degree, lived in the College Settlement for a time, and had many years of teaching experience, first in Los Angeles and then in Mexico City. She was considered fluent in Spanish and had traveled extensively, lectured, and published stories and articles.[87]

Los Angeles appeared equally well suited as a place to demonstrate the act's effectiveness. The schools had sponsored evening classes in English since the beginning of the century, and in 1906 the board had created a position of assistant superintendent in charge of evening schools. Through the years several school board members showed ambivalence toward the expansion of the evening schools, but Superintendents Foshay, Moore, and Francis had supported them wholeheartedly and had developed programs that catered to the growing immigrant population. To train teachers in immigrant education, the Los Angeles Normal School had instituted a special class taught by Ruby Baughman, a talented teacher with experience working with immigrant children in the Montana mining towns of Butte and Helena.[88]

Between 1911 and 1915 enrollment in the Los Angeles elementary evening schools almost tripled. Neighborhood schools offered unique citizenship programs and operated social centers based on settlement-house models. Graduates of the evening schools' citizenship classes were considered so competent, and the program itself so successful, that federal and superior court judges arranged with naturalization officers to grant citizenship to any alien on the presentation of a diploma. Los Angeles was the first school system in the nation where this was done. In its 1915 report the Immigration and Housing Commission singled out the program, remarking that "the holders of these diplomas are much better prepared to appreciate the values and duties of citizenship than are those aliens who pass a more or less perfunctory examination in the courts, after a haphazard individual course of study."[89]

Gibson most likely had Shiels's support from the beginning, but he had promised the board a policy of strict economy, and he had no intention of letting himself be trapped into moving ahead of the board as Francis had done. Gibson would have to convince the board that additional funds for immigrant women would be well spent. She began a campaign to sell the Home Teachers Act to the city of Los Angeles.

Since state funding had not been pushed in the effort to get the act enacted, it was essential to procure adequate local funding. Each city district would have to provide the teachers' salaries and other necessities. Gibson changed strategy to convince bureaucrats that the Home Teacher Act would benefit them financially. Working with volunteers from women's clubs and a few paid employees, she arranged for studies to determine how much money had been spent on services for the foreign-born, not only for education but also for programs to combat crime, sickness, poverty, and unemployment. They found that between 1914 and 1915 over $1,200,000 had been spent all told, but that only $40,000, or 3.3 percent, of the money had gone for education. If more was spent on education, she argued, less would be needed for other services. The researchers had prepared colored charts to use in their presentations to the Board of Education, the Chamber of Commerce, the County Board of Supervisors, women's clubs, and other civic organizations. It had a census taken and then had demographic maps drawn up to pinpoint the areas most in need.[90]

Gibson's campaign won the board's support. It accepted Chase as the volunteer home teacher for the first year and hired her the second. In Shiels's first report on Americanization to board members, in March 1917, he took care to assure members that progress had been made to protect the city from the "menace" of unassimilated immigrants before going on to suggest that the board hire home teachers on a permanent basis. "Heretofore Los Angeles has been handicapped by the fact that the teaching force has not had the supervision and experience which are required for successful immigrant education," he noted, and then referring to the class offered by Baughman, he observed: "This year has been exceptionally encouraging . . . but we cannot depend upon gratuitous services of the Los Angeles Normal School. In order that the teachers may have competent supervision and instruction so that the work may be as good or better than that of other cities, a supervisor should be appointed." He recommended Ruby Baughman as supervisor of immigrant education.[91]

Baughman left her position at the Normal School to become the first supervisor of home teachers.[92] She had come to Los Angeles the year women got the vote to begin a career as instructor in the Normal School. Her new position in the public schools was part-time, and her salary only half the amount the other supervisors received. She supplemented that by teaching summer and extension classes for the newly organized University of California, Southern Branch. By June 1918 the number of home teachers had grown to twelve. Baughman, an innovative supervisor who was well aware that many foreign women held outside jobs, arranged for the teachers to hold classes in their workplaces as well as in their homes. She urged employers to support her instruction and persuaded some to pay the cost of developing appropriate teaching manuals.[93] Yet the more she accomplished, the more she realized how much there was to do. How could a handful of teachers tackle the job of Americanizing the increasing immigrant population? In 1920 a fifth of the city's population was foreign-born, and only a handful attended Americanization classes, including home classes for foreign women. A survey that year showed the irregular attendance pattern: of the 3,448 people who began the program, 141 never returned after the first meeting, and only 322 completed the course.[94]

Something was amiss, and reformers stumbled around for a solution to the perplexing question of why immigrants were not assimilating at a faster rate. Gibson and her followers had been convinced that the Home Teacher Act was one answer, that the solution was to break down cultural patterns at their source, in the home and with the mother. Simply learning English would not Americanize foreign women; they also had to practice American middle-class customs and habits. Learning to set a proper tea table and maintaining certain standards of cleanliness became synonymous with Americanism.

Immigrants, however, did not always welcome the notion of a tea table in their homes, and their perceptions often conflicted with those of the people attempting to reform them. A tea table in a Molokan Russian home must have perplexed more than one family whose tea was served from samovars, not teapots. Molokans ate meals out of communal bowls and used wooden spoons; women ate after the men and children had finished. Although immigrants wanted their children to learn English in order to survive in the United States, they did not want them to become so Americanized that they were no longer Molokan, or Japanese, or Mexican. A proper tea table was not necessary for survival.

Most Americans viewed assimilation as a step forward. If learning to serve tea in a prescribed way furthered assimilation, then why not learn it? This conflict of perceptions between native Americans and immigrants remained unresolved and became the core problem of Americanization.

In their efforts to influence foreign women, Gibson, Chase, and Baughman devised a program they felt would come closest to their goals. The program featured professionally trained teachers, steeped in the intricacies of immigrant education. Their qualifications would parallel those of regular teachers. In addition, they required that teachers have some knowledge of household duties and child care. They also required home teachers to be well versed in the principles of government and the duties of citizenship, and all expressed the hope that the teachers would be familiar with the customs and language of their pupils. The 1916 edition of *The Home Teacher* presented a working plan for teaching rudimentary English and American-style homemaking: "We sew, We cook, You iron, You mop," in Lesson Two; "I take off the dirty sheets, I put on the clean pillowcases," in Lesson Eight. By the final lessons the women were learning how to "attractively set a tea table" and how to sing "America the Beautiful."[95]

The home-teacher program extended the first assimilation work done in Los Angeles's foreign district. The presence of Gibson, Chase, and Baughman accelerated it, and the new act institutionalized it. Whatever success the program had was attributed to Gibson, dubbed the "fairy godmother" of the Pacific Coast immigrants.[96] Susan Dorsey, superintendent from 1919 to 1929, summed up Gibson's achievements on her death in 1930: "thousands of foreign mothers in this city alone have been reduced from hopeless dependency, . . . have learned the language and have come to look upon this strange land as their home."[97]

Dorsey exaggerated, but not a whole lot. By 1923, just eight years after Gibson's act was passed, Los Angeles had forty-seven home teachers.[98] An interesting side effect of the program was the hiring of a Chinese-American in 1919 to teach predominantly but not exclusively Asian women. That was surely unusual, to say the least, considering the vehemently anti-Asian sentiment then prevailing in California. Japanese especially and Asians generally were held in contempt. Others joined the teaching staff not many years later. Katharine Chan soon joined her sister Carolyn, and both were employed by the Los Angeles schools during the 1920's; although Katharine disappeared from the *City Directory* in 1929, Carolyn remained an active teacher until 1945.[99]

One reason for the early acceptance of the Americanization programs was the support given them by Superintendent Shiels, whose experience in the New York public schools taught him the value of immigrant education. In 1910 70 percent of New York's school population was foreign-born or second generation.[100] Shiels, with a Progressive's propensity for bureaucratic reorganization, reshaped the Los Angeles evening schools in the hope that they would eliminate many of the problems an increasing foreign population might cause in the city. He had hired Baughman to coordinate the instruction of teachers. Two years later he recommended that Americanization be made a separate function of the evening schools. Shiels sought to make the program more efficient by separating Americanization classes from the regular evening classes and by hiring qualified teachers at a "living wage."[101] In 1919 and 1920 the district hired thirteen home teachers and fifteen Americanization teachers.

According to Baughman, the district held classes in labor camps, factories, canneries, and nurseries, and in less "strategic points," such as hospitals, a Red Cross salvage shop, boarding houses, and Pullman cars.[102] The determination of school people made it almost impossible for immigrants to escape some measure of indoctrination. Yet Baughman was not totally satisfied with the arrangement. In 1919 she complained in a Los Angeles school publication that "Americanization is a sideline, an addendum, an afterthought, a compromise, in too many different departments of education, social, and governmental activity." Because of its experimental nature, she urged that it be "crystallized into a definite form," with state and national support.[103]

In 1921 Baughman again pointed out some of the program's defects. Writing in the American Academy of Political and Social Science's *Annals*, she noted that the public schools' single most important task was to teach a common language. Accomplishing the job, however, had proved difficult, and she considered the task too large for the schools to handle by themselves. She blamed native-born Americans for keeping the immigrant unlettered and doomed to poverty. She saw American society discriminating against foreigners and not accepting them into their community. She reasoned that the schools were completely responsible for illiteracy among native speakers but not among the foreign-born. Local industry must become involved, if the problem was to be overcome, she said, and she cited the example of the Industrial Relations Department of the Fruit Growers Exchange, which had issued a textbook of lessons in industrial English, compiled by Baughman. The exchange also hired teachers and shared the expenses with the Los Angeles schools.[104]

In this particular industry, the teacher spent her time at the labor camp. Her duties varied from making special provisions for educating the "housemother," a designation Baughman used only for foreign women, to arranging for camp recreation. Baughman targeted Mexican workers for specific attention because she felt that they were exploited more than other immigrant groups. She believed that Mexicans, brought up to do seasonal labor, had different social values because of the temporary nature of their work. She wondered how they could adjust to shifting quarters when their homes had been the center of their life. The same could be said of other migrant peasant groups or of any other migrant immigrant community whose work depended on the capriciousness of agricultural or industrial cycles. But by singling out Mexicans, Baughman showed her concern for the one immigrant group increasing most rapidly in Los Angeles.[105]

Baughman looked to education as the only hope for integrating the alien population, and she emphasized the importance of professionalization. Teachers must be qualified through special courses in immigrant education, such as the ones she had helped organize. Like Gibson and Chase, she stressed the teaching of foreign women. Sensitive to their fears of foreign instructors, she suggested that they should meet in more familiar and less formal settings. She was also sensitive to the teachers' side of things. Unfamiliar with the cultures of immigrant groups in their schools, many felt isolated. Not until the spring of 1919 had they been assembled to discuss their common problems. Not surprisingly, when they did come together, they concluded that the economic and social obstacles their clients faced were more significant than educational ones.[106]

Baughman became a sought-after spokeswoman for teacher education throughout the state. It was not long before the recognition of her talents brought her an invitation to join the Anthropology Department at the University of Minnesota as a lecturer in its program for immigrant education. She joined the faculty in 1920.[107]

Baughman's concept of Americanization had moved beyond the confines of the Home Teacher Act and beyond most Progressives' mixture of humanitarianism and practicality. She believed foreign workers would be less exploited if they knew English and were familiar with American culture, but she also believed that they needed higher wages and better working conditions. Experience had taught her that if the program had any hope of succeeding, there had to be greater flexibility in teaching methods because of the variety of people at whom the course was aimed. All along she remained highly critical of the philosophy behind Americanization. Most of the problems she had encountered with the program had been due to a wrong social emphasis, she claimed. "Throwing the searchlight on the immigrant who is to be assimilated" ignored the mass into which he is to be assimilated. Too many people had proposed all manner of things "to do to him."[108] Quite aware that many immigrants resisted Americanization—in the 1920's, for instance, only one-half of 1 percent of the older Russian Molokans had taken out citizenship papers—she thought a more realistic approach would have neighborhood teachers work with immigrants for years and look to them for help in developing suitable programs.[109]

Gibson, a conventional reformer, could not move beyond the Progressives' prescriptions. She, too, saw the difficulties that faced the program, but her strategies reflected a less radical vision than Baughman's. While Baughman's approach was that of an alert and bold teacher and administrator, with a good understanding of her students and teachers, Gibson's approach was essentially political, practical, and public. For the record at least, she confined her criticism to insufficient resources. The most urgent needs were trained teachers and adult textbooks. In 1918 Gibson began a campaign to establish a permanent place for immigrant education within the federal government. She turned to the General Federation of Women's Clubs, whose two million members offered a large, cohesive army she might enlist. The federation proved her most valuable ally, contributing funds to print pamphlets, organize programs, and provide legal assistance.

Using tactics she had employed at the time of the Home Teacher Act, Gibson appealed to patriotism and to professionalization. This time, perhaps influenced by Baughman, she gave more emphasis to understanding immigrant cultures. And she continued to insist on highly trained teachers, noting how "sad" it would be "to trust a task of exceeding delicacy to amateurs," however "amiable," however "zealous," however—and here she used bold type—"CHEAP."[110] But now she went beyond assurances and warnings. A federal, cabinet-level department of education should be formed.[111]

The times seemed auspicious for that development. In most urban areas professionalization had swept through public schooling on all levels, and educators belonged to a myriad of professional organizations. Professionalization had restructured most urban school boards; experts advised them or administered their schools. University schools of education had become almost solely responsible for teacher education and stimulating the new pedagogy, from intelligence testing to remedial arithmetic. Professors of education had become influential leaders, who served as presidents of universities. In the circumstances, there seemed to be every reason to expect considerable enthusiasm for a separate department.[112] Gibson believed that the future of immigrant education and the advancement of female teachers in that future might be ensured by backing a federal department of education.

Gibson helped mobilize the GFWC to support a department of education in the early 1920's. But as the campaign moved into the mid- and late 1920's, the forces opposed to the bill gathered strength. The historian Lynn Dumenil explains that such diverse groups as states rights politicians, the Catholic church, patriotic organizations, and some former Progressives joined in opposition to expanding federal power in education and its concomitant, standardization.[113]

Although President Warren Harding supported adding a department of education in 1922, Senate Bill 4987, known as the Towner-Sterling bill, did not pass. Not everyone was eager to create a federal bureaucracy of educators, or to take control away from the states and local governments. The conflict reached into the ranks of education. Although the NEA campaigned for it, some educators opposed the move, including Philander Claxton, commissioner of education.*

California had a Department of Education, and there Gibson had influence. In 1917 she had appointed a Bryn Mawr graduate, Ethel Richardson, as head of the Commission of Immigration and Housing's Education Department. Richardson, a former history teacher at Bernedo Intermediate, had made the commission's educational surveys, and her professionalism had impressed Gibson. A few years later, in 1920, Richardson and her department were transferred to the state Department of Education, where Gibson felt they belonged. In that same year, the University of California's extension department set up institutes for teacher training—in Los Angeles, Fresno, and San Francisco.

Summing up what had been achieved by 1925, Gibson noted that nearly 50,000 immigrants had been taught Americanization by 1,000 teachers, and she had convinced "the best educators . . . that public schools are for the whole family."[114] The number of people the program reached continued to be small, yet Gibson felt she had met some of her goals. She had lost the battle on the federal level, but she had succeeded in her home state. The number of home teachers continued to grow—by 1928 there were eighty-three women teaching in fifty-five centers.[115] In California, where women had voted since 1912, Americanization taught by certified teachers had a secure place in public schooling, and a woman administrator, Ethel Richardson, served in the state Department of Education in charge of adult and immigrant education.

In the first decades of the twentieth century, several powerful forces influenced Progressive reformers to redesign the Los

*Herman, "Neighbors," 2: 428–31. Philander Claxton had been asked to review San Francisco's public schools in 1916. His inquiry resulted in the publication of *The Public School System of San Francisco* (1917), which included a section on immigrant education compiled by Frederick B. Farrington, a co-worker of Claxton's at the U.S. Bureau of Education. Farrington emphasized the need to Americanize foreign women.

Angeles public schools. A new city charter in 1903 reorganized the Board of Education to conform to a corporate model and proscribed superintendents from initiating policy. The line between administrators and teachers became more clearly drawn.

With changes in teaching and administration came the recognition that the common-school concept no longer fit the needs of a complex, industrial society, and some educators proposed drastic curricular changes to satisfy various groups in the city. But the self-interest of the different groups created controversy. This conflict of interest developed into a battle for political power, pitting influential citizens against each other. When the dust settled, a clear message had been sent to superintendents and to teachers: the power to make policy resided in the Board of Education.

The First World War and newly enfranchised California women between them turned the main focus of reform on Americanization. Gibson commands our attention not only because of her work in creating the Home Teacher Act, but because she represents the changing attitudes of many female reformers after suffrage. Nancy Cott notes that before they achieved full citizenship, many women reformers spoke of creating a better world. After suffrage their emphasis changed. While many continued to hope for a better world, suffrage empowered them to strike at substantive political objectives that would ensure jobs and positions for women.[116]

Teachers wanted better training for themselves and greater participation in school administration. Ruby Baughman used her position as supervisor of home teachers to become a spokeswoman for specialized teacher training. But even as she was making that move, she was speaking out ever more strongly against the Home Teacher Act's limitations. Gibson had set out to teach immigrant women English and American customs so as to reestablish order in immigrant families and to lessen disorder in society in general. In doing so, she ignored some of the major socioeconomic problems within the immigrant communities. The Home Teacher Act was a band-aid solution to a prodigious problem. When Baughman complained that American industry maintained inequitable practices in its treatment of immigrants, she had moved beyond Gibson and beyond the goals of the Home Teacher Act. Baughman addressed social and political issues that concerned all Americans. At the same time that Baughman criticized aspects of society the Home Teacher Act had not intended to change, she was enhancing her own career. The act had given her opportunities to move beyond public school teaching into administration, and, shortly, to a university position.

The varied forces that gave rise to school reorganization in these years could not overcome the endemic problem of Progressive reform. Most of the changes that reformers proposed cost money, and no one was willing to make the financial commitment that their programs required. The *Los Angeles Express* told its readers that theirs was the most expensive school system in the nation. Should they be asked to pay more?[117] School Board President Bordwell expressed the views of many when he introduced Shiels to the school principals in September 1916: "Economy in the administration of school affairs is as necessary a measure as can be. It is fairness not only to the taxpayer, but to the children and to ourselves. The people will pay almost any amount for the education of their children, but the necessity of a reduction of expense whenever possible cannot be overlooked."[118] Even Progressives were too worried about their pocketbooks to invest enough funds in the programs they claimed to love.

4
"The Best Method of Approach"

> There are experts in Americanization, men and women who have lived for many years as neighbors to the immigrants—who over a long period have studied his situation and his necessities—who understand his psychology, who know the best method of approach.
>
> —*Mary S. Gibson*

Many Americans agreed with Gibson. Americanization, fashioned on the settlement-house model and carried out in the neighborhood schools, was the best system for turning immigrants into acceptable citizens. Yet in turning to segregation, illegal in California and certainly not democratic, the schools worked against a homogeneous society, and, significantly, portrayed the importance of race in American society. The fact that they could follow both policies simultaneously suggests the complexities of the Progressives' character and the contradictions in school reform. It also says much about the ongoing tensions over who controls the schools, the issue that centers around the false notion that politics and education can be separated.

Americanization was in full swing in the Los Angeles public schools when Susan Miller Dorsey became superintendent in early 1920. Albert Shiels had resigned in December to accept a position at Columbia Teachers College. Dorsey had taught in Los Angeles since 1896. A native of the Finger Lakes region of New York, she arrived in Los Angeles in the early 1880's as the bride of Patrick W. Dorsey, a Baptist minister. Their marriage did not thrive, and in the 1890's Dorsey deserted his wife and took their only child, Paul, with him. On her own at age thirty-nine, Dorsey returned to the classroom.* Little is known of her

*Other married women taught in Los Angeles schools. Margaret Collier Graham taught in Los Angeles in the 1880's (Graham to Los Angeles Board

personal life, but a biographer suggested that she and her son did not have a close relationship and an occasional card from him meant a lot to her.[1]

Like the rest of the nation, Los Angeles felt the harsh effects of the 1890's depression, but because it came on the heels of the recession that followed the end of the 1880's land boom, the hard times seemed particularly bleak. Dorsey felt fortunate to find work in the city. Her degree in classics from Vassar College, and her experience as a teacher at Wilson College in Pennsylvania and Vassar, made her an attractive candidate for a position at Los Angeles High School. She rose quickly through the ranks; in 1902 she became a vice-principal, and in 1913 she was appointed an assistant superintendent. In 1912 the State Board of Directors elected her a member, and in 1914 the California Teachers Association elected her president. She worked under both Francis and Shiels until she took over herself and became the second woman to hold the post, the first having served briefly at the beginning of the 1880's.[2] More important, Dorsey became the second woman, after Ella Flagg Young in Chicago, to head a large urban school system.

Dorsey's rise to prominence in a profession where men held most administrative positions attests to her abilities and her political acumen. She was considerably more cautious than her sister superintendent Young and rarely jeopardized her position with the board by challenging its conservative majority.[3] Whereas Young derived much of her support from Chicago's militant teachers and Progressive friends like Dewey and Addams, Dorsey relied in the main on women's clubs and businessmen. But unlike Young, who became superintendent in the midst of the battle for school reform in Chicago, Dorsey took

---

of Education, Aug. 31, 1881, Sept. 1, 1883, Graham Collection, box 16). California law prohibiting married women from teaching in public schools was challenged and overturned in 1929 by *Dutart* v. *Woodward* (99 CA 736, 279 P 493), but there may have been an earlier provision allowing women separated from their husbands for a set amount of time to hold positions. It is not clear when the law prohibiting married women was put into effect or whether school authorities strictly enforced it. In Graham's case, her husband suffered from a debilitating disease and Margaret's work helped support the family. See Clifford, "'Daughters into Teachers.'"

over after reforms had been put in place—and after the First World War, when many Progressives had retreated. Young's support eroded by 1915, and she lost her position, a lesson not lost on Dorsey, who had witnessed Francis's fall. To keep her job Dorsey found and held the middle ground until she retired in 1929, at the age of seventy-two.[4]

Dorsey's ties to women's clubs came through her close association with Mary Gibson. Gibson, Dorsey felt, had exerted an unusually important influence on education in Los Angeles.[5] The two viewed education as the stepping-stone to the betterment of the individual and through the individual, society. Gibson, as we have seen, derived her political support from the General Federation of Women's Clubs. Key national officers resided in the Los Angeles area, including the Federation's founder, Clara Bradley Burdette. At the beginning of the Americanization campaign, the president, Mrs. Evan Cowles, and Mrs. O. Shepard Barnum, chairwoman of the Education Department, lived in or near the city.[6]

Gibson had been instrumental in professionalizing one group of female teachers by upgrading their status and by creating administrative positions for some. But in the course of doing that, she diminished the role of volunteers. Clubwomen must have sensed that professionalization would drive a wedge between professional women and volunteers. They wanted assurance that there was still a need for their work. Moreover, Americanization was too big a project to leave solely to home teachers—a group whose future was not at all secure in the conservative atmosphere after the war. An able and adroit politician, Gibson worked out a program that allowed clubwomen to continue to participate on almost all levels of Americanization except teaching. In this context, volunteers provided a safety net in case funding ceased.

Gibson gave a major role to the General Federation of Women's Clubs. With much fervor, it undertook the task of educating its members in the intricacies of Americanization work in 1918, and envisioned the job as a Second Reconstruction. According to their view, the post–Civil War Reconstruction had failed because it had neglected the very people it had set out to help. Immigrant communities now confronted what black Americans had confronted then: they had been left "unadjusted," thanks to which they constituted 40 percent of the nation's five and a half million illiterates. Federation members feared that like the blacks, the immigrants would remain an underclass, and they sought to prevent that by forming a centralized Americanization program, with themselves in command. They dedicated themselves to seeing that their "reconstruction" did not neglect the immigrants' education as the previous one had neglected the freedmen's.[7]

Such views did not translate into wishes for social equality. The federation had widely discussed the issue of black women's membership at its convention in Los Angeles in 1902, and a report in the *Los Angeles Herald* termed the color issue "vexing." Vexing or not, Progressive women like Caroline Severance, who had been an ardent abolitionist, rather than cause an irreversible rift in the organization, went along with the majority and decided to allow each state to decide which clubs to admit to the federation. Black women were excluded and formed their own separate national group, the National Association of Colored Women's Clubs.[8]

The General Federation developed an elaborate program for Americanization, always mindful that its direct application should be left in the hands of qualified teachers. In order to give female teachers a larger voice in policy-making, Gibson proposed to the federation that it throw its support to the Towner-Sterling bill to create a federal department of education. Federation members supported the bill, but it failed in Congress.

Other parts of the program were more successful, notably the arrangement of a series of seminars for members to prepare them to present their programs to local school boards. Ethel E. Robinson, assistant superintendent in charge of Americanization for the California Department of Education, helped prepare the seminars.[9] In 1917 Gibson successfully applied to the California Council of National Defense for funds for the Americanization program. She assigned specific tasks within the immigrant communities to specific women's organizations. The

Women's Christian Temperance Union conducted a housing and recreation survey, the Daughters of the American Revolution arranged patriotic meetings, the Native Daughters of the Golden West organized foreign-language speakers, and the Association of Collegiate Alumnae surveyed working conditions in factories. The program also included projects for industry to be carried out in conjunction with local chambers of commerce.

Gibson brought John Collier to Los Angeles in 1919 as lecturer to Americanization teachers and placed him on the Housing and Immigration Commission as the director of community organization. Known in Progressive circles for his work in New York settlement houses, and later as a crusader for Indian reform, Collier and Gibson became fast friends. At her memorial service, he eulogized her as one who had changed the lives of immigrants.[10]

Gibson designed her program to accommodate a wide range of views. Yet for lack of a comprehensive theory, not unlike the American Legion's "100% Americanism," the federation's Americanization program was fraught with problems, the immigrants' refusal to abandon their native languages and customs being foremost. To its credit, the federation compromised on this issue. The object of cultural hegemony was never in doubt, but to imply that under Gibson's leadership the federation had no sympathy with the immigrants would be untrue.

Gibson's 1918–19 federation pamphlet, *A Suggested Program for Americanization*, reveals that she understood many of the complexities of immigration but had little feel for the economic realities of immigrant life. She thought the analogy of Americans living abroad sufficed to explain the universal peculiarities of immigrants and to illustrate the many ambiguities of people caught in an alien culture: Americans congregating in foreign cities explained the clannishness of immigrants of every kind. Noting that the official outlawing of native languages had proved unsuccessful elsewhere, for instance, with French speakers in Alsace-Lorraine, Gibson suggested that teachers earn the confidence of their intended pupils by learning the culture of the foreign groups in their cities—a rather unrealistic request in the polyglot cities of the early twentieth century.

In Los Angeles the California branch of the federation's Americanization Department organized a "Homeland Exhibit of Arts and Crafts." The pageant, held in Exposition Park in the spring of 1921, charged no admission and reportedly included exhibits from all nations. The public schools also participated. Madilene Verenka, supervisor of kindergartens and primary grades, helped in the planning and she represented her ethnic heritage in the Czechoslovakian exhibit. In a newspaper interview, Gibson pointed to the pageant as an example of what a city could do to promote foreign artwork, and spoke of how the immigrants' economic importance and talents had added to the richness of the city.[11]

The pageant resembled events staged on a much smaller scale by settlement workers and teachers in neighborhood schools to acknowledge what Addams termed "immigrant gifts." The federation's leaders in Americanization, and their friends in the schools, reiterated the old themes of respect for foreign cultures without yielding an inch on the need to assimilate aliens. While Congress debated the implications of the scientific theories of racial superiority and the failure of assimilation because of genetic differences, many influential Angelenos still relied on the old melting pot to render immigrants into good Americans.

The general federation prepared its pamphlets on Americanization at a time of intense xenophobia. The success of the Bolshevik Revolution only heightened the passions stirred up by the war. The threat of socialism from abroad, as well as at home, resulted in the deportation of aliens and the curtailment of Americans' civil liberties. In Los Angeles citizens came before the Board of Education to bring up such questions as whether the United States should recognize Soviet Russia and whether that new government was sending ten million dollars into this country to subvert democracy. Angelenos had a special interest in Mexico, and many thought that the 1910 Revolution had socialist underpinnings that made it unwise to recognize the Mexican government.[12]

These fears coincided with the national educational community's reassessment of pluralism. The Los Angeles *Educational Journal* reported that the Commission on the National Emergency, which reportedly represented "thousands of loyal and patriotic teachers," believed that instructing children in a foreign tongue was "un-American and un-patriotic."[13] The General Federation thought that its members should be made to understand the need for some pluralism in the early stages of settlement but must also understand that its prolongation posed a threat. Unassimilated aliens could not be loyal Americans. To avoid further conflict, the federation reasoned, the country must assimilate the immigrants it already had and control unregulated immigration. This attitude led many California members to advocate Japanese exclusion by 1920.[14]

During Dorsey's tenure interest in Americanization heightened as she and her colleagues continued their crusade to assimilate foreigners. Throughout the 1920's, a decade associated with exclusionary policies, reformers pursued the goal of Americanization in the city schools; specifically, they continued the ideas pioneered by the settlement-house leaders Jane Addams, Dana Bartlett, Mary Gibson, and Amanda Chase. During the period of nativism that followed the war and the Red Scare, and the drive to exclude "unassimilable" aliens, Los Angeles school administrators worked to provide the kind of Americanization that they felt would be most effective and would least antagonize the city's foreign-born population.

Americanization in the 1920's

In 1921 the *School Journal* published a series of articles by teachers in the Americanization program. They are of inestimable value in showing not only how the work progressed but also the wide spectrum of viewpoints that existed among those most closely involved in the Americanization effort.

The junior citizenship program at Central Junior High School represented eleven nationalities and had students whose ages ranged from thirteen to forty. Most of the younger pupils attended all day; the working adults came for half a day. The curriculum emphasized written and spoken English, introduced American customs and holidays, and described civic institutions. Students took field trips to exhibits at local parks and to hear the Philharmonic Orchestra. One teacher noted that some students enjoyed certain events more than others. "Mexicans, Polish and Russians enjoyed rehearsals of the Philharmonic," while "Chinese, Korean and Japanese students received the most pleasure from a visit to the different departments of the Hall of Records."[15]

Another teacher, Margret Dooher, told what happened in her class on "Christening Days":

> Orientals received names teachers may pronounce and names that make them feel "at home." They often choose names they like from the sound, and the teacher says, "Now you are Warren," and the deed is done. On one occasion a Chinese boy said, "I will be Jacob," but in a week he returned with the following: "This name is no good. I have another." "Is Herman good?" a Korean boy asked. The several German girls joyously exclaimed, "Yes, yes; it is good. It is German!" A Mexican girl watched these proceedings several times, and finally when a new Japanese boy arrived, she frantically waved her hand and asked, "Oh, may I be the godmother of the China?"[16]

Dooher's innocent description hardly jibes with Maxine Hong Kingston's accounts. According to her, this kind of Americanization often alienated children from the school and/or the children from their parents. Many times the family chose to ignore the new name, and the children used it only among their English-speaking peers.[17]

In 1920 the Board of Education redesigned the course of study for citizenship. To make the program more efficient and bring it into line with the national model, naturalization became a function separate and apart from the functions of the evening schools. In establishing two departments, Immigrant Education and Naturalization, Los Angeles followed the pattern set by the federal government, where the Bureau of Education, within the Department of Interior, and the Bureau of Naturalization, within the Department of Labor, vied for authority in the campaign to Americanize the foreign-born.[18] But since the Los Angeles system had proved its leadership by being allowed to make school diplomas sufficient proof for naturalization, the new department had little effect on actual procedure.

With the creation of the two departments of Americanization, the old-line Progressives still had the opportunity to carry out their Americanization programs through neighborhood schools, and citizenship training became the sole responsibility of the Department of Naturalization. The division also gave teachers and principals autonomy over their classrooms and their schools by diverting official attention away from the day-to-day details of Americanization. William M. Bell, for example, who worked with adults in San Pedro, had the leeway to construct his classes as he saw fit. Bell's class met twice a week for ten weeks; over 200 men and women completed the course and became citizens.

From his article in the *School Journal*, we gain some insight into why certain immigrants chose to become citizens. A variety of ethnic groups lived near the harbor. "Dalmatians and Jugo-Slavs" were the most numerous, followed by Swedes and Danes and then Englishmen and Canadians. Many of the men were fishermen, and "the law of the state requires that no man may be the captain of a boat even though he be the owner, unless he is a citizen." Bell wrote that he could "not generalize as to the merits of these different nationalities," though he was convinced that even the poorest graduate had more knowledge of American institutions than the average native-born citizen. All the same, he singled out Mexicans as "the least inclined to become citizens. Their easygoing habits preclude the industry necessary to become a factor in the government under which they are living."[19]

Not all teachers shared Bell's bias. Josephine Ringnalda at Albion Street School told a far different story.[20] Her district had a foreign population of 90 percent, mostly Sicilians and Mexicans, but with a sprinkling of Greeks, Slavonians, Serbians, and Japanese. Far from just teaching rudimentary English and citizenship, her job entailed renovating homes in the rundown area. The demographics of the district had changed since 1907, when Italians had predominated. By 1921 Mexicans had come in such numbers that "whole streets that once were settled by Italians are now occupied by Mexicans." Ringnalda found them "educated and self-supporting," and thus not a "problem."

The Mexicans in the Albion district, like the Molokans in the Utah district a decade or so earlier, shared houses with their countrymen, but within a few years many Mexican families were able to purchase their own homes. The prosperous war years had allowed immigrants some economic independence but had also produced inflation. Rents rose, and housing became scarce. Ringnalda feared that if the unemployment that preceded the end of the war continued to rise, her district would suffer. Nevertheless, she concluded that Albion's communities "truly" were "upward striving."

Much of this success she attributed to Albion's Americanization program. Several years earlier, presumably before the program's expansion, she found that the houses and the children had a neglected look. But by 1921 fences and houses had received a fresh coat of paint, and sidewalks had been repaired. She approvingly reported that some of the people had acquired such items as pianos, bedspreads, rugs, and even electric washing machines. Obviously, Ringnalda believed that Americanization was a complete process, not only a plan to rid foreigners of their languages and cultures but also a snare to hook them on the American Dream. To be sure, Ringnalda would undoubtedly not have employed the ironic tone. She felt that Americanization had worked at Albion; immigrants had become American consumers.

Reformers like Ringnalda saw the acquisition of household goods in another light also. Material items made the home more attractive, as well as more important in the immigrants' lives. Reformers had seen the loss of family cohesiveness as one of the effects of immigration. As the second generation became Americanized, it grew away from the family. Gibson had argued for home teachers in order to mitigate this trend. She wanted immigrant mothers to learn English and American customs so they would again have the respect of their Americanized children. Reformers perceived the rise in crime in the immigrant communities and the high percentage of criminals, both adult and juvenile, as evidence of family deterioration. If the home was made more commodious, with more American possessions, family life would center there; children would be less likely to be on the streets and less likely to engage in unwholesome pursuits.[21]

Ringnalda's commentaries provide a window into the changing society within the city. She based her remarks on a close association with her neighborhood, and for this reason she epitomized the type of teacher Gibson and Baughman described as one of the "experts in Americanization." It is also clear from her remarks that, in 1921, the school's Americanization program continued in much the same way as before. The program revolved around the neighborhood school and around a home teacher who combined the skills of a social worker, nurse-practitioner, precinct captain, psychologist, and surrogate mother. Ringnalda assures us that, in 1921, school people continued to employ the Progressives' methods, manifested in the settlements and in the neighborhood schools.

Ringnalda went so far in her role of teacher as to arrange for the Board of Education to rent a house for a large immigrant Mexican family, on condition that the family repair it. The family did. Unfortunately, the remodeled house then became so attractive that the owner—an Italian—decided to sell it for a nice profit, and the hardworking renters were forced to move. After that fiasco, the board became reluctant to move into the home real estate business.[22]

Another view of Americanization comes from Nora Sterry, principal of Macy Street School. Sterry's reputation extended beyond the city's limits; she published articles and was a sought-after speaker on Americanization.[23] Under her leadership Macy Street had become a neighborhood-school showpiece. It was one of the first schools to provide penny lunches and nursery care, and the very first to have an elementary evening school devoted to Americanization. Nevertheless, in the late 1920's immigrants still used the school's facilities to preserve their languages and traditions, as they had since the program began in 1911. In December 1922 Sterry addressed the board on behalf of a group of Syrians in her district. They had written to her to request the use of Macy Street's auditorium so that they could discuss various ways to teach their children Syrian language and customs.[24]

Using the schools as neighborhood centers had many advantages. Schools could be enlisted into the campaign for school bonds, for example, as they were in 1921–22. The Bond Committee, of which Sterry was one of three members, unveiled its plan for the foreign district. The committee suggested that teachers check the lists of parents at City Hall and visit the homes of unregistered citizens in order to persuade all those eligible to register and vote. Teachers sent children out to parade with banners and placards informing neighbors of their schools' overcrowding and half-day sessions. In class they wrote poems in favor of the bond campaign. A popular one was set to the tune of the familiar wartime favorite "Over There":

Vote the Bonds, Vote the Bonds!
Have a heart! Do your part! Vote the Bonds![25]

Sterry, along with many Los Angeles educators, believed that if immigrants viewed the schools as centers of the communities, when they became citizens they would be inclined to cast their votes for educational measures. She was especially concerned about the Chinese community's lack of participation. As a group the Chinese did not petition the schools for space to conduct language or cultural classes; nor had any of the volunteer organizations expressed a particular interest in teaching them English. A combination of Protestant churches and Chinese societies ran language classes on their own and did not seek support from the outside community. Some Chinese women did attend English classes, to be sure, but Sterry wanted more than that. One-half of her precinct was Chinese, and Sterry anticipated that within a few years these people would have an impact on local elections. She was convinced that the more responsive the schools were to the needs of the Chinese community, the more the Chinese would support the schools.[26]

Sterry found that most Chinese children had artistic talent and were conscientious students, although their families had come from China's "unlettered class." More than half the children, thirty of fifty-six, had been born in China and were "badly retarded" to begin with, but after they learned English "they were more thorough in their work than the other foreign children and made steadier progress." Most of the children did not meet the Health Department's standards; Sterry attributed this to the long hours they spent in Chinese language school after their day at Macy Street.[27]

Sterry showed more insight on the source of the Chinese children's health problems in a 1922 article, in which she described Chinese housing conditions as the worst in the city.[28] Another interesting clue to the children's poor health may have been the fumes emitted by the nearby Los Angeles Gas and Electric Corporation plant. The fumes became so offensive that residents petitioned the city health commissioner to do something about them; he in turn asked the Board of Education to look into the matter. In July 1921 Sterry informed the board that, indeed, the industries in her district, including the Gas and Electric Corporation and various packing houses, produced unpleasant odors, but she declined to say whether or not they caused physical harm.[29]

The procedure here is particularly interesting. The Health Commission's turning the matter over to the Board of Education illustrates the extent to which the schools had become a dominant force in the community. The commission assumed that the schools had more influence with the gas company than it had.

Whether the fumes actually contributed to the poor health of the Chinese children is a matter of conjecture. Since new outbreaks of tuberculosis, influenza, and smallpox threatened Macy district, along with other poor areas of the city, educators certainly had cause for alarm. However, someone as interested in Americanizing foreigners or their children as Sterry was might be overeager to lay their ill health to too many hours spent on studying their own language—a convenient scapegoat and more easily remedied than poverty and squalor.

By the 1920's most educators believed that schools should help develop the body as well as the mind. Schools promoted and encouraged all manner of games and competitive sports, but Sterry noticed that few Chinese children participated. The older generation of Chinese immigrants placed a different emphasis on play, and participation in American sports did not seem important. This does not imply that Chinese youngsters avoided American games; indeed the difference in generational perceptions added to the tensions within the Chinese community. A recent article in *Gum Saan Journal* testifies to the eagerness with which Chinese children participated in American games when they were allowed to, focusing on the baseball team that proudly defeated a champion Japanese team in 1927. The authors bemoaned the fact that the Chinese community had only one baseball team while other groups had many. The Japanese, for instance, had twenty teams, all sponsored by local merchants. The Chinese team was unsponsored, which meant that the players had to find the money to equip themselves. According to a former member of the 1927 team, the Chinese elders did not support the team because they could not understand why boys were playing strange games instead of working.[30]

Sterry was an astute observer, but the core of her findings made assimilationists uneasy. She found that although acculturation was making inroads into the Chinese community, most Chinese, even the American-born, had more loyalty to China than to the United States. And she also thought there was a good reason why the Chinese adhered so tenaciously to their traditional loyalties. "We have no right to condemn a non-loyal attitude on their part," she wrote in 1923:

> The Chinaman is intensely proud of his blood and traditions, supremely aware that his civilization, despised by us, has stood the test of centuries while ours is still in the making. Stung by our contempt, it is natural that he does not consider himself one of us but turns toward his native land. . . . The loss is ours as well as theirs. They are a permanent part of our nation.[31]

Sterry wrote out of conviction that if America did not draw the Chinese into the society, they would remain "a stumbling block in the path of our national development." The neighborhood school had great potential for avoiding that.

What Sterry and other school people envisioned as more comprehensive Americanization programs required additional financial support: not only funding from the Los Angeles Board of Education but from Sacramento as well. Not all officials agreed. In 1923, following a national trend to cut Progressive programs in general, the Los Angeles schools faced drastic cuts in many of their most cherished services, including many in neighborhood schools. The conservative Republican governor, Friend Richardson, appeared to be no friend of the schools; his proposed budget slashed 60 percent from the request for operating costs for the next two years and called for the dismantling of the state Office of Assistant Superintendent of Americanization. Dorsey expressed particular concern that the governor undervalued the Americanization programs. She asked whether he thought Americanization was so small that it did not require the time of one administrator to coordinate it. Dorsey foresaw the work of assimilating immigrants grinding to a halt.

Dorsey felt that Los Angeles had more than its share of immigrants, and the responsibility to educate them could not be handled by the city alone. The state and federal governments should contribute to the cost of education:

> The first duty of education is to equalize opportunities for every child; and this cannot be done unless the State and the nation help bear the burdens of education. For instance, it is unfortunate and unfair for Los Angeles, the third largest Mexican city in the world, to bear that burden alone of taking care educationally of this enormous group.[32]

Dorsey's remarks did not fall on deaf ears. Before the Principals' Club in 1923, Walter Crane, principal of Ramona Street School, spoke for many of his colleagues when he called for guidelines from Sacramento for the vexing problem of rising numbers of immigrants and decreasing state support. He noted that California had become "one of the great foreign ports of the world. Foreigners are being smuggled in here by the hundreds." None of the many education problems California faced had so much "importance as that of Americanization."[33]

The Los Angeles schools were struggling under the burdens of increased enrollments. Dorsey put the rate of increase at 20,000 per year between 1919 and 1923.[34] According to the 1920 census, a little less than a fifth of the city's population (112,057 in a total of 576,673) was white foreign-born. To get a truer picture of the foreign impact on the city, however, one needs to look more closely at the data. Adding in the numbers of those whose parents, one (86,808) or both (53,541), were foreign-born, and the Japanese (11,618) and Chinese (2,062) brings the total to 266,086, or almost half the city's residents. The number of naturalized white foreign-born was 22,946; only one of five immigrants had become citizens.[35] Little wonder that Americanizers felt concerned over cuts in their programs.

The Fight for Control of the Schools

The national and state trend towards conservatism manifested itself in isolationism, restrictive immigration laws, and a reluctance to rely on government for social reform. The tensions engendered by these tendencies often extended to local levels. In Los Angeles they came to a head during a bitterly contested school board election in June 1923. Teachers and administrators openly vied for power and influence, and fought each other's attempt to impose restrictions. The battle supposedly centered on teachers' salary raises but quickly moved into the arena of school board politics. Fundamentally, it boiled down to a question of who was going to control the schools. That the battle became heated is hardly surprising, for there was so much to be gained by that control, as David Tyack and others have shown. Winners held the power to set the political, social, and cultural standards for the city's school population.[36]

Paul Peterson has argued that after teachers became active members of reform associations and better trained, their quest for professionalization led to conflicts with school boards and administrators over salary increases and policy-making.[37] Both issues were at work in the 1923 campaign.

The election came in the midst of a three-year battle teachers waged for salary increases. Although teachers had received annual increases from 1916 to 1919, they had had none since. A 1921 American Federation of Teachers survey showed that among seven cities with populations of 100,000, Los Angeles ranked sixth and fifth in high school and elementary salaries, respectively. Early in 1920 some 4,500 city teachers organized a campaign for community support. They hired a lawyer "courted by the press," advertised in newspapers, and in keeping with their locale, hired a publicity agent and propagandized their cause with movies. Although teachers felt they had gained community support, Superintendent Dorsey and the board—and the *Los Angeles Times*—remained unmoved.[38]

The drive for higher wages and the backing of liberal board members brought on a vicious campaign between teachers and the *Los Angeles Times*. The vindictiveness of the *Times* precipitated a rift between a majority of the city's teachers and the Principals' Association. Teachers supported board candidates who were likely to be sympathetic to their cause. Among them were two Progressive incumbents, the Reverend G. Bromley Oxnam, pastor of the Church of All Nations, and Marcus Bettinger, a former teacher and principal, and the first superintendent of immigrant education and the evening schools. Oxnam, serving out his first term, was an enthusiastic supporter of Americanization. His work brought him in close contact with the city's Mexican community. He also was an outspoken critic of the local police, in particular of police brutality toward the Industrial Workers of the World during a 1923 seamen's strike on the San Pedro docks. The incident became particularly noteworthy after the chief of police, Louis Oaks, had been unmasked as a member of the Ku Klux Klan. Oxnam had appeared on a podium with the novelist and socialist Upton Sinclair, where both urged an investigation of police behavior. Sinclair and his followers organized a branch of the American Civil Liberties Union the following year.[39]

The publisher and editor-in-chief of the *Times*, Harry Chandler, made Oxnam and his running mates targets of a personal vendetta. Oxnam's philanthropic work brought him considerable attention, some of it political. His suggestions for better enforcement of housing laws, for greater power vested in the city's Housing Commission, and for a relief system targeted at the

Mexican community all required municipal funding and were anathema to powerful conservatives who were not interested in expanding government.*

The *Times* found a powerful ally in the Better America Federation. The Better America Federation, an arm of the Merchants and Manufacturers Association, was organized in Los Angeles in 1922 to conduct aggressive lobbying against Progressivism and regulatory commissions in general, and unionism in particular.[40] Under the leadership of two prominent businessmen, H. R. Haldeman and E. F. Watkins, the organization turned into an anticommunist crusade. The Better America Federation kept vigil for any sign of communism in the city, and by the 1930's it used its influence to warn right-thinking people about the dangers of Communist infiltration in all levels of society. Louise Ward Watkins, president of the Friday Morning Club in the early 1930's and wife of E. F. Watkins, referred to the organization as "a private intelligence agency."[41]

Chandler's tactics knew no bounds. He tried to discredit Oxnam in every way. The *Times* printed articles implying that the minister was unpatriotic and surrounded himself with "disloyal Americans" who had opposed the war. These allegations led to Oxnam's repudiation by many of his former supporters in veterans groups and by influential fellow ministers such as Robert Schuler.

The *Times* labeled Oxnam and Bettinger the "Teachers' Ticket." In an effort to undermine their support, the paper not only implied that former Assistant Superintendent Bettinger was incompetent, but attempted to link the liberal board candidates with a move to oust Dorsey. This ploy was intended to divide the teachers, for staunch as they were in their campaign

*Oxnam, "Mexican in Los Angeles." Some of the city's conservatives, including Chandler, under the guise of patriotism, hoped that Governor Richardson's leadership in Sacramento would return to them the reins of control from "fuzzy-headed" Progressives, not a few of whom they suspected of harboring dangerous socialist ideas. Richardson, a former state treasurer, had campaigned on a platform of limited government and fiscal economy and had attacked Progressives as "spendthrift politicians." In his 1923 inaugural address, quite out of character with the tradition of inaugural addresses, he berated his predecessors for their "orgy of extravagance." (Putnam, *Modern California Politics*, p. 9.)

for salary increases, most were unwilling to attack Dorsey. The so-called leading contender for her position, E. J. Lickley, president of the High School Teachers' Association and an assistant superintendent, along with L. E. Thomas, the chairman of the Better Schools Committee of Citizens and Teachers, denounced the *Times* and the Better America Federation for falsely accusing the teachers of wanting to oust Dorsey.

The teachers knew that the fundamental issue was the control of the schools. To clarify their position, Thomas took to the pages of the *School Journal* to ask, "Shall the control of our public schools be placed in the hands of certain selfish interests?" And if so, would this group "inaugurate the teaching of reactionary principles in our schools" and "nullify the progressive measures which the people have been able to secure during the past years?" The Teachers' Association charged that the same selfish interests that had supported Richardson for governor were behind the campaign to dismantle programs in the Los Angeles schools.[42] The Principals' Association, co-sponsors of the *Journal*, objected to the teachers' use of the magazine as a vehicle for their partisan views. The principals threatened to withdraw from the *Journal* altogether, accusing the teachers of underhandedness in publishing the minutes of their meetings so as to avoid the editorial policy against partisanship.

The *Times* and the Better America Federation proved too powerful adversaries. The Progressives lost the election, and teachers were not granted raises.[43] After the defeat the teachers promised to keep their political views off the *Journal*'s pages. Both school groups apparently became reconciled, but conservative forces unconditionally controlled the school board and the *Journal*. No matter how well organized the Los Angeles teachers were, they were rebuffed in their demands for higher wages and a voice in school board affairs, and given the message that partisan activities by teachers were not allowed.

For the next several years the Better America Federation tried to influence the schools and rid them of what they considered subversive elements. It succeeded in one respect. The board canceled the schools' subscriptions to the *Nation* and the *New Republic*, and turned aside repeated efforts of teachers and librarians to reinstate the magazines.[44] The Better America Federation also sponsored an oratorical contest and awarded lucrative prizes for speeches applauding the Constitution.[45]

Still, the conservative tone set by the Better America Federation, the Chamber of Commerce, and the American Legion must certainly have been felt. The "100% Americanism" espoused by the American Legion, the slogan "America First," the pressure to rid the United States of "hyphenated Americans," as Theodore Roosevelt had so elegantly put it a few years before, all helped create a conservative, if not a reactionary, atmosphere throughout the nation. But fiscal conservatism in the schools worked against super-patriotism. Without large outlays of money to shape the schools in the image they would have wished, super-patriots could only go so far. Many aspects of Progressivism remained, seeping through the cracks they left unclogged. Above all, Dorsey, in her belief that Americanization should center in the neighborhood schools, continued to support them. That aspect of Progressivism and many of the programs associated with it remained completely intact to meet the needs of the changing city.

Continuation of the Neighborhood Schools

As the immigrant population grew, so did the assimilation efforts. The foreign-born totaled 278,964 in 1930, but again, if one includes the native-born with one or both parents born outside the United States, the figure rises to nearly half the population—576,762 in a total of 1,238,000. The black population also rose during the decade between 1920 and 1930, from 15,579 to 38,894.[46]

Between 1922 and 1924 the number of home teachers remained at forty-seven, two more than in 1921; by 1927 the city employed sixty-three. There were also twelve teachers of Americanization. The major expansion came in the home teaching centers, fifty-five in 1922 and eighty-three in 1928.[47] The schools' major effort to assimilate immigrants thus came through the tried-and-true system of community involvement based on the models first articulated by the settlement workers.

A playground near Chinatown exemplified Americanization in the mid-1920's. Until 1924 the nearest playground to Chinatown was several miles away, in Echo Park. Margret Cope, a Macy Street schoolteacher, set out to remedy the situation. In a stunning example of persuasiveness, Cope worked out a deal between Southern Pacific Railroad representatives and the city to buy land for a local playground. The site, a former stable behind what became the Union Station, was located in old Chinatown. By the 1920's the stable had deteriorated, and the owner, Southern Pacific, agreed to sell the city its land. Macy Street students worked to clear the site. The playground, Apaplasa, became the home field for the Chinese baseball team that proudly defeated a champion Japanese team in 1927.[48]

Much else remained the same, as is attested by a 1927 *School Journal* devoted to neighborhood schools. Principals Sterry of Macy Street and Ethelda Drake of Ann Street, in one of the poorest Hispanic communities, reminisced about the early days of penny lunches and day nurseries, when regular teachers and principals had cooked and cared for the children.[49] Most articles in this issue described Americanization in 1927, but without the date it would be difficult to tell when they were written. The preoccupations and concerns they voice hearken back to the days when schools took their direction from the settlement houses, with their emphasis on uplifting and social welfare.

For instance, Gladys Patric Shahovitch, a physician with the school's Health and Development Department, expressed concern that Americanizers paid too little attention to the cultural differences among the immigrant population. She feared that uninformed teachers would have little success. She noted that personal cleanliness differed among foreign groups. Many had not been accustomed to bathtubs, but she added emphatically, "neither have our grandparents." She pointed out the different bathing habits, the contrast between the Latin concept of modesty and the Baltic peoples' communal baths. She also acknowledged particular dietary habits and the endurance of a "patriotism of the stomach"; "dishes of the native land cling long after an honest allegiance to the American flag has been pledged." Shahovitch felt that Americans would have success if they showed patience with the immigrants' reluctance to cast off all of their old-country traditions. Nevertheless, her concerns were with Americanization; she wanted the immigrants to learn American bathing habits and to cook what she called "practical diets."[50]

Edna Manley, principal of Soto Street School, reiterated the various roles expected of a teacher of Americanization: interpreter, scribe, negotiator, intermediary. In one incident a Soto teacher was asked to compose a letter for an illiterate Spanish-speaking immigrant, a Mr. Montalvo. With the help of his English-speaking children, the teacher wrote to the State Immigration Office and explained that an Imperial Valley bank had stopped payments due him from a land sale. Within a short time the payments resumed.

Manley told of two kindergarten teachers who visited every home in their district where a death had occurred, making over 400 visits in one year. The Soto Street nursery ran an extended day-care center for working mothers; it cared for children over nine months of age until they reached kindergarten. Manley cited another case in which emergency aid was given to a family with eleven children when the father went to prison. Not infrequently home teachers were asked to intervene in family quarrels. Example after example testifies to the teachers' active role in their communities and their emphasis on humanitarian involvement rather than the cold, businesslike method of naturalization that characterized citizenship classes.[51]

Another indication of the schools' determination to continue the human side of Americanization came from Flora D. Smith, Baughman's successor in the Department of Immigrant Education. Smith noted that the home teachers in Los Angeles had grown from one, Amanda M. Chase, in 1915 to fifty in 1926. Yet the average attendance of 1,018 out of an enrollment of 3,116 suggests that the program had only limited success; educators must have questioned their effectiveness. Smith made no comment, but clearly home teachers were not reaching enough people. Nevertheless, Smith found that American-born women indicated that they liked some of the programs.

American women petitioned to use a model cottage for their women's club. American and foreign women alike found handicraft classes attractive, and Smith felt that this type of activity built racial understanding.[52] Her descriptions are those of the old-time Progressives. They could have been written in 1919 by Ruby Baughman, in 1911 by Dana Bartlett, or in 1906 by Bessie Stoddart. The formula used in the mid-1920's was the one worked out years before by settlement workers.

To ensure the program and her position, Smith suggested a still-greater involvement for home teachers. She foresaw the home-teaching program expanding as a larger part of a modern approach to child-rearing. The Modern Parenthood Conference met in Los Angeles in late 1927, and to stimulate interest in the meeting, the Council of Jewish Women arranged for speakers to talk before groups of foreign women. In conjunction with the Child Guidance Clinics, a study of the schools' child-training classes was also arranged. Naturally, Smith expected the home teachers to participate in both the study and the conference. California, the first state to recognize the importance of educating foreign-born mothers by legalizing the role of home teachers, must continue to encourage their efforts, Smith said. She envisioned broadening the scope of their efforts, "contacting both native-born and foreign-born mothers, literate and illiterate and all races and creeds in [an] attempt to help mothers meet the problems and responsibilities of our complex civilization."[53]

Through the whole course of Superintendent Dorsey's tenure, Americanization programs continued to expand. The separation of immigrant education and naturalization in 1920 helped alleviate some conflicts within the program. Since most American conservatives supported naturalization, as long as the citizenship classes continued to turn out new Americans, few would bother with the diurnal Americanization in neighborhood schools.

Dorsey appears to have been what one historian calls a pragmatic progressive,[54] walking the line between the earlier reformist impulses and the conservative attitudes of the times. She and her lieutenants withstood conservative attempts to curtail the Americanization program of the neighborhood schools.

Not all of her motives were altruistic, to be sure, as a 1923 remark betrayed: "We have these immigrants to live with, and if we Americanize them we can live with them."[55] Nevertheless, without her support the program would have collapsed.

Segregation in Los Angeles

Alongside Americanization and its supposed promise for democracy, blatant, undemocratic segregation settled in on public schools in the 1920's. In its darker form it institutionalized racial segregation. As nonwhite urban populations increased, so did the practice of segregating children by race. In New York, Chicago, and Los Angeles, white communities pressured school boards for separate schools for nonwhite children. School boards reacted in varying ways and with varying results. In Los Angeles the board's slowly formulated policy produced a clear pattern of institutional segregation by the end of the decade. Three nonwhite communities, Japanese, Mexican, and black, illustrate both the dilemma and the complexities of school segregation.

Segregation was not new to Los Angeles. A school for nonwhite students existed in the city until 1880, when the California legislature declared that black and American Indian children might attend schools with white children. Desegregating Chinese children was not part of the package. Nevertheless, in Los Angeles, where the Chinese school population totaled only nineteen in 1890, compared with 434 in San Francisco, Chinese children attended an integrated public school.[56]

The city's Japanese population was also small; 126 Japanese children attended school in 1905.[57] Though San Francisco began to segregate Japanese students in 1906, Los Angeles did not. Writing of the San Francisco policy, Superintendent Ernest Moore said that Los Angeles educators found the Japanese "quiet and industrious" and "such good students that our principals and teachers believe them to have a most helpful influence upon the other pupils." Moreover, he "bitterly" regretted San Francisco's actions, and thought it "wholly unnecessary" and "not representative of public opinion in California."[58]

By the early 1920's a few Los Angeles elementary schools were effectively segregated because of residential patterns. The East San Pedro School on Terminal Island, where Japanese families fished and worked in canneries, was completely Japanese. Lemona School in the San Fernando Valley, where Mexican fieldworkers lived, was entirely Mexican.[59] In the mid-1920's the board institutionalized segregation.

Los Angeles's nonwhite school population grew faster than the board had anticipated. The Mexicans increased more rapidly than any other nationality, and even by conservative estimates, the growth was spectacular—from 5,632 in 1910 to 21,653 in 1920. If the number of Mexicans were added to that of other people of color—the Chinese, Japanese, Indians, and blacks—the nonwhite population would stand at 141,866, or nearly a quarter of the total.[60]

The nature of the ethnic growth varied in different parts of the city, as did the reaction to it. In the Albion district, as we have seen, home teacher Ringnalda found the Mexican newcomers to be upwardly striving, and she accepted the change in ethnicity from mostly Italian to predominantly Mexican as part of a pattern of economic mobility. Others disagreed. Many viewed their new neighbors as invaders. This reaction produced petitions to segregate children by race.

The efforts were initially concentrated on the fastest-growing group—the Mexican children. One of the earliest attempts to segregate them occurred in late 1916, when people in the Sherman School district petitioned the board to separate the Mexican students from the others. Sherman School, situated in East Hollywood near the Pacific Electric Railroad Camp, had become the host school for the children of the Pacific Electric workers, most of whom lived at the camp. In 1911 the number of children with Spanish surnames in the school could be counted on the fingers of one hand. But by this time there were five or six in each grade. The 1916 petition contended that the Mexican children carried communicable diseases. Superintendent Shiels and the board directed the Health and Development Department to examine the group in question. Their findings convinced Shiels that the Mexican children had "neither vermin nor skin disease," and the board could not "dictate in the matter in question."[61] Sherman School solved the problem in 1921 by directing all but a handful of Mexican children into an "ungraded" class, set up to instruct non-English-speaking pupils.[62]

At Belvedere School in 1918 a group of Austrian parents petitioned the board to relieve overcrowding by purchasing a bungalow for the Mexican children's use. Presumably the Austrians would keep the original building. The board answered that it was against state policy to segregate by race. It is not clear what, if any, other steps the board took, but twenty years later 914 of Belvedere's 1,134 students were Mexicans, and there were only seven Austrians left.[63]

In the San Fernando Valley petitioners from Owensmouth were the first in that area to ask for segregated classes. Los Angeles had annexed Owensmouth in 1915, after the completion of the Los Angeles Aqueduct opened the valley for development. In 1918 board members reported that the valley schools were well equipped and large enough to warrant bringing the Mexican children in the area into them. One school had so many vacant rooms that teachers asked to use them as their temporary domiciles.[64] The Owensmouth community seemed not to mind teachers living at its school, but having Mexican children attend classes there was not taken well by various groups. A 1921 petition asked the authorities to take "immediate steps to segregate Mexican pupils in the grammar school." The petition, signed by the Owensmouth Chamber of Commerce, taxpayers, and patrons of Owensmouth school, bypassed the Board of Education and instead went to the Los Angeles City Council. Doing so did them little good, for the council simply referred the matter to the board.* The issue finally ended up in the lap of the board's

*Board, *Minutes*, 32: 158–59. The city clerk, Robert Dominguez, the highest-ranking city official with a Spanish surname, sent the communication to the board (*Notables of the West*, 1 [Los Angeles: International News Service, 1913], p. 695). Dominguez, a descendant of a veteran of Gaspar Portola's 1769 expedition who was one of California's earliest land-grant holders, was fluent in Spanish and English and had served as Gov. William Howard Taft's secretary and interpreter on the Philippine Commission between 1900 and 1902 (W. Robinson, *Land in California*, pp. 10, 45–47).

Teachers and Schools Committee, whose chairwoman, Bessie Stoddart, the former College Settlement crusader for health care and playgrounds for the immigrant poor, reported that her committee was "inclined to make every effort legally possible" to meet the petitioners' requirements. She hoped it could be done "without unduly increasing the number of problems."[65]

To conform to California law, which had no provision for the segregation of Mexican children,[66] and still accommodate the petitioners was not an easy task, but with the help of the Mutualista Sociedad Benito Juárez and its spokesman, Bulmaro M. Lona, the board succeeded. The Mutualista owned a building in a "convenient location" that it agreed to rent to the board after contacts were made by Flora D. Smith and Harry H. Shafer. Both Smith and Shafer had important jobs in the Americanization program.[67] The newly acquired building, called an annex or branch of Owensmouth Elementary, had all the characteristics of a settlement house, from the janitorial services to the evening classes, and included a baby clinic and a center for afternoon classes for women. The board's minutes do not mention a regular day school on the premises, so it is not clear whether Mexican children were taken out of their classrooms and moved to the annex.[68] But that does seem to have been the intent.

The Mutualista played an interesting role in the Owensmouth case, raising the intriguing question of whether leaders of the Mexican community traded school services for segregation. Mutualistas developed in Mexico around 1850 to protect workers from exploitation, and they became popular among artisans wherever they moved. In the United States they were collective and voluntary mutual-aid societies, similar to those formed by other immigrants. Many were highly nationalistic, and in some cases they stressed the importance of Mexican schools.[69] The historian Mario García has observed that the generation of Mexicans living in the United States during the 1920's expected to return to Mexico and therefore in effect created Mexican cities in a foreign land; and the contemporary educator George I. Sánchez acknowledged that often times Spanish speakers encouraged segregation for their children.[70] In the building donated by the Mutualista, Owensmouth's Mexican children would have had less contact with English-speaking children and be better able to resist acculturation.[71]

The second request for segregating the schools in the valley came from San Fernando. Although it remained a separate city, its schools were annexed to Los Angeles in 1920. The following January the San Fernando Chamber of Commerce wrote to the Board of Education requesting that the board segregate Mexican children; it cited as precedent letters from the towns of Covina and Monrovia, northeast of Los Angeles, where segregation had been effected.

Stoddart's committee noted that it knew of the large number of Mexican children in one school and was well aware of the problems growing out of their presence. The board was of the opinion that the law did not recognize segregation, but it was disposed to make a satisfactory arrangement whenever possible for individual pupils.[72] The board accommodated those pupils so thoroughly that San Fernando School was soon entirely Mexican. No new school was built for non-Mexican children at this time, so school people found another way to make segregation feasible: allowing those children who wished to do so to be transported to outlying schools. At first local entrepreneurs petitioned the board for the right to charge parents to transport children in their cars; as the practice increased the board set up guidelines. The San Fernando Valley, with its vast area and scattered population, developed a reliable school transportation system. It became so efficient, in fact, that, when parents petitioned the board to open a new school in Pacoima, adjacent to San Fernando, they were turned down and told to continue using the existing transportation.[73] In this way the board managed to avoid a full discussion of the matter.

Just two years after the San Fernando parents' initial request, in 1923, the *School Journal* reported that the San Fernando School "[was] attended entirely by Mexicans, and [had] an enrollment of six hundred, with a steady increase each year."[74] The point the writer wished to make was that the children would be better served if the school emphasized vocational training. The school had recently been enlarged with the construction of ten new classrooms; additional plans included changing the school's name to fit that proposed purpose—to the Mexican Industrial School. The name remained unchanged; the board did not want to emphasize that it had sanctioned segregation.

Whatever views the San Fernando Mexican community had, it did not express them to the board. Some may have accepted a trade-off of new school facilities for segregation. Sánchez and García have suggested that some Mexican communities approved of separation. Others argue that Mexicans, fearful of losing their jobs, kept quiet rather than challenge school policy.[75]

Writing from today's perspective, historians are quick to criticize vocational education because it set too many restrictions on upward mobility. Seventy years ago attitudes and expectations were quite different. Lawrence Cremin reminds us that in the interwar period most colleges and universities were elite institutions for the upper and middle classes, and slow to change.[76] Very few Americans planned to send their children to institutions of higher learning. Learning a skilled trade in a vocational school had more appeal to poor, unskilled workers than preparing their children for college.[77]

The board's motives for segregating Mexican children and its failure to take action against any other group at this time reflect a growing prejudice in the city as the number of Mexicans swelled. Throughout this period the *School Journal* repeatedly mentioned the "problems" schools faced because of the growing Mexican population. In 1922 the National Educational Association held a national conference on illiteracy in San Francisco. Assistant Superintendent Smith, representing Los Angeles, was not surprised to learn that Mexicans in the Pacific states constituted the largest numbers of illiterates.[78]

Still, it was not long before other groups became the focus of segregation efforts. In 1922 the Chamber of Commerce of Gardena, an agricultural suburb whose schools had been incorporated into the city's system, asked the board to segregate the Japanese children there. The board reiterated its stand that segregation was illegal.[79]

The Japanese presented a dilemma for school people. Japanese Americans excelled in schools, and their parents took great interest in their education. (That interest extended to the school grounds as well. At Terminal Island's East San Pedro School some years later, the Japanese Fishermen's Association donated play equipment and built a pagoda on the playground. In Lomita, a farming area, the Japanese Vegetable Growers Association contributed lumber to erect a shed at the local school for classes in mechanics.) More important, the Japanese government had been outspoken in its opposition to the segregation imposed in the San Francisco public schools a few years before, and the board sought to avoid adverse publicity from a strong foreign government. Moreover, the Japanese population in Gardena was small; providing a separate school would be costly.[80]

African American children also faced segregation during this period, though in this case the push for it involved not elementary pupils, as with the Japanese and Mexican children, but high school students. The issue surfaced in 1921, when a Mr. B. T. Zeller communicated to the board his concern that although a person, no matter what his race, was entitled to equal rights, "it [was] disastrous to property values to plant a person of different color" in a community. Property values had depreciated in the area adjoining Jefferson High School because blacks had settled there, he wrote, and he hoped that the board would take notice and "keep the north of Jefferson and the south of Jefferson districts separate by keeping any school away from the Jefferson Street line." The board commented that it was not considering building a new school at that time, but it would place Zeller's communication on file for future consideration.[81]

By the time Zeller wrote to the board, black Americans lived in several of the city's poorer areas. But as an increasing number of blacks began seeking better housing and moved into white middle-class neighborhoods, Zeller's comments were repeated. A contemporary community study reflected the resentment and racism in a changing neighborhood. Some residents, like Zeller, sought protection from white-dominated institutions and took their complaints to the Board of Education.[82] The board reacted in due course, and in 1927 a new school opened. John C. Fremont High made institutional segregation possible. Instead of drawing students from adjoining districts, white students were directed there, and nonwhites were sent to Jefferson.

Black Americans in Los Angeles and New York City experienced institutionalized segregation in schooling in a similar manner. In both cities elementary school segregation resulted from forces beyond the control of school authorities. By and large the cities adhered to the law in the elementary schools, but secondary school segregation resulted from unofficial policy; black students were assigned to particular high schools and to particular courses within those schools.[83]

In Los Angeles, as elsewhere, restrictive covenants in housing —not struck down until 1953—assured the de facto segregation of many elementaries and eventually led to the 1962 ruling of Judge Alfred Gettleson that mandated school busing in the sprawling city.[84] Such covenants covered all sorts of racial and religious groups. As a condition of purchase, home owners agreed not to resell their property to blacks, Asians, or Mexicans in Los Angeles; elsewhere Jews and other groups were singled out. Although on the books in Los Angeles since the beginning of the century, covenants were not commonly observed until after 1918, when the increase of nonwhites reactivated them. In 1948 the Supreme Court in *Kelly* v. *Kraemer* and *Hurd* v. *Hodge* ruled that the enforcement of restrictive covenants was in violation of the Fourteenth Amendment and the Civil Rights Act of 1866. In 1953, in a case originating in Los Angeles, *Barrow* v. *Jackson*, the court thought it had closed the last loophole.[85]

Leaders of the city's black community kept a watchful eye on board policy. The community was growing and attracting national attention. The *California Eagle*, a weekly founded in 1881, became its self-appointed watchdog. The *Eagle* followed the national Republican Party line in the 1920's, running photos of Calvin Coolidge on the front page for months before the 1924 election. But it was not slavish in its Republicanism; it criticized former California Governor and then Senator Hiram Johnson for his failure to appoint blacks to prominent jobs within his administration. In 1932 the *Eagle* switched its allegiance to Franklin Roosevelt and the New Deal, and its intense opposition to segregation in public schools continued.* Segregation

*In the 1950's the *California Eagle* took a further turn to the left; in 1952 the editor, Charlotte Bass, became the first African American woman to run for vice-president. Supported by two prominent black activists, the educator

meant, as it editorialized in 1926, "the Negro school gradually becomes a school only in name—a sort of excuse to say to the outside world, 'Yes, we have [a school] for the Negroes.' "[86]

In March 1927, aware of a $23,000 bond issue to build a separate school for Mexican children in the nearby community of La Verne, the *Eagle* warned: "If these Mexican children are segregated then what will the future hold for us—just watch and watch closely."[87] Yet the *Eagle* was not always sensitive to minority groups that competed with blacks for jobs; it urged subscribers to write their congressmen in support of Japanese exclusion laws and immigration quotas, and considered Mexicans non-taxpaying aliens who ought to be brought under the quota act.[88]

All the petitions to the Los Angeles Board of Education requesting segregated schools, or at least separate classes within a school, were aimed at nonwhite students. If any other groups were targeted for segregation, the board's minutes do not say so. Prejudice is not confined to any one group, and at different times many people have felt the bigot's sting, but clearly in Los Angeles schools it was most obviously felt by nonwhites. Reformers like Stoddart and Smith, who had devoted their energies to making life pleasanter for immigrants by providing welfare services through the schools, bowed to community pressure, and in some instances bowed to segregation.

War, socialist revolutions abroad, fear of socialism at home, and increased immigration created a form of hysteria in Los Angeles that complicated the goals of Americanization. These factors turned many school people away from assimilation and toward segregation and a national policy of exclusion. The dilemma of assimilation versus segregation plagued school people and underlined the significance of race in society.[89] For various reasons school board members on both sides of the issue rejected some persuasive attempts at segregation, but their own racial biases precluded a complete rejection.

Whether the outcome would have been different if Oxnam

---

and writer W. E. B. DuBois and the opera star Paul Robeson, she ran on the Progressive Party ticket with the San Francisco attorney Vincent Hallinan.

and Bettinger had won the 1923 school board election we will never know. But it seems fair to assume that in the atmosphere created by the Better America Federation, school people like Stoddart, Shafer, and Smith were frightened enough by the attacks on liberals to fear for their own positions.

Some historians have noted many of the negative results of the reform period.[90] Yet another view has recently emerged that suggests the Progressive Era must be looked at carefully, each reform separately, in order to form an accurate picture. In San Francisco, as Terrence J. McDonald and Paul Peterson have shown, many Progressives integrated their interest in efficient government with their interest in upgrading public schools, even though it meant spending more on public services than they may have anticipated.[91] In Los Angeles no matter how strong the highly visible conservative tide ran, critical pragmatic aspects of Progressivism remained. Americanization continued because school people deemed it necessary.

5
In Search of Efficiency

> Today the entire child goes to school to be trained physically and spiritually. To develop the best possible individual into the best possible citizen is the object for which our public schools are established and maintained.
>
> —*Susan Snapp, 1923*

By the mid-1920's administrative Progressives in Los Angeles had succeeded in remaking their school district on the model of the scientifically managed corporation. They had transferred control to a centralized board, administered by a superintendent friendly to their cause, Susan M. Dorsey. With support from powerful political allies like Harry Chandler and H. R. Haldeman, they had fought off a so-called teachers' revolt during the 1923 school board election. And they continued to hire specialists, philosophers, psychologists, and curriculum experts from prestigious university schools of education to aid them in their task.[1] Nevertheless, the issue of who controlled the schools was far from settled. Conflicts continued to erupt, pitting teachers against principals, principals against superintendents, and teachers and principals against the school boards. Many of these centered around the theme of professionalism. Two school policies—on the access of ethnic groups to school facilities and on intelligence testing—reflect this theme.

Much as the Americanization programs of the 1920's resembled the earlier ones, they had taken on a different form. The new shape reflected the impatience of old-stock Americans with the slow pace of assimilation. At the prodding of Albert Shiels, the school board had decided to separate immigrant education and naturalization into two departments, allowing Progressive administrators to continue the humanitarian concerns of Americanization, particularly in the neighborhood schools. At the same time the board consolidated the political process of citizenship under the title of naturalization. Periodically the two overlapped. After all, Progressives believed in Americanization and wanted immigrants to become citizens. Ruby Baughman's fears about assimilation were not shared by the majority of reformers. Most saw no contradiction in helping immigrants and expecting them to conform within a homogeneous society. Therefore, when the recipients of their aid, the immigrants, had not evolved into typical Americans, when they continued to speak their own languages, to form their own societies, and to cling to their traditions, reformers were both dismayed and puzzled.

Educators, like many Americans, wanted an affirmation of American values and a sense of community, at a time when society had become diverse. The board reacted by becoming less willing to make schools available to immigrant group gatherings. At the same time, influenced by psychologists and other advocates of intelligence measuring, it introduced group intelligence testing. It expected testing to simplify the teaching of vastly diversified groups of children by identifying those with special talents and those with learning defects. Group testing soon became one of the most controversial of the schools' policies because it raised issues neither psychologists nor educators could answer.

Principals, Petitions, and the School Board

Before the First World War, in response to petitions by ethnic groups and to encourage assimilation, the board had willingly given immigrants access to public school facilities. The board assumed that closer ties to the schools would narrow the gap between ethnicity and acculturation. During the 1920's the board became convinced that it had erred; assimilation lagged in many immigrant communities. Los Angeles immigrants revealed their resistance to conformity by their repeated petitions to use school facilities to maintain their own cultures and languages. The board's previous open policy changed, and for the first time many of the requests were turned down. But that policy was thwarted to a certain degree by the simultaneous opening of a new avenue of access, the office of the principal. Most of the requests for the use of school facilities now came not by direct petition but by way of the principals, who consequently won a stronger power base within their communities.

At the Fifth Street School in San Pedro, for example, the evening school principal, Grace Briggs, requested the auditorium for the tenth anniversary celebration of the Mexican organization, the Benefica Recreativa Sociedad. On another occasion, she requested that a local Mexican group be allowed to hold a paid entertainment program in the auditorium and stated that the group agreed to donate a percentage of its earnings to the school. In both instances the board granted the requests.[2] But two different Mexican societies in San Pedro had their petitions turned down; in both cases the organizations petitioned the board directly.[3] In neighboring Wilmington Serbians asked for a room in which to teach fundamentals of arithmetic, reading, and writing in their native language. The board denied their petition on the grounds that the group constituted a private school and as such could not use public school buildings.[4]

At San Fernando the principal, Callie Darnell, noted that Mexicans needed school facilities to hold their Independence Day celebrations since no park was available in that area. The request was granted. Principal Sterry at Macy Street requested the school's auditorium for Syrians in her district who wanted to retain their children's native language. The request was granted. The principal of Lafayette Junior High requested space for a meeting of the National Association for the Advancement of Colored People. The request was granted. But the Molokans at Utah and Belvedere schools neglected to use proper channels when they petitioned for rooms to teach Russian, and in both cases they were turned down, again on the grounds that this would amount to establishing a private school.[5]

In central Los Angeles a local athletic club petitioned to play soccer on the school grounds on Sundays. The club proposed to "educate and Americanize their members by athletic games and exercises," and to that end requested the use of Jefferson High's playing fields. The club was willing to assume all responsibility for any damage to school property. Nevertheless, the board denied the request, saying that it was contrary to the board's regulations that "school grounds should be rented exclusively by an outside organization." Furthermore, the board members felt that the results had proved "objectionable where the experiment had been tried."[6]

One might think that if the California Commission of Immigration and Housing petitioned the board to let the Mexican club, Circulo Social Deportivo, use the auditorium at Polytechnic High for an entertainment program, the request would be granted. According to the publication *School and Society*, in 1923 Polytechnic had the largest registration of evening school students in the nation—an exaggeration but also an indication of how the city's Americanization programs had expanded. Nevertheless, the board turned the commission down, noting that the use of school property for paid entertainment for a group's gain was prohibited.[7] The commission might have requested that the club contribute some of the proceeds to the school, but it did not. The board may have decided that Americanization should be channeled through the evening school, where it was in control, instead of through a sports club, where it was not. Many board members, along with their conservative supporters, the Better America Federation, opposed Progressive state commissions epitomized by Immigration and Housing. Board members owed allegiance to the anti-Progressive elements in the city who had elected them to office in 1923, and, therefore, had decided not to sponsor an activity supported by Progressives from outside the area. Nevertheless, the only discernible difference between the Circulo Social Deportivo's request and the requests that were approved in San Pedro is that the San Pedro ones came through the principal.

There were exceptions, of course. The secretary of the YMCA, Colored Branch, petitioned the board directly to use Lafayette Junior High for a mass meeting to launch a building campaign in June 1923. The board agreed but with certain stipulations: the group had to be nonsectarian, open and free to the public, cause no damage to school property, and place a policeman on duty at all times.[8] The Y, whatever color, had sufficient political clout to command the board's support.

This subtle but important shift reflected the growing conservatism of society in the decade following the war; it also reflected the changes taking place in Los Angeles. Nativism reached new heights in the 1920's, stimulated by the reaction to the war, to the socialist revolutions abroad, and to the unrest at home. The anarchist bombing that led to federal raids on "subversive" groups under the authority of the U.S. Attorney General, A. Mitchell Palmer (the so-called Palmer Raids); the rise of the Ku Klux Klan in the cities, including demonstrations in and around Los Angeles;[9] and restrictive immigration legislation all reinforced the fears of native-born Americans that the United States had allowed in too many unassimilable aliens.

After 1923 the majority of the board seemed to share this view. The members had pledged to rid the schools of subversive elements, and they tried hard to fulfill their campaign promises. As we have seen, they banned both the *Nation* and the *New Republic* from the school libraries. During this period the virtues of Americanism were being promoted in a week of constitutional study. Students vied for prizes in essay writing and oratorical contests. Both the Los Angeles Chamber of Commerce and the Southern California Branch of the American Civil Liberties Union presented a program to the school board for this study week. The board, not surprisingly, chose the more conservative one proposed by the Chamber of Commerce.[10]

Nevertheless, the board had not retreated completely from its policy of permitting the use of school facilities to individual groups. Board members surely were not above political back-scratching. They expressed confidence in granting petitions directly to the principals, many of whom had supported their election—in contrast to many of the teachers who had not—and seemed well disposed to the board's objectives.

Yet if the board looked to the principals as a safe port in which to anchor their conservative policies, in some cases they must have been disappointed. One can hardly imagine two principals whose professionalism was more tightly woven into the fabric of Progressivism, or more dedicated to Progressive reforms, than Sterry at Macy Street and Briggs at Fifth Street. Both women had been influential in the early "betterment" campaigns in their districts and had their positions of power firmly based in Americanization campaigns. Furthermore, there is every indication from reading the board minutes and *School Journal* articles that their views on Americanization had survived. After all, in a manner reminiscent of earlier Americanizers, the principals were closer to immigrants than the board was, hence more sympathetic to their wishes and less doctrinaire in their approach. Therefore, much as the board may have wished to shut off ethnic-group access to the schools, it could not do so. Principals gained more control of their schools by circumventing board policy, acting as intermediaries for the immigrants and negotiating directly with the board.

The interaction between the board and the principals, and between the ethnic groups and the principals, shows the manner in which principals asserted themselves. More significantly, it shows a greater degree of local control than some historians have suggested. Even though the board set policy, that policy could be and was changed. The corporate model had been put in place, but there was flexibility. Private organizations had access to the schools under some circumstances, provided that they knew how the system worked and could reroute it.

Undoubtedly there are other reasons for the board's less open policy besides anti-Progressivism and nativism. For instance, the board's conservative nature dictated that it keep a tighter hold on school budgets. Moreover, as the city grew, both numerically and physically, ethnic groups had some choice of meeting places; the board probably no longer felt obligated to meet this particular need. It did still grant access where there was no other suitable space, as we saw in San Fernando and other less-developed sections of the city. Likewise as the city's recreation facilities expanded, athletic groups could use public playing fields and playgrounds instead of the schools. And, then, there simply seemed to be less need on the part of some groups to use the schools. For example, Jewish groups, which had frequently asked the schools for rooms to teach Hebrew and Yiddish, along with Jewish culture, no longer petitioned with much regularity. As the city's Jewish population expanded, Jewish organizations built meeting places to accommodate their growing membership.[11] Neighborhood synagogues proliferated during the 1920's, including the imposing Wilshire Boulevard Temple. Most of these buildings had facilities for after-school classes.[12] On the other hand, the requests from Mexicans increased. Their population expanded so rapidly in the 1920's that their societies could not keep up with their needs.

Intelligence Testing

During this era of conservatism the policy to tighten the public purse strings emanated from Sacramento and Governor Friend Richardson's office, filtering down to Southern California. Nevertheless, the Los Angeles Board of Education saw fit to expand one of its most expensive programs, intelligence testing. In 1920–21 the board spent $14,212.30 for the operations of the Department of Psychology and Educational Research; by 1923–24 the sum had risen nearly 50 percent, to $21,225.15. (These sums cover the cost of the test materials and the salaries of administrative and clerical staffs; they do not include the teachers' pay.)[13]

The promise of efficiency implicit in testing made it relatively easy for the board to depart from its tight fiscal policy. The administrative efficiency the board saw for itself, it hoped to transfer to the day-to-day workings of the schools with help from intelligence testing. As expensive as the program was, the board accepted the expense because the promise of efficiency seemed to more than equal the investment.

Science and Efficiency

Science, efficiency, and professionalization went hand in hand and became the cornerstone of Progressive education. "If science promised nothing else," Lawrence Cremin observes, "it promised efficiency; this ultimately was the plum educational scientists dangled before the taxpaying public."[14] The principles of scientific management when applied to school administration reflected the education community's interest in efficiency and standardization, and these same principles were now applied to curriculum diversification and grouping by intelligence.[15]

Perhaps no area of science affected the attitudes and policies of the Los Angeles schools more than the work of psychologists, particularly those who concentrated on the measurement of children's intelligence. Intelligence testing offered educators the ultimate in efficiency. It would be a grave mistake, however, to think of all Progressive education as a mere attempt to make schools more efficient. Although certainly an objective, such a generalization negates many of the school people's positive, humane goals. Progressive educators under the guidance of John Dewey stressed individualized school programs to educate the whole child.

Nevertheless, some might argue that IQ testing fit nicely with concepts of individual education because it offered ways of tailoring curriculum to meet the needs of students according to their supposed abilities. Tailoring curriculum to meet individual needs resulted in a myriad of programs, including classes for the physically handicapped, remedial work for slow learners, vocational education, and specialized courses for the academically gifted. After the war and the formation of the Progressive Education Association in 1919, the emphasis changed more toward efficiency than reform.[16] Mental testing stands at the apex of the time-management syndrome.

Diagnostic testing held much appeal for Progressives in other institutions besides the schools. David Rothman found in his study of prisons and asylums that the reformers' interest in devising ways to classify patients was stimulated by their hope that diagnostic tests would lead to effective systematic treatment. Psychiatrists placed emphasis on diagnosis rather than treatment, says Rothman, "because psychiatrists remained uncertain of how to translate their understanding of the deviant into specific recommendations for cure."[17]

The problem confronting the reformers in schools, prisons, and asylums alike stemmed from the fact that not all of their charges followed the pattern administrators had carefully cut out for them. In the schools many pupils simply were not progressing at the expected rate. Labeling these students subnormal, moving them into special rooms, supposedly enabled teachers to concentrate on specific learning disabilities. It also gave them a reason to divert poor students into various types of vocational training. The process of channeling students had begun with the introduction of junior high schools, and now it would be done scientifically. A staff member of the Los Angeles schools' Psychology and Educational Research Department expressed many of the school people's feelings when she wrote in 1924: "The problem of the education of subnormal children is one of the vital social and economic problems the public schools have undertaken in recent years."[18]

Not only in Los Angeles, but throughout the United States, educators turned to mental measurement as the panacea for this problem. The late nineteenth and early twentieth centuries witnessed the expansion of the public schools to include all children. In the United States and in many Western European countries and Japan, lawmakers pressed compulsory attendance laws and inaugurated a system to punish offenders—truant officers joined the list of school employees. California enacted its first compulsory attendance law in 1874, amended it in 1903, and instituted penalties for noncompliance.[19] The added numbers of pupils, many of them poor, provided a challenge to school people, who readily accepted any method that promised to simplify their task.

Educators in France and Great Britain faced similar problems. In France administrators turned to Alfred Binet. Born in Nice and first trained in the law, Binet had successfully shifted to experimental psychology, concentrating particularly on the measurement of reasoning abilities. His institute at the Sorbonne was highly regarded on the Continent and in Great Britain. In 1904 the Paris Minister of Public Education employed him to find ways to identify children whose slow school progress needed special attention. Binet assigned a grade level to specific tasks and located the mental age at the point where a child could no longer do the next task. If a gap was found between the mental age and the chronological age, that supposedly signaled a child in need of special help. Binet did not envision the use of his methods to test the general school population. As early as 1905 he feared that schoolmasters with "exaggerated zeal" would use his measurements as a convenient excuse to rid their classrooms of "children who trouble us." He went on to write, in what Stephen J. Gould calls a self-fulfilling prophecy, "It is really too easy to discover signs of backwardness in an individual when one is forewarned."[20]

While Binet unwittingly set up the mechanism for the school-testing program, it was the U.S. Army's group mental testing that provided the model the schools adopted. The military's emphasis on group tests rather than on individual tests appealed to schools. They had used testing before 1917, to be sure, but the postwar proliferation of that instrument can be tied directly to the army's experience. The army's alpha and beta tests were devised by a core of psychologists under the direction of Harvard's Robert M. Yerkes, then president of the American Psychological Association. The army's interest in alpha tests began not as a method to measure intelligence as such, but as a means of finding men qualified for Officers' Candidate School. Later it expanded as a way to sort out recruits in general. Since many of the recruits were illiterate in English, the Yerkes group developed another test that supposedly required little fluency in English. Alpha tests were given to literate, English-speaking soldiers, and beta tests to illiterates, or at least those illiterate in English. From 1917 to 1919 over 1.7 million men were tested. As one might expect from culturally biased tests, the least-assimilated groups—in 1918 that meant most Southern and Eastern European immigrants and black Americans—scored consistently below the IQ scale median of 100; most of them scored about 80.[21]

These tests were not without serious shortcomings. Both tests were not only culturally biased, but sufficiently distorted to favor the better educated; the beta pictorial tests required enough knowledge of English to understand the oral directions and enough familiarity with American culture to answer the questions. Yerkes was persuaded by Madison Grant's popularized arguments for Nordic racial superiority, but he also could not dismiss the correlation between scores and years of schooling. Putting two and two together, he came up with one: immigrants and Negroes lacked schooling because they were less intelligent.

The publicity from the testing created interest among all sorts of educators, women's clubs, immigration restrictionists, and many others. In 1920 the Rockefeller Foundation's General Education Board gave $25,000 to the National Research Council to develop a similar program to be used in schools.[22] As Paula Fass notes, psychologists "suddenly found themselves in a lucrative business with skills very much in demand." Many companies rushed tests into production without ample time to check their reliability. Between 1922 and 1923 one testing firm specializing in developing and distributing sold 2.5 million tests.[23]

With the backup of scientific data, the army's testing program reinforced what had heretofore been only notions of racial inferiority. But the greatest worry stemmed from the recruits' generally low scores. Some scholars even questioned the desirability of democracy in a nation where 60 percent to 70 percent of the population had a distressingly low level of intelligence. Professor of Sociology Harry Elmer Barnes of Smith College found truth in the "old Aristotelian dogma that some men are born to rule and others to serve."[24] Other educators went on record to declare that, since only a few of the country's young people had the mental capacity to learn, expending resources on the others was a waste. President George Cutten of Colgate University stated in his 1927 inaugural address that "only fifteen percent of the people have sufficient intelligence to get through college."[25]

Hindsight provides the advantage of recognizing many of the inadequacies of IQ testing. Many theories of the hereditarians Henry H. Goddard, Robert Yerkes, and Lewis M. Terman, along with less illustrious testing originators, have been discredited. Advanced study has shown that they based their assumptions—their mooring deeply rooted in cultural and racial biases—on faulty premises; intelligence is not an independent function of heredity, as they insisted, but a combined function of heredity and environment. We also recognize that testing for intelligence is at best a dubious undertaking, and that school performance and intelligence do not necessarily go hand in hand. Nevertheless, IQ testing offered school officials more efficient methods than any system they had previously used.

By the turn of the century, motivated by increased enrollments, many school systems had introduced special classes for physically and mentally deficient students.[26] Superintendent James Foshay had established "ungraded" classrooms in Los Angeles in 1901. The ungraded rooms benefited "those pupils who required more individual training" and relieved "the busy teacher [in] the crowded classroom." Many of the children had specific deficiencies. Rose Hardenburg noted: "A bright little second grader . . . could read as well as any grown-up but he had never had number work, and he was a very poor writer. He studied only these two branches, and will soon be ready for the fifth grade." Foshay wanted to segregate "troublesome children who were 'very poor' in deportment." Hardenburg, principal of Sentous Street School, the first to use ungraded rooms, reported: "At the time the class was organized, we were fortunate enough to find no one in the building who could be classed as incorrigible. Later two such were added with very satisfactory results."[27]

The board integrated other specialized programs into the curriculum in the early 1900's. Through the years the programs expanded to reflect the Progressives' theories of ability grouping and core curricula. All of the programs cost money, and by the 1920's, in keeping with the spirit of fiscal conservatism in Sacramento, the Los Angeles board talked retrenchment. Teachers, too, caught the spirit. They openly discussed their fear of funding cuts and the loss of salaries. They felt that they were required to make better use of public monies and suggested that they help develop relevant programs to fit students' needs.[28]

Nevertheless, the promise of efficiency overcame other concerns. In 1922 the Board of Education hired a specialist from the University of Chicago, J. Franklin Bobbitt, to reorganize the curriculum. Bobbitt, who had studied with G. Stanley Hall at Clark University,* became a proponent of applying business principles to school programs. He preached the gospel of good

*Shortly after his graduation from Indiana University in 1901, Bobbitt moved to Manila, where he taught in the Philippine Normal School and helped devise the curriculum for the Philippine school system. In 1907 he entered Clark University to study with Hall and wrote his Ph.D. dissertation on the growth of Filipino children. Bobbitt admired the work of Frederick W. Taylor and adapted many of his theories to education. (Longstreet, "Bobbitt.")

management, stressing that both schools and business should practice the principles of efficient administration. He served as an assistant superintendent from January to April 1922, and again for those same months in 1923.[29]

The ultimate outcome of the main testing program depended on a curriculum revision to allow for variations in mental abilities. If IQ tests could predict which children would be best suited for a particular subject, how much easier to place children in specific classes from the beginning rather than rerouting them at a later stage. Bobbitt's emphasis on curriculum differed from the emphases of many of the earlier school people and reformers. In Cremin's opinion, he typified the change in Progressive education in the 1920's. Bobbitt took a more pragmatic approach than his predecessors, one that continued to hope for a better society but depended on good management and left nothing to chance. In the *26th Yearbook of the National Society for the Study of Education*, he wrote: "The school is not an agency of social reform. Its responsibility is to help the growing individual continuously and consistently to hold to the type of living which is the best practical one for him."[30]

Bobbitt's pragmatism may have developed, in part, from a sense of disillusionment after the war. In February 1923, in an address to a group of Los Angeles educators, he stated his reasons for a curriculum overhaul in terms of global failures: "The world's education of ten years ago was not very good for that period as proven by the inability of men and women so to manage their affairs as to avoid the awful disasters of the past decade." He continued: "Education is primarily of interest to adulthood, not to childhood. We simply utilize childhood as the time of preparing for the fifty years of adulthood. And, when we know what men and women ought to do, and do well, then we have before us the things for which we should educate them."[31] Whether or not he was in the vanguard of the 1920's peace movement and disarmament campaign, Bobbitt clearly demonstrated a certain resolve to try to change the conditions that lead to war.[32] The official school publication took a similar stand but not until 1928—the year in which the United States joined fourteen other nations in signing the Kellogg-Briand Pact renouncing war as an instrument of national policy and five years after Bobbitt's statements. That year's *Courses of Study* devoted a section to what the writers called an "Outlawry of War."[33]

Bobbitt's book *Curriculum-Making in Los Angeles* had been well received, and the Psychology and Educational Research Department welcomed Bobbitt with open arms.* The *Educational Research Bulletin* declared: "The course of study committees have been appointed, enthusiasm is tense and Doctor Bobbitt will arrive soon. Let's get under way!"[34] Bobbitt differed from most hereditarians in his emphasis on the importance of experience in one's education. After making allowance for the heredity factor, he believed that the education of any person was essentially determined by the person's past experiences. He favored ability grouping. The department discussed the advantages of grouping and noted that children progressed five to seven times more rapidly in equal groups than in unequal ones.[35]

Lewis Terman

No single person in this country is associated with IQ testing more than Lewis M. Terman. Like Bobbitt, he had studied with the eminent psychologist G. Stanley Hall, of Clark University, whose theories on adolescence and child development greatly influenced education in the first half of the twentieth century.[36] During his years of studying, Terman contracted tuberculosis and, like many other health seekers, he came to Southern California to recuperate. In 1906, after a year teaching in San Bernardino, he accepted a position at Los Angeles State Normal School. After settling himself and his family in Los Angeles,

*The Department of Educational Research began its work for this study in the autumn of 1921. Over 300 administrators and teachers participated in the project, which was coordinated by Bobbitt; committees were formed to study particular areas of curriculum. It is not clear whether Bobbitt made a trip to Los Angeles in 1921, before he was hired as assistant superintendent in January 1922, or whether he directed the early stages of the project from Chicago. The book was published in June 1922, before the various committees had made their final changes, in the expectation that outside educators who read the book would offer their own suggestions on curriculum. These suggestions would then be taken into account in designing a new curriculum during the following year, when Bobbitt would return for another three-month stint as assistant superintendent.

he arranged for his friend and fellow psychologist from Clark, Alfred Gesell, to join him on the staff. Terman taught at the Normal School for four years, before moving to Stanford University, the place where he did his major work.[37]

Terman's enthusiasm and innovative theories of intelligence measurement influenced the corps of students he trained both at the Normal School and at Stanford. Not only did many of his students teach in the city's schools, but some held positions in the Department of Psychology and Educational Research. One was the department's statistician, Ellen Alice McAnulty, who had worked as his research assistant. Terman was also close to Dr. Arthur H. Sutherland, the department's director of educational research. In 1922 Sutherland outlined the workings of the department in a booklet entitled *Intelligence Tests and School Organization*. Terman, a member of the Commission on Revision of Elementary Education that prepared the booklet, wrote its preface.[38]

Terman's work on the American version of the classic IQ test transformed Binet's concept of age-mentality, and he was one of the first to popularize the term "intelligence quotient," which expressed the relationship of an individual's mental age to his chronological age. The Stanford-Binet became the model for all other IQ tests, including the achievement tests conceived by E. L. Thorndike and his students: arithmetic (1908), spelling (1910), handwriting and drawing (1913), reading (1914), and language ability (1916). Terman attributed mental retardation to "inferior mental endowment" and discounted irregular attendance, the use of foreign language in the home, malnutrition, bad teeth, and adenoids as major causes of low IQ. In his 1919 work, *Intelligence of School Children*, he announced that, contrary to the theories of some educators, "educational reform may as well abandon, once and for all, all effort to bring all children up to grade."[39]

From the beginning, Terman's theories provoked controversy. Dewey criticized the hereditarian underpinnings of mental testing in 1922. The IQ, he wrote, "reflects not upon the innate mentality of the mass but upon the acquired intelligence of men in high positions. It shows how their education, that given by their surroundings as well as their schools, has fixed in them the disposition to judge by classification instead of discrimination." Dewey opposed using the tests as the sole standard for dividing or grouping children. In his view the IQ was at that point "at most an indication of certain risks and probabilities. Its practical value lies in the stimulus it gives to more intimate and intensive inquiry into individualized abilities and disabilities." Terman's basic concepts were thus simply wrongheaded.[40]

In that same year the writer Walter Lippmann initiated a debate with Terman in the pages of the *New Republic.* Lippmann attacked Terman and the army testers for ignoring the purpose of the tests, which was to aid classification, not to measure intelligence. Leveling his most heated criticism directly at Terman, he wrote: "The claim that we have learned to measure hereditary intelligence has no scientific foundation. We cannot measure intelligence when we have never defined it, and we cannot speak of its hereditary biases after it has been indistinguishably fused with a thousand educational and environmental influences from the time of conception to the school age." Although Lippmann saw the tests as having the potential for achieving a homogeneous grouping of schoolchildren, he felt they needed to be "administered with skepticism and sympathy."[41]

Not to be outdone by the environmentalists, Terman counterattacked. But he never confronted the crux of the argument: where was the scientific evidence for the psychologists' claim that intelligence was determined by heredity, let alone the claim that it could be divorced from life experiences? The only study Terman mentions, one undertaken by his graduate student, attests to some of the contradictions of the tests. The study found considerable variations in the IQs of Japanese and Portuguese children in California; the average among the Portuguese was around 80, whereas the Japanese child "soon develops an I.Q. not far below that of the average California child of Nordic descent." Having no explanation for the discrepancy and wanting to make light of Lippmann's criticisms, Terman suggested that the children's native languages might have something to do with it. "It is conceivable that the more liquid Latin tongue exerts a sedative effect on infants' minds as compared with the harsher Japanese language, which may be stimulating in comparison."[42]

By the late 1920's the environment-versus-heredity controversy had come under severe criticism by psychologists themselves. Younger, non–Anglo Saxon psychologists like Samuel Kohs, author of the Kohs Block Test, had already been questioning the rationality of the hereditarian theories for some time. Then, in 1925, William Chandler Bagley published *Determination and Education*, the first book-length criticism of the practice of basing educational opportunity on intelligence tests. At the National Education Association's 1928 meeting, Terman's hereditarian views were challenged by three educators, Bagley of Columbia University, and Frank Freeman and Charles Judd of the University of Chicago. Although the debate provided no winners, clearly Terman's views were not universally accepted. Finally, in 1937, Terman revised his Stanford-Binet tests to include the environmental factors that affected test scores. Whether the adverse influence of Nazism, or pressure from his own discipline, or the work of American anthropologists and other scientists, or the Depression (or some combination of these) caused that shift is another question.[43]

Much of the controversy surrounding the testing programs stemmed from the implication that certain ethnic groups are genetically inferior. Not only on the army tests, but on school-administered IQ tests, most of the new immigrants in the industrial cities of the Atlantic seaboard and the Midwest scored around the eighty-fifth percentile.[44] Kimball Young noted similar scores in groups of Northern California "Latin" schoolchildren. Young, a graduate student of Terman's, conducted a study of Portuguese, Southern Italian, and Mexican schoolchildren in San Jose in 1919. He lumped the three nationalities together as Latins and found that these immigrant groups scored considerably below non-Latin students. Young de-emphasized language as a handicap: language was an impediment only for the very young and the "newly immigrated." He stood "firmly on the ground that the cause of school difficulties must be found in the more innate intellectual difficulties."[45]

In another study Bertha Boody found that Jewish immigrants tested at Ellis Island in 1921 held the most "certificates for mental defects." African Americans sometimes surprised the examiners. In a 1924–25 Massachusetts report, black students scored higher than Portuguese children. Moreover, in these Massachusetts schools, with mixed ethnic populations of French-Canadians, Italians, Poles, and Portuguese, blacks had the highest percentage of IQ scores over 120.[46]

Around the same time the Los Angeles school district published two studies showing that both black children and Jewish children scored, on average, as high as, or higher than, native white pupils. One study noted that Jews as a group scored consistently high. As in other cases of ethnicity, Los Angeles researchers failed to note whether the Jewish children were first-, second-, or third-generation Americans, or whether their forebears came from Eastern or Western Europe.[47] During the late 1920's many of the studies on the IQ of Jewish children confirmed the Los Angeles findings, so that even the racist Young was forced to admit grudgingly that "Hebrew" IQ scores were comparable to those of Northern Europeans.[48]

Scholars have noted the inconsistencies in the immigration restrictionists' arguments for a halt to Jewish and Asian migration. Young claimed that immigrants from inferior nations lowered the general IQ of the nation. Yet he quoted studies confirming that the IQs of Jews and Asians were similar to those of native-born white Americans.[49] It might follow that these particular groups should be allowed to enter unfettered. But deductive reasoning was not the restrictionists' strong point. Never to becloud their arguments with contradictory evidence, expert witnesses called to testify before the House Committee on Immigration and Naturalization during the 1920's used prewar army tests and studies such as Boody's to substantiate their views. Unlike many of the subsequent inquiries on schoolchildren, those materials ranked Jews, along with other new immigrants, near the bottom of the IQ scale.[50]

There is no question that studies like Young's reinforced social and ethnic theories and were used to persuade Congress to restrict the flow of immigrants from certain parts of the world. Young's attitudes are particularly important to this study because, as an acolyte of Terman's, he reflected many of his master's views. Young was blinded by his prejudices, while other testers, including those in Los Angeles, were simply myopic. They failed to recognize that if American middle-class culture had not filtered into the homes of many of these children, those children could hardly decode it on an IQ test.

In recent years studies of immigrants and their experiences with American institutions, along with new interpretations of the testing programs, have led researchers to conclude that the old, culture-based tests were inadequate measures. In the heyday of testing, however, most of them believed the data and drew their conclusions based on their own racial and cultural biases. Generally, most immigrants scored lower on culturally biased tests than white, native-born Americans. One writer suggests that the combination of social scientists and Progressive educators, the instigators of testing, victimized Hispanics in Los Angeles and throughout the Southwest.[51] Chicano children in Los Angeles usually scored near the bottom of the spectrum, and since the scores were used as an important criterion for determining the type of education a child received, most Hispanic children were channeled into some form of vocational education at best and at worst into schools and classes for the retarded.

The tests, however, were not the only criterion used for classification. In "neighborhood" schools—in those schools where 50 percent of the population was foreign-born—principals and teachers actually made most of the decisions concerning grouping.[52] There is no denying that some were infected by the period's prevailing racial attitudes. But the assumption that their racism so blinded them that they never questioned standardized testing on the Chicano community has too many exceptions to be the rule. School administrators in fact went to great lengths to find suitable tests for non-English-speaking Mexican children. Numerous articles in school publications indicate that many educators were concerned about the low scores of Mexican children and tried to analyze the situation in order to find ways to improve the scores. The official organ of the

Psychology and Educational Research Department, the *Educational Research Bulletin*, devoted many pages to discussions of testing.

Admittedly, the writings in the *Bulletin* or in the *School Journal* are not necessarily indicative of the extent of school people's social biases. Whatever their inner thoughts, few expressed them for the record. One does not find any statements so explicit as those of Ellwood Patterson Cubberley, dean of Stanford's School of Education, in any official Los Angeles publication, for example.

Cubberley's concern was not the Mexicans so much as immigrants from Southern and Eastern Europe. He saw those groups as a national problem and placed the responsibility for assimilating them directly on the schools. To him Americanization represented the only hope of protecting the nation from the onslaught of inferior immigrants. Southern and Eastern Europeans "were of a very different type" from Northern and Western Europeans—"largely illiterate, docile, often lacking in initiative, and almost wholly without Anglo-Saxon conceptions of righteousness, liberty, law, order, public decency, and government." Their coming, he feared, had "served to dilute tremendously our national stock and to weaken and corrupt our political life."[53]

The Institutionalizing of IQ Testing in Los Angeles

On the surface Los Angeles educators appear to have been hereditarians. During the 1920's Los Angeles school counselors administered mental tests to nearly the entire school population. But some school people were dissatisfied with the standard IQ tests. Many of the educators who worked with immigrant children—particularly with Hispanics—found the tests an inadequate gauge and turned to achievement tests.[54] Some felt strongly that all areas should be examined and insisted on testing such diverse skills as music, art, and handwriting, as well as the conventional ones of reading, spelling, and arithmetic.

Sixty-first Street School stands out as an exception to the district's seemingly uniform mental testing program. As early as 1922 the Sixty-first Street staff rejected intelligence tests and gave only "educational ones." The principal, Adele Mossman, observed that Sixty-first Street preferred "that pupils unconsciously classify themselves according to mentality by our revised project tests." The project tests were given independently to each child when that child showed a readiness to be tested.[55]

The "revised project tests" she had reference to were based on the so-called project method, a pedagogical approach, or at least an expression, first given currency in 1918 by William Heard Kilpatrick. Kilpatrick, a colleague of Dewey's at Columbia University's Teachers College, envisioned education developing out of socially useful acts. Children would prepare for life in urban, industrial America by "whole hearted purposeful acts carried out amid social surroundings." In examples reinforcing the gender attitudes of the times, Kilpatrick demonstrated that girls learned by the "socially purposeful" act of making a dress, and boys learned by publishing a school newspaper. The teacher was central to his scheme, providing the correct atmosphere, steering the project, and, finally, "if we believe in democracy, eliminating himself or herself from the success of the procedure."[56] Historians have noted that the project method, though it allowed some teachers a little more freedom in the classroom, never threatened the hierarchical power structure.[57]

The Sixty-first Street staff also favored achievement tests. Since the school was classified as a "normal" school, with few if any foreign-language-speaking children, Mossman's decision to use other forms of testing was not based on language difficulties, the problem commonly faced by administrators in neighborhood schools. The preference for project and achievement tests over IQ tests indicates that at least some Los Angeles school people questioned the comprehensiveness of the latter, although not necessarily the premise of testing or the hierarchical structure of the testing program.

Assistant Superintendent Emma Raybold reported on one of the earliest group tests on the Mexican population in June 1925.* This test was not to assess intelligence but to determine

*In describing the participants of the studies, I have used the department's designations. In no case did the testers differentiate between Mexican-born

the most reliable test for future measurements. The previous fall school counselors had administered a series of intelligence tests to two groups of "unselected" first-graders in the San Fernando Valley schools. The groups consisted of Spanish-speaking Mexican children at San Fernando and English-speaking children at Lankershim. There is no mention of the ethnicity of the Lankershim students. The series of tests included two versions of the Binet Individual, the Detroit First Grade Intelligence, and the Pintner-Cunningham. At San Fernando School the counselor added the Kohs Block test because she felt it was "the best tool to use with such a group." As a nonverbal performance test, in which children were asked to fit blocks of various colors together into set patterns, the Kohs would not require fluency in English.[58]

The correlation coefficients for most of the test scores were quite high; however, the Mexican students' Kohs scores correlated poorly with their scores on the verbal tests: .53 with the Detroit, .57 with the Binet, and .59 with the Pintner.[59] Unfortunately, Raybold failed to report the range and standard deviation of any of the test scores. In addition she did not mention whether she performed statistical tests to determine if the differences between the correlations were statistically significant. Finally, and most importantly, she failed to give the Kohs test to the Lankershim students, thereby obviating several valuable comparisons. All we know is that the school people passed over the Kohs in favor of verbal tests.

The test results caused confusion. Testers had assumed that the Kohs test would be most suitable for non–English speakers. When they found that the Mexican children's Kohs scores correlated poorly with their verbal scores, Raybold concluded that the Kohs test "was not as reliable with a primary group of Mexican children who cannot speak English as is a test involving language factors." The Detroit test, however, correlated highly with the other verbal tests, and from that she concluded that

---

and second- or third-generation Mexican Americans; the same is true for Japanese nationals and Japanese Americans. The term "American" referred to white native-born children. "Unselected" probably meant random.

"Mexican children actually understand the English language more than we realize." The Detroit test became the standard for testing Mexican children.[60]

In rejecting the Kohs test and accepting the Detroit test as "reliable," educators preserved the cultural and economic bias of the testing program. In this case they failed to realize that a nonverbal test would correlate less well with verbal tests than the verbal tests would with each other, and that the nonverbal test would provide a different but no less valid view of students' mental abilities.

Raybold expressed surprise that the San Fernando students understood more English than the counselors imagined; yet instead of taking this newfound information and using it in a constructive manner, the testers misinterpreted it. The Hispanic children were what educators now call "limited English speakers," with an English vocabulary of about a hundred words. They could identify common objects but not enough of them to raise their IQ scores much. The children knew just enough English to confuse the psychologists and give the impression that they were not as handicapped in language as their examiners believed.[61]

Raybold and the psychologists operated under two faulty assumptions: first, that intelligence was a single entity, and second, that the Stanford-Binet measured it well. Although Raybold had some intuition that the primary testing at San Fernando School was not giving perfectly clear results, she relied on the traditional view of intelligence and the traditional methods to explain the results. Racism may have influenced her conclusions; few teachers could escape the biases of their backgrounds. It is possible that the Hispanic children scored higher on the nonverbal Kohs than on the verbal Binet. But since the Kohs did not correlate as highly as the other verbal tests did with the Stanford-Binet, and the lower scores perhaps fit in better with Raybold's and the staff's perception of where Mexican children would score, they decided to reject the Kohs test. This was most likely a monumental error; the Kohs showed how far off the verbal tests in fact were.

At any rate, satisfied with the Detroit test, the psychologists decided to use it with first graders at Belvedere School the following October. They felt that the Detroit test not only pointed out individual differences better than either the Binet or the Pintner, but lent itself more readily to a translation into Spanish. It is unclear why the department chose to use a Spanish translation of the Detroit test at Belvedere. Located east of the central city between Boyle Heights and East Los Angeles, it was in a more urban district than San Fernando and had a somewhat more ethnically mixed population. Over the years new industrial opportunities and cheap housing had attracted an increasing number of Mexican laborers to Belvedere and other districts east of the Los Angeles River,[62] and by this time they may well have had a better command of English than their San Fernando counterparts. But they may not have been much different, either, for in ethnically mixed schools, Mexican children tended to stick together and speak Spanish on the playgrounds. This was in no way peculiar to Mexicans, to be sure. Before the First World War the same was true of the recent Eastern European Jewish immigrants in New York City. A school supervisor, Julia Richman, an assimilated, second-generation Bohemian Jew, concerned that Jewish children in the Lower East Side were not assimilating rapidly, forbade the children to speak Yiddish. She suggested that teachers wash out the offenders' mouths with soap! We can only speculate about her success.[63]

There is nothing to indicate that anything so drastic as mouth washing occurred in Los Angeles, but that does not rule out the use of such procedures. Many school people viewed the retention of foreign language as an obstacle to becoming proficient in English. Some also regarded it as an indicator of low mental capacity. Edith Heim had that in mind when she proposed the Spanish translation of the Detroit test, and she wanted to prove her theory. The Belvedere counselor wrote that the translated test would determine whether language was the handicap or whether, as she expected, "language difficulty is often indicative of mental deficiency."[64]

The translated Detroit test clarified little; above all, it did not identify the children's abilities. Tests were often translated into a form of the language not totally familiar to the children. The

Detroit test was undoubtedly translated into Castilian, which would have captured few of the idioms of the language used in the barrios or poor Mexican neighborhoods. Some educators recognized the unreliability of translated tests and wrote their own. Hershel T. Manuel and his staff at the University of Texas's Department of Education developed and administered their own version of the Stanford-Binet in the early 1930's.[65] The Texans had found that a direct translation ignored cultural biases—those beyond the simple biases of language. Even if the children used Castilian, the same cultural partiality that existed in the English version would continue in the translation.

The same criticism applied even more strongly to a nonverbal test. For example, the now largely abandoned 1919–20 Haggerty Intelligence Examination, similar to the beta test but for primary grades, is a completion test. Some of the pictures are easily completed, but others rely on past experience. After all, a story about zoo animals in either English or Spanish would require prior knowledge, a trip to the zoo or at least a glimpse of a book about animals. One has to be acquainted with a telephone to add a cord, and an American hearth to add a screen, and to have seen a live elephant or a picture of one to add a trunk.

Heim felt that the Spanish translation had only one section where the Mexican children might be at a disadvantage, the one asking them to mark "five things which we dig out of the ground." It is not clear whether her worry was that the "correct" answer involved fruits and vegetables not familiar to Mexican children; at any rate, since this item was only one out of fifty, or one month out of the mental age, she did not see a wrong answer as much of a handicap.[66]

The Belvedere counselor favored holding non–English speakers back until they knew sufficient English to take the test in English, and she suggested that children attain the mental age of six before they entered the first grade. She wanted to see the special class, C1, already in operation on a limited basis, expanded to meet the need of a larger non-English population. She hoped the C1 class could act as a bridge between kindergarten and first grade, avoiding the problem in which "2 or 3 semesters of either drifting or drowning result in indolent, uninterested pupils who become the problem and despair of even the best teachers."[67]

Heim exemplified the way a lower-level administrator could make school policy. By selecting particular tests and administering them in Spanish, and then, developing a program of language arts based on the results, she and others working in the field had the ability to initiate school policy. Rather than the board dictating to Heim how to interpret testing, she took it on herself to suggest a multilevel program for non–English speakers and limited–English speakers in order to prepare them for entrance into mainstream classrooms.

In many ways the school personnel acted out of a sense of frustration. In trying to develop a test that would record a realistic score for non–English speakers Heim and her co-workers showed a certain sensitivity to the language problem. What they failed to understand is that even though the Mexican schoolchildren in Los Angeles were becoming bilingual and bicultural, they had not acquired sufficient knowledge in either the language or the culture to have much effect on a test that was geared to English-speaking, middle-class Americans. Standard IQ tests translated into Spanish would not give any more realistic results than those in English. The real problem with the testing program, whether in English or in Spanish, was that the tests had been devised for a middle-class population, or at least a population that aspired to the middle class. American middle-class values did not appeal to many immigrant families. The petitions to the Board of Education illustrate that ethnic communities were as interested in retaining their own culture and language as they were in adopting those of America.

Heim, like Young and many others in the profession, viewed the lack of English as a manifestation of low mental ability, not a simple unfamiliarity with a new language and culture. But at the same time she proposed that intensive exposure to English in the C1 class would overcome the problem. She stressed homogeneous grouping to hasten the learning process; that would allow the teacher to concentrate on English instruction. Heim's solution exemplifies the contradictory thinking of many Los Angeles school people. On the one hand she argued that English difficulties reflected low mental ability, and on the other, she wanted to solve the problem by total immersion in special English classes.

In December 1925 the central school administration ordered another test of Hispanic children. This time it chose to test at Palms School, an integrated setting. The results were published in the *Educational Research Bulletin* under a title indicative of the view that many in the community took of the influx of Mexican children—"The Mexican: An Educational Asset or an Educational Liability?" Palms's principal, Mrs. Leo Gamble, refuting what she called the "feeling of unfairness of dubbing [the Mexican child] 'lazy' or of feeling him a liability without first measuring his efforts," chose to administer two different tests, one to measure intelligence and the other to measure achievement.[68] (Note, again, how Gamble, like Heim, asserted her own policy, becoming the final arbiter of the groups to be tested and deciding to use achievement tests along with IQ tests in order to obtain more realistic scores.)

Palms School administered tests to 250 children in the third through eighth grades, twenty-two of whom were Mexican. Gamble viewed the Mexican families as upwardly mobile; half owned their own homes, and five had automobiles. Most of the children were American-born and not one had immigrated after the age of two. Many of the families spoke some English, but not all of them. Gamble noted that with so few Mexican children in the school, all of them spoke English, and none had a language handicap. Nevertheless, the IQ test results were disappointing, tending to reinforce established biases. The average IQ of the testees was 100.25; the Mexican children scored an average of 78.75. The achievement scores told another story. The Mexican students consistently scored more highly in achievement relative to their IQ scores than the rest of the students.

What Gamble failed to note, and what a careful examination of the tests may reveal, was that even though the school's Hispanic community seemed upwardly mobile, the tests imposed cultural biases against them. The fact that some of the parents spoke English and that English dominated the schoolyard conversations did not guarantee that the children knew enough

English to perform well on a verbal IQ test. Another reason for their lower test scores may be that they entered school a year or so later than the English-speaking children. The average age of the Mexican first-graders was 8.5 years, compared with 6.9 for the average "American" child. The ratio of mental age to chronological age that defines the Binet IQ would automatically favor the younger group. Nevertheless, Gamble's use of achievement tests to find a more reliable testing method for the Mexican students' ability shows a continuing sensitivity on the part of Los Angeles school people to the shortcomings of IQ testing.

Another indication of the educators' reluctance to rely solely on IQ tests to gauge mental abilities appeared in the *Bulletin* in the fall of 1926.[69] This case once again illustrates how principals and teachers assumed command of the testing process and tried to make sense out of what they saw as arbitrary policy. Principal Joseph Kendall of Lemona Grammar in Van Nuys, a newly constructed, completely segregated Mexican school, reasoned that little significance should be attached to the low intelligence scores because the measure used, the National Intelligence Test, presupposed reading ability in English. Kendall sought tests that would not penalize children who lacked skills in English. He chose other versions of the National Intelligence Test. Although one tested reading comprehension, the others tested spelling and arithmetic. The entire school personnel directed their efforts at improving the standard scores.

From the beginning the Lemona educators realized that nonstandard procedures needed to be employed if they were to attain their goals. In fact, the school's previous scores had been higher than some expected, considering that so many of the pupils lacked fluency in English. For example, in arithmetic the students almost met the city norm; they were a little less than a year behind in reading comprehension, and a little more than a year behind in spelling. However, since many of the children were old for their grade, the retardation rate was calculated at two and a half years. Their average IQ was 75.

The Lemona staff put together a program to raise the scores. Without allotting extra time for fundamentals, the teachers combined standard materials with ones that they had designed themselves; these obviously stimulated the children. Collectively the IQ scores rose to 81, and Kendall noted that the change "was of course due to the fact that the added knowledge of the English language which the pupils had acquired and the greater reading ability caused them to register to a closer degree their real intelligence."[70] In the teachers' eyes the real gains came in achievement. In only seven months the students' overall gain amounted to fourteen months, or a 100 percent acceleration rate. They gained thirteen months in arithmetic, ten months in reading comprehension, and a remarkable twenty months in spelling.

Kendall imagined what progress could be made if the school was integrated. Although English was spoken in the classroom, on the playground the children spoke Spanish and "continued to think in the Spanish language."[71] "If such results can be achieved with a group of foreign children unleavened by the presence of English-speaking mates," he wrote, "what might we not expect if similar enthusiasm and equally efficient teaching methods were applied in schools where our foreign children have the added advantage of hearing English on the playgrounds and having associations with children skilled in the customs our schools must teach to our newer citizens?"[72] Later advocates of school integration would repeat Kendall's question.

The Lemona example illustrates the potential for conflict between the hierarchy in the Department of Psychology and Educational Research and rank-and-file teachers and principals. The central school administrators expected to choose the tests, to administer them, and to interpret them. The Lemona staff had its own agenda. Kendall and his teachers wanted to control their school program by choosing and administering other tests and, then, interpreting them. In these instances professionalization—the authority to choose the test—and its concomitant—enhanced status in the profession and in the district—collided. The psychologists and the Lemona staff both wanted to make the decisions.

The Lemona example also illustrates a continued belief in the goals and values of Americanization. Kendall viewed assimilation as the key to solving the country's problems as well as the immigrants'. The study clearly shows that he and his dedicated teachers worked for the betterment of their pupils, at least their betterment in terms of higher scholastic achievement. To this end they discouraged expressions of Mexican culture and the Spanish language, expressions of biculturalism and bilingualism many advocates of pluralism value in the 1980's. If the Lemona educators were familiar with Horace Kallen's theories on the importance of "cultural pluralism," they rejected them.* Kendall's biases extended toward the Mexican culture and language but not toward the ethnic group itself. In true melting-pot rhetoric, he implied that once rid of their nationalistic baggage, immigrants would be just like everyone else.[73]

Los Angeles educators also questioned the relationship between IQ scores and educational attainment. Teachers wondered why some students had successful school careers, and others did not. In 1928 Winifred Murphy, a counselor at Belvedere Junior High, decided to analyze the problem to determine which factors led some students to advance to senior high and others to drop out after junior high. She wondered whether the board should institute restrictions on who should attend high school. Obviously Murphy was weighing the merits of educating masses of children beyond eighth grade, yet her study presents some interesting insights into her own sensitivities to cultural differences within the immigrant community. Murphy underscored the influence of family expectations on continued schooling. Fifteen- and sixteen-year olds were expected to take care of their own needs, and this assumption led many to choose work over school.

Murphy found that native capacity had little to do with

*Kallen, a Jew and former student of the philosopher William James, began writing on the subject when he sensed that assimilation would result in the loss of Jewish identity. He broadened his concepts to include other ethnic groups because he perceived a universal determination among the foreign-born to retain their traditions. He suggested that instead of melting into one Anglo-Saxon tradition, each group should maintain its own heritage. Though his following was small, he became the first major writer to articulate some of the deep psychological implications involved in assimilation. (See his article "Democracy vs. the Melting Pot," 1915; and his book *Culture and Democracy in the United States*, 1924.)

whether or not students entered senior high, since the number of dropouts with low and high IQ scores formed a normal distribution curve. Moreover, the correlations between IQ and matriculations were too low to be significant, as were those for age and grades. Correlations between effort and IQ and between cooperation and IQ proved insufficient also. The counselor had to conclude that since none of the criteria used correlated with each other, another method should be adopted. Her remarks indicate the ambivalence that IQ testing had created. Since test scores apparently had little predictive usefulness, their professed value became suspect.[74]

The September 1928 *Educational Research Bulletin* published a study of the methods used to classify students into groups. Questionnaires were sent to all elementary schools: "regular," where the majority of the children spoke English; "semi-neighborhood," where 30 percent were non–English speakers; and "neighborhood," where 50 percent were non–English speakers. In the neighborhood schools only, principals' and teachers' judgments received priority over test results in determining grouping. It is not possible to know how test scores influenced their decisions, but placing the final responsibility for ability grouping or tracking with those educators most closely associated with immigrant children clearly indicates that many of the central administrators had listened to the teachers' and principals' reservations, and were aware of and concerned about the unreliability of the testing program.[75]

A more comprehensive example of the growing suspicion about the adequacy of IQ tests as a means of classifying students appeared in the *Bulletin* in 1929. The studies conducted in 1926, 1927, and 1928 were based on over half the elementary schools in the city. The results were predictable: the percentage of mentally retarded—IQ lower than 70—was highest in the neighborhood schools; the percentage of children scoring above 130 was highest in the normal schools and lowest in the neighborhood schools. Ellen Alice McAnulty, the Department of Psychology and Educational Research's statistician, noted two factors that influenced these results: (1) the tests required a reading knowledge of English when a very large proportion of children in the city were foreign; (2) a number of younger and brighter children had been promoted to junior highs, leaving the elementary schools in foreign neighborhoods bereft of their superior scores. McAnulty planned another study to determine to "what extent the use of group tests have failed to predict the intelligence quotient, as later determined by individual Binets, for the various groups, foreign and native, found in our schools."[76]

Another indication that the department found the testing results questionable is found in a study done by McAnulty and Clara Schmitt in 1931.[77] At this time they tested groups of subnormal children, eight- and nine-year-old Mexican and American students whose IQs ranged between 60 and 69. They wanted to find out whether Mexicans failed the language test more often than Americans. They were not disappointed. American students succeeded 84 percent of the time, the Mexicans only 57 percent. The students with the greatest problems took another test, which could have been Kohs Block, the Haggerty Completion, or a translated Detroit. On the nonlanguage sections the results were very close. For example, Mexicans had success at counting up to twenty 94 percent of the time, against 90 percent for the others; Mexicans succeeded in finding likenesses 88 percent of the time, against only 72 percent for the others. McAnulty and Schmitt concluded that the six Binet tests "may be a test of racial differences, but examination of the items indicate that they are the ones most affected by language."[78] They decided that Mexican children had a mental age at least a year higher than was usually computed for them.

Blacks received less attention in the literature than the Mexicans. As the *Bulletin* published these and many other studies of Mexican children in the years 1923–32, it carried only one study of black children, although it promised more.[79] This almost certainly had to do with the relative sizes of the two groups. Although the black community grew during the 1920's, it never rivaled the size of the Mexican community. Blacks, like other Americans, lured by the promises of temperate climate and economic opportunity, flocked to the City of Angels mostly in the two decades following the war. But even in 1940 they numbered only 63,774.[80]

It may also be that educators felt blacks had fewer learning disabilities than Hispanic children. Lawrence DeGraaf has found that until the 1930's, when poorer Southerners migrated into the city, most black residents were part of a nascent middle class.[81] Two earlier studies reinforce DeGraaf's analysis. In both, black children were found to score as well as or better than their white counterparts. The *Bulletin*'s one study, published in 1923, reported on the testing of 500 black children in five elementary schools and how they compared with the children from fifteen schools that the psychologists felt represented the city as a whole. On the National Intelligence Test the black children's median score was 104.7, the "representative" children's 106.0. Likewise, their scores on achievement tests compared favorably. True, on a sixty-word spelling test the black children scored almost a year below grade level, but as Assistant Supervisor Willis Clark noted, the situation was not materially different for the rest of the school population.[82] Ten years later McAnulty promised another study of black schoolchildren, but that study did not appear in the *Bulletin*. It was to be part of a three-part study of Mexican, Japanese, and black children to determine whether these minorities "measured up to the norm." McAnulty reminded the reader that the standardized tests had been devised for white children. She failed to mention that it was devised for middle-class white children.[83]

McAnulty may have had in mind making Hazel Whitaker's three-year survey of Los Angeles's black population, completed in 1931, part of the promised study. The first black to receive a regular teaching assignment at Los Angeles High, Whitaker wrote a master's thesis at the University of Southern California on gifted black children. Herself a successful professional, she married Leon Whitaker, the first black deputy district attorney. Using the files of the Psychology and Educational Research Department, Whitaker found that black and white children from the same social class and geographic area had similar IQs. Irving Hendricks has noted that the one difficulty Whitaker encountered was "finding one hundred gifted white children living in the community with blacks."[84] Most of the whites were recent immigrants and poorer than their black neighbors. They also scored lower on the tests. Whitaker recommended encouraging talented African Americans rather than trying to dissuade them from further study. She found the school practice of admonishing bright blacks against advancing academically one of the "most reprehensible . . . to be found among educators."[85]

Yet as we have seen, Los Angeles began segregating black high school students at this time. The IQ tests played little or no part in that decision. There is ample evidence to prove that the board bowed to community pressure and set out on this policy in the late 1920's regardless of test scores. In the case of Jefferson High, and later Jordan High, the board redrew some school boundaries,[86] and in other cases school staff directed African American students into vocational education classes.[87] Some of the classes fitted them into subservient occupations; for example, no other high school except Jefferson offered a course in how to become a maid.[88]

Los Angeles's Japanese students, the city's only other sizable nonwhite group, apparently posed no particular educational problems. As with black students, school people found the Japanese students' IQs on a par with whites. McAnulty reported in the January 1932 *Bulletin* that both groups tested out at an average of 105. She noted that the results appeared unusually high for both groups but did not question them further.[89]

The Japanese community had grown from just a few at the turn of the century to over 35,000 in 1930.[90] The larger and more prosperous the community became, the greater the antagonism toward the Japanese. The 1913 anti-alien land legislation had been specifically aimed at curtailing the success of the Japanese farmers. No other group faced the kind of organized hate campaigns mobilized by the Anti-Asian League. The Ku Klux Klan never had the open backing of people in power as the Anti-Asian League did. Its membership rolls included even so notable a Progressive as Hiram Johnson. The former governor and senator, along with other influential West Coast restrictionists, succeeded in excluding Asian immigrants entirely from the 1924 quotas.[91] This could not have been on the familiar grounds of mental inferiority, for there are no data to suggest that Japanese children were ever labeled defective. On the contrary, teachers praised their Japanese pupils' scholastic aptitude. A librarian from the Boyle Heights branch of the city library remarked: "The Japanese are not to be forgotten. We have many of them, and the Japanese children are great readers. The children are good students and make the most of their opportunities."[92] Yet at the same time that teachers and librarians commended Japanese students, other school people opened their facilities to events sponsored by the Anti-Asian League. Japanese children had no role models on the school faculties; one would be hard pressed to find a Japanese name in the *Teachers' Directory*.

Several factors may explain the success of Japanese children despite the society's overt racism. When Japan opened itself to the Western world, it adopted many of the West's features, including public education and baseball. In 1900 81 percent of the children in Japan were enrolled in primary schools, and in 1910 the figure reached 98 percent. Ronald Dorn, in *The Diploma Disease*, notes that Japan accepted education with the same eagerness with which it adopted other forms of modernization. Moreover, in the early twentieth century, the most sought-after positions were in civil service and not in business; entrance into civil service required formal education.[93] The Japanese viewed education as a step on the ladder of success. Japanese immigrants brought these attitudes, along with their other cultural accoutrements, when they arrived in the United States. The literacy figures of the Los Angeles Japanese community reflect that tradition: in the 1930's 96.6 percent of the males and 91.2 percent of the females over ten years old were literate. John Modell shows that 22 percent of Nisei males attended college in the 1930's; the figure for native white males was 21 percent.[94]

Japanese parents expressed their support for the schools by their continual efforts to provide extra help. As we have seen, at East San Pedro School the Japanese equivalent of the PTA, the Fu Kei Kai, raised money for many projects, including renting land for a park, landscaping it with trees, flowers, and grass, and providing playground equipment. In other areas of the city Japanese societies donated their time and their building materials to provide better facilities at school sites.[95] Japanese natives excluded from citizenship wanted their children to learn as much as they could about their adopted country, and to live by its laws and customs, in the hope that they might thus protect themselves and their families from future harassment.

Another factor helping to explain the Japanese children's success is that by the 1920's many of their parents had entered the middle class, or at least aspired to the middle class, and were familiar with American middle-class culture and competent in English. Consequently, on an IQ test geared to a middle-class, English-speaking audience, they could be expected to score as high as other children of the same class and language group. Some authors have noted that many Japanese were "secondary migrants," people who had stopped in other places in the United States or Hawaii before they arrived in Los Angeles and had already picked up some English. This may apply to many of the men but not to the women. The majority of women entered the United States as "picture brides" from Japan; and their children, like the children of other immigrants, probably spoke Japanese before they spoke English. In part, because of the large number of picture brides entering the United States after the 1908 Gentlemen's Agreement supposedly cut off immigration, members of the House Immigration Committee targeted the Japanese for total exclusion under the 1924 Immigration Act.

Racism reached a zenith during the 1920's. Nationally the Ku Klux Klan grew to over 5,000,000 dues-paying members, and racist restrictionists managed to pass immigrant quotas through Congress. The restrictionists directed their efforts at Southern and Eastern Europeans as well as at Asians. Some wanted Latin Americans excluded too, but they lacked the nationally organized support to ram that through. Campaigns against further Latin American immigration never equaled the frenzy of those directed against "new immigrants" or Asians. Latin Americans were not included in any of the quota acts of the time, although in 1917 the government initiated a form of head tax to try to control the flow from south of the border.[96] Also in the late 1920's, the California attorney general advised that although Mexicans were Indians, they were distinct from native North Americans and therefore not entitled to the same protective legislation. And in 1930 the U.S. Census Department created a special classification for Mexicans, lifting them out of the "white" category.[97]

All the same, it is too easy to point to the obvious racism of the period as the reason why so many Hispanic children fell into the school's category of mental defectives. As we have seen, most test supporters and critics alike recognized the language problem. Fewer recognized the cultural biases of the tests. Even the so-called nonverbal Kohs depended on some familiarity with color patterns. As Stephen Gould has so clearly explained, without some familiarity with American culture and English language, foreigners generally score poorly on IQ tests. Most of the Mexican children came from poor neighborhoods. And children from working-class families generally score lower than children from middle- and upper-class families.

An additional reason may be the children's unfamiliarity with schooling in general. Most Mexican immigrants came from poor agricultural or mining areas where there was little or no opportunity for education. Even where schools existed, such as in the mining district Ricardo Romo described in "Mexican Workers in the City," poverty forced Mexican children to leave school at an early age to help support their families.[98] Most of their parents were illiterate. Book learning had not played an important part in their traditions. They were not unique in this. Most of the southern Italian, Hungarian, Slav, and Greek immigrants were also illiterate; so were most of the Irish who arrived during the years of the potato famine. Except for the Irish, who came early enough to escape the IQ net, most of the children of these immigrants faced the same problems of low test scores as the Mexican children in Los Angeles. With the exception of one 1930 study, the *Bulletin* neglected to publish the test results of most European ethnic groups, so little local comparison can be made.[99]

Whether the labor patterns of Mexican farmworkers played a role in the lower test scores cannot be determined because of an absence of data. However, in studies throughout the Southwest, school officials and researchers noted that poor attendance constituted a major problem in the education of Mexican children since so many missed up to six weeks of school.[100] In the San

Fernando Valley Mexicans worked in the walnut groves and kept their children out of school to work with the family. Routinely, teachers remarked in the *School Journal* that Mexican children entered late each fall. Generally, if students miss a considerable amount of class time and do not receive special instruction to make up for the loss, they will score lower on standardized tests. Six weeks is over a quarter of a semester, and that is a considerable period to be absent from a classroom. The problem is compounded if the absence comes at the beginning of the school year, when acculturation begins. The first few weeks are devoted to learning desk assignments, names, and the important particulars of each classroom; for instance, the location of pencil sharpeners, cloakrooms, lavatories. These details are critical for young children, especially those from immigrant homes. To enter school in November and miss out on this orientation might well make a child who already felt insecure in a new situation feel very much an outsider.

It is difficult to estimate what effect Mexican nationalism had on assimilation, including schooling. Undoubtedly the ease with which Mexicans crossed back and forth to their native land played a part in their desire to remain Mexican nationals. Moreover, the steady infusion of newcomers into Los Angeles helped renew the older immigrants' feelings of patriotism and uninterest in assimilation. The largest Spanish-language newspaper, *La Opinion*, saw its readers as potential repatriates. The paper opposed Americanization in the schools and stressed the retention of Mexican traditions and the Spanish language because it expected "children of Mexican extraction to be Mexican patriots." The Mexican consulate distributed textbooks in Spanish to be used by the city's Mexican children.[101] Since ethnic groups often cling to their traditions more tenaciously when they feel discriminated against by the dominant society, all these factors should be considered, along with the obvious class bias of the tests, to explain the effect on Mexican children's education.[102]

By the mid-1920's Los Angeles educators were openly criticizing the biases of the tests. Ethelda Drake, principal at Ann Street School, who had worked in Americanization for many years and who was as keen an observer of human foibles as one can find, expressed her disapproval in the form of a satirical letter published in the *School Journal*:

> Dear Fellow-Principals:
>
> . . . On the long stretch through the Indian Ocean I conceived the brilliant idea of giving mental tests to the children of the various countries wherein I might visit. Fortunately, I was supplied with samples both for group and for individual tests. Through the ship interpreter I have had them translated into the different languages—Chewrashee Tchuk-cha, etc., and have had the necessary numbers printed in each language. It is true that a translated test cannot be considered truly valid; yet it is analogous to the situation that confronts a foreign child in American schools, and we all know that test results under such circumstances are infallible.
>
> I have just finished with the children of Krasnovodka. It is difficult for me to write without sympathetic tears. Every child I tested is definitely feeble minded.
>
> Such a simple task as writing the word that makes the sentence comprehensible in "A —— is made up of an engine and coaches"; "Mother —— doughnuts," in every instance remained unattempted. Fancy a child, as I found out by subsequent questions, who had never seen a train or a doughnut! It is sad in a way to think that actual mentality depends on such fortuitous circumstances.
>
> I shall continue this testing as I travel leisurely from country to country, for however disheartening it may be when one considers those benighted lands, it is wonderfully inspiring to know that American children have such measurably higher intelligence quotients than any foreigner can possibly have.
>
> Yours in the interest of research,
> Ethelda Drake[103]

Another indication that the testing movement was under assault came from Superintendent Dorsey. Addressing the National Congress of Parents and Teachers in Oakland in the spring of 1927, Dorsey stated:

> In the first place, the test does not measure intelligence, but achievement. It does not measure brain matter nor brain capacity so much as brain opportunity. It is a test of mental experience, rather than mental ability. For example, a child born in the mountains, when questioned about wharves, piers, and fishing shacks, might display but little intelligence, but if the questions were directed toward forest trails and rangers, to mountain lakes and woodcraft, he might be found to be 100 percent intelligent.[104]

Anne Reynolds, a teacher at Hollenbeck Junior High, conducted a study for the U.S. Office of Education in 1933 on Spanish-speaking students in five Southwest states. Her conclusions reflected the influence of reformers such as Ruby Baughman. Reynolds called for specialized training for teachers who taught Spanish speakers and for an increase in the number of Mexican teachers within the schools. She noted that few Mexican children finished high school and, therefore, few qualified for college training to become teachers. She also mentioned the encouraging preliminary results of an experiment in New Mexico where children were taught Spanish for one period a day. Her remarks on IQ testing suggest the growing tendency of Los Angeles school people to question the test results, especially when applied to Mexican children:

> Formerly persons writing on the subject showed considerable agreement in assigning a relatively low place to Spanish-speaking pupils along intelligence achievement, and school progress lines. This is not true at the present time. The trend of thought expressed by research students and school people generally is in favor of postponing judgment as to the relative status of members of this group until much more information is available, based on far greater equalization of economic, social, and educational opportunities than at present obtains.[105]

In fact, as I have shown in the preceding pages, many teachers refused to accept test conclusions as infallible. Educators who worked with children of limited English-speaking backgrounds had seen some of the inadequacies of testing; they found the IQ tests to be inconclusive indicators of potential ability. They also began to change educational policy. When Kendall and his Lemona teachers disregarded IQ tests, used achievement tests, and, finally, incorporated enrichment programs to improve the scores of their Hispanic students, they were making policy. By rejecting standard IQ tests and publishing their results, the Lemona staff pointed in a new direction and hoped others would follow.

The expansion of the Psychology and Educational Research Department, culminating in IQ testing, exemplified the way "administrative and pedagogical Progressives" joined forces in the drive for efficiency and conformity. Experts hired to teach new "scientific" business methods and techniques tested almost the entire school population, and in some cases catered to the schools' largest immigrant group by administering Spanish translations of standard IQ tests. The IQ programs signified the ultimate in progress. At the same time, to ensure more homogeneity within the schools and within society, the board tried to curtail ethnic groups' access to school facilities. Conflict developed as teachers and principals, and in the case of IQ testing, counselors like Murphy and Heim, tried to retain some influence and control in their profession and within their schools. Some rejected the dictates of the board and the hierarchy in the Department of Psychology and Educational Research, and asserted themselves in policy-making.

Progressives hoped to make the schools more responsible to each child's need. In practice the results worked contrary to their aims. In some instances educators used IQ tests to justify segregating students, but not always. None of the requests for segregating students by race mentioned test results, and the board's decision to confine nonwhite pupils, particularly blacks, to Jefferson High had little if anything to do with IQ. There is also some evidence to suggest that during the early years of testing, IQ may not have been used as much as a determiner for "tracking" or ability grouping among immigrant children as has been generally assumed. By the mid 1920's, even though the Psychology and Educational Research Department applied more pressure on the board to have students' classifications based exclusively on IQ scores, the teachers and principals of the neighborhood schools continued to exert the most influence on student placement. Consequently, IQ was less of a criterion for classification in schools where most of the children were from immigrant homes. This is not to say, of course, that test results had no influence on their decisions.

Teachers and principals would not abandon their beliefs in progress, clinging to their ideas that science would solve their problems with new labeling methods and specialized curriculum.[106] Moreover, even though testing proved less efficient than expected and created more problems than educators had bargained for, negating its value would have been tantamount to refuting the wisdom of university schools of education, a thought repugnant to most of them.

In some cases, such as at Lemona and Palms schools, achievement tests were administered to supplement IQ tests. Nevertheless, even though achievement tests measured accumulated learning rather than supposed innate ability, those tests, like the IQs, were firmly grounded in middle-class, English-speaking culture. Lower-class, non–English speakers' test scores reflected that bias. Too often the tests penalized poor children and held them in remedial classes; those who were considered normal were channeled into vocational education. As a result very few attended college, and fewer still entered the professions.

Educators have been accused of using testing to exploit Anglo-Saxon perceptions of superiority. Many undoubtedly thought that intelligence tests measured differences between races and nationalities, but others did not. Yet the schools continued to rely on the tests to overcome the dilemma imposed by mass education, immigration, and industrialization, and they hoped to solve the dual problems of reaching slow learners and enriching the curriculum for the gifted. Educators were left with the hope that the tests would provide scientific answers to questions of educational efficiency.

Current thinking would have it that the placement of minority children depended exclusively on IQ tests. But evidence from Los Angeles school publications indicates that teachers and supervisors, such as those at Lemona School, were highly sensitive to the shortcomings of those instruments and took a keen interest in the welfare of their students. By the mid-1920's, during the zenith of the testing drive, teachers and principals in neighborhood schools controlled placement decisions. This is not to suggest that the teachers and principals wholly ignored the tests or that tracking was not an essential ingredient of education. It is to suggest, however, that criteria other than IQ scores entered the picture. Los Angeles educators did not rely as slavishly on the supposedly scientific results of IQ testing as some would have us believe.

6
Modern Urban Schooling

Los Angeles is America. . . . It is the essence of America.
—*Louis Adamic, 1932*

By the 1930's the public schools had become Los Angeles's foremost institution for acculturation. From the 1880's onward services had been established to integrate the poor into American society and to turn foreigners into acceptable middle-class Americans. Whereas Progressive reformers, often volunteers, had been in the vanguard of initiating services at the turn of the century, volunteers had given way to professionals, and by the mid-1930's almost all services had become institutionalized. The result was a restructured school system that was, on the one hand, more responsive to community pressure and, on the other, more assertive in the need for conformity. In 1935 Pauline Young, whose work on the Molokan Russians continues to illuminate the assimilation process of ethnic groups in Los Angeles, was convinced that the process had been completed. The schools had become the premier tax-supported agencies for social reform. "These agencies have now passed their experimental period," she declared, "and are now part of the established order."[1]

As agencies for social reform the city schools certainly had passed the experimental stage. So completely had they accepted the responsibility for change that the earlier methods they developed to accomplish this change had become institutionalized, and educators began to use these models to solve different problems. The ascendancy of the schools in areas of social reform depended on their acceptance by ethnic communities. Without the cooperation of minority groups, the schools' preeminence could not have occurred. The continuation of service in the 1930's and the involvement of ethnic groups warrant careful scrutiny.

Institutionalized Services

The Depression of the 1930's created an unprecedented economic crisis in public schooling, forcing educators to rethink, restructure, and differentiate among the programs they wanted to support and those that must be discontinued. This rethinking so changed the attitudes of elected officials, as well as school people, that many now took pride in the very services that had been a source of controversy only a few years before. The uncertainty of the times worked in favor of retaining most services. Los Angeles's ethnic groups continued to turn to the schools for help, partly because the schools had been open to their requests in the past, and partly because they recognized the important role the schools played in their communities. Finally, as their community grew in size, black Angelenos challenged some of society's inequalities and brought their grievances to the city's schools.

Young noted that settlements had played a vital role as social experiment stations and as instigators of change during the early decades of the century. Yet as a sign of the changing attitudes of the 1930's, she admitted that many of their attempts at "social control" had been based more on good intentions than on an understanding of the local situation. The new thinking was, she said, that settlement workers had been overzealous in the effort to Americanize immigrants, and that "given the opportunity and intelligent guidance," immigrants could "best Americanize themselves when left to their own devices and to the skills and ingenuity of their native leaders." Nevertheless, she applauded the settlement workers. She noted, for example, that when local studies revealed undesirable conditions, settlements experimented with methods and institutions to correct them. To soften the realities of urban living, settlement workers created kindergartens, open-air schools, playgrounds, and health centers, plus a variety of other "preventative agencies." The proof of the value of these activities was that they "were taken over by public tax-supported organizations which could promote them on a large scale and make them available for the masses."[2]

The services offered by the schools expanded. A reader of

the *School Journal* could find an article headlined LEGAL AID CLINIC SERVES AS ATTORNEY TO THOSE IN NEED. The head of the University of Southern California Law School expected Los Angeles teachers to channel the indigent parents of their students to the law school's legal clinic. The clinic had increased its hours from one night a week to two and announced that its doors were open every afternoon, including Saturdays.[3] One could imagine that the schools, or at least the PTAs, would soon take active part in the clinic and eventually have a law clinic of their own. That did not happen. But teachers did assist their students and the parents of students and direct them to this and other places to get legal advice. Nor was it out of order for the vice-president of Security First National Bank of Los Angeles to commend the teachers and principals of Los Angeles who "inspired leadership in work that builds character." Vice-President William Russell Morehouse had set up a savings section for the city schools, and the character he referred to was the kind that came from having grade-school children maintain savings accounts; the money was collected at school and deposited by the school.[4]

The Cafeterias

One service that expanded significantly was the school cafeteria. By 1934 the cafeteria system that grew out of the old penny-lunch program had a centralized board to coordinate its operations. A new organization, the Los Angeles City School Cafeteria Association, expected to simplify operations by scientifically regulating the menus, by cutting expenses through large-scale buying, and by hiring only personnel qualified by civil service examination.

Yet accommodations were made for differences within the system. Each cafeteria planned its own menus and prepared its own food. One of the new association's first steps was to publish a cookbook, appropriately titled *Reliable Recipes in Large Quantities*. The home economics teachers who had written the cookbook tried to make the menus as appealing as possible and at the same time adhere to the latest nutritional advice from academia. A chef could concoct stews and potato salad for seventy-five, and follow recipes for Mexican ham loaf, Mexican spaghetti, tamale pie, and Danish coffee cake in similar proportions. The general introduction reminded readers to bear in mind the nature of the school's population, dietetic principles, and the need for variety, along with seasonal changes and the limitations of their equipment. It noted that lunchroom managers "must recognize racial food tastes,"[5] but it left to their imagination what they should do about this. The teachers never forgot the necessity of pleasing the eye as well as the palate, and they happily suggested adding garnishes of parsley and olives whenever appropriate.

Professional attitudes governed other aspects of the operation as well. Ethnic women were no longer sought out as workers. By 1934 the cafeterias had such community-wide acceptance that they did not worry about enticing their patrons and no longer needed to hire immigrant neighborhood women to bring in foreign students for a hot lunch of soup and bread. Now they directed their concerns at regulating and Americanizing their help. They still hired immigrant women, but these women had to be citizens or permanent residents, qualified by civil service examination. The new requirement must have eliminated many immigrant workers.

The reorganization took many of the operational procedures out of the principals' hands and relieved them of financial responsibilities, although they still had the final say on the scheduling of lunch periods. By centralizing, the school board hoped to achieve economies of scale. In principle, anyway, small schools with little purchasing power would be able to buy at a cheaper cost because of the quantities purchased by the central system.[6]

The Kindergartens

Since the time Caroline Severance introduced kindergartens to Los Angeles in the 1870's, early schooling had been the goal of many reformers and educators. As we have seen, by the turn of the century kindergartens had been made part of the established order. The supervisor of kindergartens recorded her remarks to the superintendent in the board's 1902–3 annual report, along with her fellow supervisors of music, drawing, and physical culture.[7] As the years passed, establishing kindergartens became routine. Any group of twenty-five parents who lived within a mile of an elementary school could petition the Board of Education to establish a class for their four-and-a-half-year-olds there.

The kindergarten appeared to have secured a solid position within the educational structure, but the stock market crash quickly eroded that support. During the Depression many cities eliminated kindergartens from their curriculum altogether.[8] Los Angeles's program was hard hit. In 1933 the *School Journal* reported that some kindergarten teachers had been dismissed.[9] But the institution as such was not dismantled, even in the face of shrinking tax revenues. The state of California, faced with the same shrinking tax base, stepped in to try to preserve kindergartens and at the same time save money. In 1933 Governor James Rolph, Jr., signed the Green Act, raising the kindergarten age from four-and-a-half to five. Many educators opposed the new act, and the *School Journal* published statements from public school teachers and university professors voicing the fear that more cutbacks would mean the demise of the kindergarten.[10] That fear turned out to be groundless. Though the Green Act reduced the kindergarten population, it left the service intact, so much so that in 1939 a long-time goal of kindergarten advocates passed the legislature. The 1939 bill eliminated the one-mile residence restriction for forming kindergartens.[11]

The Repatriation of Mexicans and Mexican Americans

An analysis of some aspects of repatriation and the city schools gives new insights into the complexity and variety of the Mexican community in Los Angeles. No sooner had the schools institutionalized their newest services than some of the recipients of those services presented a different need. The 1921 and 1924 exclusionary acts changed the way already resident immigrants viewed living in the United States. Many began to rethink their commitment to America. No longer could certain aliens afford to leave the United States, return to their native lands, and re-enter if their plans at home proved elusive. For many immigrants affected by the quotas, it meant a lifelong commitment to America.

A combination of the exclusionary laws and the pressures that American officials and advocates of Americanization brought to bear on aliens influenced many to become citizens. Theodore Saloutos has noted the important role new immigrants played in activating traditions and languages in older immigrant communities. But since few new immigrants came during the 1920's and the Depression, there was now much less chance of new arrivals reinforcing old-world traditions and languages. As a result, Americanization had more success in this period than in the previous decades.

Historians of the immigrant experience like Saloutos and Andrew Rolle have shown that for certain immigrant groups, returning to their homeland was a continuing theme of American history.[12] Many industrial and agricultural foreign workers went home during slack seasons, some with plans to return to the United States, others not. The process was common enough that expressions developed to explain their unusual way of life. For example, the Italians termed their migrant workers "Golondrinas," or swallows, and these "Birds of Passage" crossed the Atlantic many times between Italy and America. Rolle, noting that Alfred Stieglitz's famous photograph "The Steerage" depicts immigrants leaving America, not immigrants arriving, observes: "Our dreams of triumph have so swamped reality that most Americans scarcely consider that America's woebegone newcomers could ever have wished to return home."[13]

Mexicans came and left California even more often and in greater numbers than the Golondrinas. What makes their migrations noteworthy for this study is the involvement of officials on both sides of the border to repatriate them, and, more important, the participation of the Los Angeles schools in the process.

The idea of repatriating unemployed Mexicans during the Depression was not particularly novel. Returning home was easier and less expensive for Mexicans than for other immigrants because home was so close. Moreover, after 1924 federal immigration policy allowed Mexicans to come and go more freely than many other nationalities. Questions of repatriation surfaced in Los Angeles as early as 1923, when railroad building had slackened. The *Los Angeles Times* reported that two Mexican nationals, A. M. Villareal and C. Sánchez, representing several hundred Mexicans, had asked the Southern Pacific to help pay for the repatriation of the now-unemployed workers. Villareal and Sánchez also wrote President Warren Harding to explain that between 300 and 500 Mexicans who had been brought to Los Angeles by the railroad company now desired to return home. Their idea was to have the company pay the workers' fares to El Paso with the final phase of the journey picked up by the Mexican government.[14]

In early 1931, a little over a year after the 1929 crash and soon after President Herbert Hoover appointed William N. Doak Secretary of Labor, a new repatriation policy took shape. The stock market had not rallied that year, and the nation sank deeper into depression. The Hoover administration offered little federal funding for relief; it was up to charities to look after the unemployed. Doak believed that the country's woes would be corrected if Americans replaced alien workers in the job force. Doak employed methods similar to those used during the Palmer Raids a decade or so earlier. One of his first ventures in "alien baiting" came in New York City, when twenty Department of Labor agents and about the same number of New York policemen broke up a dance given by the Finnish Workers' Educational Association. Swooping down, blocking the entrances and exits, the authorities lined up more than a thousand terrified guests and asked each to show proof of his citizenship status.[15]

Denunciations came swift and loud from the press and other critics, but Doak was not deterred. He rather enjoyed the publicity, putting immigration officials throughout the country on notice that he was looking for deportable aliens. In Los Angeles the large numbers of Mexicans on the relief rolls provided immigration authorities with a sizable group for deportation. Not all the Mexicans who left Los Angeles were deported, however; many went voluntarily.

In Los Angeles during the early years of the Depression, before the federal government allocated money for relief, whatever aid there was came either through the state or through the county. The state granted aid to orphans, half orphans—a now-forgotten term for children with one deceased parent and the other parent unable to work—and in particular cases, children of tubercular fathers. Recipients had to have lived two years as legal residents of California and not have entered the state in a dependent condition. These restrictions excluded many Mexican families. Los Angeles county relief was administered almost exclusively by private charities, the Outdoor Relief Division of the County Charities Department, and the Community Chest. In 1928 Mexicans received 25 percent of the combined state and county aid even though they represented only 11 percent of the county population.[16]

Inadequate relief measures placed the burden of support on city and county officials, who in turn sought ways to cut back on assistance. Transporting Mexicans back to Mexico turned out to be cheaper than providing aid to the unemployed. In 1934 Emory Bogardus, professor of sociology at the University of Southern California, described the three ways Mexicans were repatriated:

> (1) those who have voluntarily packed up their belongings and returned by car or train; (2) those who have returned under polite coercion; (3) and those who have been deported. The second group is composed of many Mexicans who have been told by county or other public welfare agencies that if they would depart their transportation expenses would be paid, but if they did not accept this proposition they would be denied further welfare relief.[17]

Between March 1931 and April 1934, 13,332 Mexican nationals and some American-born children left Los Angeles County.[18] Most of these "repatriados," a term Mexicans used to describe compatriots who lived in a foreign country and returned home, were on the county's relief rolls, and the county paid their way back to Mexico. Abraham Hoffman suggests that perhaps an equal number repatriated themselves or were helped by the Mexican consul in Los Angeles. In April 1931, for example, only 800 of the 1,150 Mexicans who departed by train from the city had their fares paid for by the county; the other 350 managed to pay their own way by one means or another.* As early as 1932 the U.S. Labor Department's Commissioner of Immigration concluded: "It is certain that all Mexicans will seek to return when employment and business conditions improve, as our country is the promised land for these people."[19] Whether or not they saw America, or more specifically California, as the promised land one might debate. Nevertheless, it is a fact that significantly fewer Mexicans repatriated themselves after 1934.

Surprisingly, the city schools' attendance figures give little indication that repatriation had much impact on the Mexican school population. One might suppose if substantial numbers of Mexicans either left Los Angeles voluntarily or were forced to leave in the 1930's, the city school population would reflect that change. Yet evidence suggests that was not the case. The accompanying table shows that in the period 1929–38, the student bodies in four elementary schools with large Hispanic populations (at least 90 percent of the children) in fact increased, as did those in the three schools with no sizable Mexican representation (less than half of 1 percent) that were sampled for the sake of comparison.† Note that the two schools with the

*Hoffman, *Unwanted Mexican-Americans*, p. 88. The movement of returning Mexicans was not unlike the movement of "dust bowl" migrants coming to California. One imagines the two groups passing each other near Barstow: families with their belongings, including animals, crowded into old cars heading toward Mexico, and another caravan of families in similar old cars heading into California. Los Angeles relief agencies and the Labor Department cheered the departing Mexicans, and at the same time local authorities tried to stop the "Okies" from entering California. In 1934 Los Angeles Chief of Police James Davis set up blockades at points along the Colorado River, where the American migrants were interrogated. The police tried to turn back any who were indigent. When John Anson Ford became a county supervisor, at the end of 1934, he stopped this illegal harassment of citizens (Ford, *Thirty Explosive Years*, p. 14). In 1941 the U.S. Supreme Court overturned a state law allowing authorities to transfer vagrants or paupers across the state line (*Edwards* v. *California*, U.S. Supreme Court, *Report of Cases*, 314 [Oct. term, 1941]: 160–86).

†The board's *Nationality or Racial Background Survey*, the source of the 1938 data, had its own way of differentiating the students. Most Jewish children

Comparative Growth of the Populations in Heavily Mexican and Non-Mexican Schools, 1929–1938

Elementary school	1929	1934	1938 Total	1938 Mexican
Ann Street[a]	411	494	454	411
Brooklyn Avenue	864	1,028	1,272	1,256
Lemona Street	178	162	195	195
San Fernando	609	719	860	773
Carthay Center	523	834	889	0
Eagle Rock	491	451	523	2
Leland Street	539	611	628	35

SOURCES: 1929, 1934 (based on average daily attendance), Board of Education, *Auditors' Annual Financial Report, 1929*, pp. 39, 42, 44, *1934*, pp. 28, 31, 33; 1938 (enrollments), Board, *Nationality or Racial Background Survey*.

[a] This school, unlike the others, included the 7th and 8th grades. The fall-off between 1934 and 1938 may well be due to children of these ages (12–15) dropping out to go to work in the depths of the Depression.

largest increases were Brooklyn, almost all of whose students were Mexican (1,256 of 1,272 in 1938), and Carthay Center, which had no Mexican students.

These data can be interpreted in a variety of ways; they do not necessarily indicate that the Mexican student population had stabilized or that repatriation played no role. It is entirely possible that the school populations were unstable. That is, the schools may have been revolving doors with one family going out and another taking its place. Or it might be that most of the people who were repatriated were single men or that when families repatriated themselves they left one or more of their school-age children in the care of others until they were settled in Mexico or until they could return to Los Angeles. What the data do show is that in a number of schools, the Mexican or Chicano school population grew during the Depression years, rather than declined.

These results are puzzling and stir interesting speculations.

seem to have been classified by religion rather than by their parents' nationality. Carthay Center had 515 children of English background and 347 Jewish ones. Eagle Rock had a majority of English children, 427, as did Leland Street, 447. At Leland Street Mexican children made up the largest non-English group, 35, and Scandinavians the next-largest, 27, with 29 "others."

Did the repatriation campaign affect some segments of the Mexican population but not the entire group? Were the most recent arrivals the most vulnerable, and families with American-born, school-age children less susceptible to the upheavals? At the least, this new information suggests the complexity of the Mexican community in the city. It was not a homogeneous group, but a community in various stages of assimilation, multilayered, changing with each additional immigration.

The Mexican government showed an interest in repatriating its nationals, but its timing was off. In 1934 the Mexican government assigned Miguel Bracho of the Agricultural Department to cooperate with Los Angeles county officials. Bracho submitted a report on the feasibility of settling Mexicans in three or four northern Mexican states. Manuel Gamio, a Mexican anthropologist, aided Bracho and gathered information for the fourteen-page report.[20] During the height of the Mexican immigration to the United States, the Social Science Research Council had asked Gamio to investigate the migration from south of the border. He presented his first survey in September 1927, and two months later the Mexican government agreed to collaborate with the research council. Gamio's study was the first of its kind, and he became an expert on Mexicans in the United States. Not only did he detail their occupations, living conditions, and social and benevolent organizations; he also collected their songs and poems.[21]

From the content of Bracho's report, it seems clear that the Mexican government wanted skilled agricultural workers and thought that many of its nationals had achieved a measure of economic success in Los Angeles. It assumed that a fair share of the repatriates owned property and wondered whether the county would dispose of those properties. It also hoped that the county would either deduct the property tax on them immediately or make arrangements with the owners to pay the taxes after they had gotten established in Mexico.[22]

The Mexican government hoped to profit from the repatriation of its skilled nationals in various ways. The repatriates were thought to represent "a standard of education, preparation, discipline, initiation, activity, aspirations, economic sense [above] what our laboring class offer." Their contribution "to our country will represent an important step in [its] economic betterment," socially and intellectually, "contributing in this way to the rapid progress of our country."[23]

Bracho expected Los Angeles County to provide the vital statistics and to arrange with a transportation company to transport each repatriate. For its part, the Mexican government would provide them with land and tools, and would have the Agricultural and Public Works Department launch a propaganda campaign to explain the reasons for the repatriation. Bracho also wanted to see the Department of Colonization form a special division to study further ways to bring Mexicans from California.[24]

In the end the Mexican government did not succeed in its attempts to lure back many of its nationals. By the time it had established a National Repatriation Board, in late 1934, most Mexicans living in California had decided to stick out the miseries of the Depression rather than uproot themselves again and take a chance in Mexico. Nevertheless, in 1937 President Lázaro Cárdenas renewed his interest in repatriating Mexicans. The Department of Publicity and Propaganda sent officials to Texas and California to entice Mexicans to come home. But caution prevailed in the governing circles in Mexico City, where talks centered on what to do with the repatriates once they returned. Finally, in 1939, the Cárdenas government announced a plan, similar to Bracho's, to organize a farming colony in northwest Mexico for the returnees.[25]

It is not clear how successful that government initiative was, but two years later Supervisor John Anson Ford saw fit to make a trip to Mexico in the hope of renewing the Mexican government's interest in the matter. Armed with information compiled by Los Angeles officials, Ford and members of his family arrived in the Mexican capital in December 1941. In a letter to his Los Angeles staff, Ford made it clear that even though the Mexican government had expressed interest in his official visit, he had received little attention since his arrival. In fact, interest in Ford appeared so lacking that only after four attempts was he able to meet with the chief of the federal police. Nevertheless, Ford had convinced himself of the importance of his visit and felt that he could "see more and more clearly that there is all too little mutual understanding of our respective social problems; and we are only a little better off in matters of culture, particularly folk culture. And these fields—social and cultural—are the ones where real mutual understanding must be developed."[26]

The information Ford gleaned came from many sources. He had sent out inquiries about Mexicans to county officials. The surveys included school attendance statistics, juvenile delinquency, adult crime, welfare and relief, and economic, health, and housing conditions. The majority of his information came from a 1941 report entitled "Notes on the Mexican Population in Los Angeles County," by William Burk, of the county Coordinating Council's Information Division. In a cover letter to the council's director, Herman Stark, Burk emphasized that although the report considered the "general problem of our Mexican population," it failed to portray the community in a realistic light: "The data covers the activities and conditions that require attention. It does not and, unfortunately, cannot cover the very many fine characteristics of these people, their very great usefulness in our economic system, and the personal likableness that make them many times the kind of citizens that we would like to be ourselves."[27]

The Coordinating Council noted that the county's Mexican students enrolled in elementary schools but failed to graduate from high school. In areas where Mexicans represented a large majority, notably in the Belvedere and Watts districts, difficulties arose because of juvenile gangs. The report blamed the development of gangs in part on the schools. Burk remarked that "the curriculum of our public schools, and especially of our high schools, is in many cases poorly adapted to the actual needs of young men of this race, and is one in which they find it difficult to maintain an interested participation."[28] But, he noted, educators were aware of the problem, and through research they expected to solve it by revising the curriculum.

Ford sent a letter to Vierling Kersey, the superintendent of schools, to inform him of his proposed trip and of the county's plan to repatriate Mexican aliens and their children. Ford wrote that he wanted materials that would allow him to demonstrate to the Mexican authorities the extent to which the schools provided educational services to both children of alien parents and those whose parents had become naturalized. "My purpose in asking for this," he said, "is to lay before the Mexican authorities evidence of our goodwill. Likewise, to show them in spite of some obstacles we are treating their nationals as equals and giving them great benefits when they become integrated into our community life." Ford was eager to see more cooperation between Los Angeles County and the Mexican government in the hope that "our efforts will perhaps be in favorable contrast to some undertaken a few years back."[29]

Kersey replied several days later. His letter serves as a critique of the services Los Angeles city schools offered their students and reinforces Young's view that they had taken over the role of caretaker from the settlement houses. Kersey indicated that the schools had incorporated services of every description into their program, a far cry from the meager ones introduced on a limited basis in 1900. He noted that educators recognized that Mexican children required special instruction to serve their needs, and he assured Ford that "there is no city school system providing more extended programs of home cooperation, school and community service, vocational counseling and guidance, and personalized instruction than our schools." Moreover, the schools had not only provided the tools to assure Mexican students a place in the city's work force, but created a climate in which to overcome society's racial biases. "We have created a consciousness on the part of the employers in this community that for the work [to] which they are particularly suited, a trained Mexican becomes an employee of loyalty, faithfulness, and efficiency. With this spirit now prevailing, we have no difficulty in placing all of our Mexican youth who are sufficiently trained to warrant recommendation." Kersey neglected to explain just what work "particularly suited" Mexicans; nevertheless, he added that the percentage of job placements of Mexican graduates was exceptionally high.[30]

Kersey's letter reaffirmed that the schools did not overtly treat

Mexicans as "unwanted Americans." He wrote that his school district spent great sums to give the impression that Mexicans were indeed wanted. Kersey further indicated that he had some interest in the Mexican community when he expressed the wish that Mexicans provide leadership from within their ranks.

As it turned out, Ford's data-gathering effort had little impact on the county's effort to repatriate Mexican aliens. Interest in repatriation had peaked, and his 1941 effort appeared little more than a postscript to the 1930's movement. The bombing of Pearl Harbor and the country's declaration of war changed any plans the county had for repatriating potential workers.

John Anson Ford and Japanese-Language Schools

Ford's involvement in Los Angeles's ethnic communities ran deep. His district, the third, stretched from Hollywood to the east side of the Los Angeles River and included Wilshire, Westlake, Silver Lake, and the downtown areas. In anyone's terms, the third supervisorial district was unwieldy, not only for its size but for the diversity of its people. The area encompassed the mansions of Hancock Park and Adams Boulevard and the ramshackle houses in the poorest, working-class neighborhoods, where many of the immigrants lived. It also contained noted tourist attractions, such as the evangelist Aimee Semple McPherson's Angelus Temple, the Plaza Church at Olvera Street in old Los Angeles, and Chinatown.

The city's multiethnic community considered Ford its man on the Board of Supervisors. Minority constituents often wrote to him requesting help, from passing immigration laws more favorable to Chinese to hiring a Jewish manager of the unemployment relief bureau in Boyle Heights. Certain requests reveal the discrimination in employment that some minorities felt. For example, Shuji Fujii, the editor of *Dotto,* described as a "Progressive Japanese bimonthly for equality, peace, and progress," wrote Ford in 1938 asking him to find some way to get more "federal and state funds (WPA, NYAM, SERA, etc.) [allocated] to give vocational cultural and Americanism training to citizens of racial minorities, who because of their race are barred from most general fields of employment." He also urged an elimination of racial bias in the selection of applicants for civil service posts.[31]

The requests also illustrate some of the ways immigrant communities tried tailoring school services to fit their own needs. At times they succeeded, at others they did not. The request that Fujii went on to make serves as an example of one that failed. He wanted the supervisor to use his influence to have the Japanese language taught as part of the regular curriculum in schools with large Japanese American student bodies. He also wanted the board to grant schoolrooms for after-school language classes: "a knowledge of the Japanese language is essential to the Japanese American in order to supplement his cultural background with the heritage of his forefather's country and thus become a better American."

Fujii's letter reflects an emboldened spirit among Japanese Americans. Now, as natives and citizens, they expected to be treated with more respect and recognition than had their foreign-born parents. It is also indicative of a campaign on the part of many Japanese Americans to separate themselves from the policies of the Imperial Japanese government and to declare their opposition to Japan's bellicose actions in China. Fujii acknowledged that there were many Japanese-language schools in the city, so it might appear that there was no real need to include Japanese in the public school curriculum. He allowed, however, that many of these private schools might have been teaching subversive notions. "It is true," he wrote, "that there are many private institutions in California disseminating this knowledge but it is appallingly true that much of this propaganda of the present Japanese fascist-militarist nature is being instilled in the minds of the growing future Americans who are attending these schools. The need, we say is great, because the teaching of Japanese in public schools would eliminate this undesirable element."

For his last argument Fujii picked economics. He wrote to Ford: "Furthermore, the economic burden that would be lifted off the shoulders of the students' parents would aid considerably in raising the standard of home conditions. Traditionally ethnic organizations carried the burden of hiring instructors and renting space for after-hours language and cultural schools. In Los Angeles most Japanese schools operated under the direction of the Japanese School Organization of Southern California. Each school was organized on a cooperative basis, with the community paying for the equipment, educational materials, and teachers. In hard times the tuition could be steep. Each parent paid five dollars a month per child in 1933, though exceptions were made when there were several children. For instance, a family with four children would pay twelve dollars a month and a family with three, ten. Customarily communities donated extra money toward the schools' operation for special occasions, such as the death of a family member, or the birth of a child, or when relatives returned from a trip to Japan.

What Fujii does not argue may be, in fact, the real reason behind his campaign to include Japanese in the curriculum. It has been suggested that the Japanese community was facing the unhappy prospect of closing many of its schools because of indifference on the part of students and parents. A study of a Japanese neighborhood in Los Angeles found that that community, with a population of only 200, had two Japanese-language schools. But no one attended them regularly. Many of the children, particularly the older ones, resented having to participate. The researcher wrote: "The children themselves regard these language schools as distinctly supplementary, and in many cases would prefer not to attend, a point that has special significance, as Japanese children have an exceedingly deep desire to become proficient along educational lines."[32] Even some of the parents viewed the schools as a remnant of an earlier stage of immigration. One parent noted that she did not mind if her children attended a Japanese school, which they did not, but added: "It is almost impossible for them to learn a great deal about the Japanese language, when the English language is so much more familiar to them. They haven't the time to learn both languages."[33]

No matter how strong Fujii's argument, neither Ford nor anyone else could have changed the school curriculum at this time to include Japanese in the language program. Anti-Japanese feelings, never very far below the surface in California, were rising, not declining. Ford, a former high school teacher, replied that he was in favor of "any and all language courses which will better serve the community from which pupils come."[34] Nevertheless, no course in Japanese was adopted into the school curriculum in the late 1930's, and after Pearl Harbor the matter was a dead issue.

It may be that in 1938 Japanese American children resented spending their afternoons learning Japanese, as their parents' generation had done. It also may be that the older members of the community recognized that their young people needed an incentive to study their ancestors' language and therefore hoped to have it placed in the curriculum. By the late 1930's many of those young people were interested in school clubs and sports, not Japanese culture and language. They saw themselves as Americans of Japanese heritage, not as many of their parents perceived them, as Japanese who lived in the United States.

Americanization had worked well in the Japanese community, and school-age Japanese Americans had absorbed the lessons. Japanese Americans had participated in school activities before the First World War; a 1910 Los Angeles school yearbook noted several Japanese names on the rosters of school clubs. By the 1930's Japanese Americans had become school leaders. Nowhere was this more true than at Roosevelt High School in the eastern section of the city. Of Roosevelt's approximately 3,000 students in 1938, 10 percent claimed Japanese ancestry, including the student body president.[35] The Japanese Students' Club had 150 members, whose avowed purpose was to "foster good fellowship among the Japanese students of the . . . school, to be of service to our school and community and to build good American citizenship."[36] This is not to say that these good citizens did not study the language of their parents. They may have attended the Japanese-language classes held in the public schools on Saturdays.

Institutionalized Language Classes

The mechanism that allowed the Japanese community to use school facilities on Saturdays had been set up at the turn of the century. By the 1930's the common model had been institutionalized, and after-school classes were included on the Master Calendar. Many ethnic communities no longer needed to petition the Board of Education to this end. The hours varied to suit the mutual needs of the groups and the schools. For example, the Japanese-Language Class of Southern California used two classrooms at Oxford Street School for six hours on Saturdays. The Greek Community of Los Angeles and County, Inc., used seven schools and conducted classes in three of them five days a week. The others held classes two or three days. Taking advantage of the light hours in the early fall and spring months, the classes started at 4:00 P.M. and ended at 6:00. In the winter classes began at three o'clock and ended at five. German-language classes had been reinstated during the 1920's, and in 1936 students studied German in six different rooms at Seventeenth Street School for three hours on Saturdays. The Armenian Educational Society held classes at Stevenson Junior High for six hours every Saturday, and the Yugoslav American Education Society met at Cabrillo Avenue School in San Pedro after school.[37]

Other groups whose names did not appear on the Master Calendar may have arranged for their own language classes. Some chose not to use school facilities. For instance, the Chinese community had access to seven language schools, none of which used public school facilities. The Chinese Consolidated Benevolence Association ran three of these schools, and Protestant and Catholic churches the others.[38] By the 1920's Jewish groups that had previously petitioned for facilities had built classrooms in synagogues for language instruction. We might reasonably suppose that an ethnic group's use of public schools in one neighborhood did not rule out its using other, more convenient private facilities in a different district.

International politics played a role in some of the language schools. Shuji Fujii addressed the problem within the Japanese community in his letter to Supervisor Ford, and politics and ideology defined Italian classes, too. Four different Italian societies vied for Italian American students during the mid-1930's: the Guglielmo Marconi Italian American, the Italian Pascoli Society, the Giovanni Pascoli Italian, and the Italian American.[39] Gloria Ricci Lothrop, remembering her youth in Los Angeles during the 1930's, tells us that Vice-Consul Ernesto Arighti had appointed her mother to the local governing board of the Giovanni Pascoli schools, which were administered by Dr. Spadea, the daughter of the president of the University of Rome. According to Lothrop, though the Italian government provided the books and paid the teachers' salaries, the schools were free of political overtones until Italy aligned itself with Nazi Germany in 1938. After that, relations between the board of the Giovanni Pascoli schools and the Italian government deteriorated. Dr. Spadea no longer was welcome at some schools, including those in San Pedro. The schools closed before the United States entered the war. A California legislative committee conducted hearings into allegations that the Italian schools fostered Fascist propaganda, but no formal charges were ever made.[40]

By 1933 the State Board of Education had codified procedures to eliminate the cumbersome task of petitioning the local board each time an organization wanted space. As in so many other things, the Los Angeles schools continued to set precedent; their model was increasingly emulated by educators in other districts. The correspondence that arrived in the administrative offices indicates that the city's innovative policies had become known in many quarters far beyond the county or state boundaries. From Seattle and Baltimore and closer to home, from San Diego, Superintendent Frank Bouelle, Dorsey's long-time associate, and his staff fielded inquiries on procedures to grant requests and the costs to the board; one wanted to know if Los Angeles had a policy regarding the use of schools by "communist organizations or any other radical agencies."[41] While the correspondence from Los Angeles remained silent on "Communists and radical agencies," Bouelle noted that in fiscal 1933–34, 21,061 groups met in the public schools, and that custodians and heating engineers received $28,598 in additional salaries. Writing to a Seattle superintendent, he added: "As a result of the Depression, the board has extended the use of school premises by outside groups considerably, particularly in the case of pay entertainment for charitable purposes."[42]

By 1940 the Los Angeles administrators needed their own clarification. Assistant Superintendent C. L. Craig had requested information on the applications of the Civic Center Act of the State Education Code. The issue concerned a religious organization's use of the public schools. The state had redefined its restrictions in 1933 and 1935, but as more requests poured in, school officials wanted clarification from the county counsel. The counsel reiterated: schools could not be used for religious purposes. Yet sometimes the lines between religious use and secular use blurred. Beach Vasey, deputy county counsel, tried to illustrate the complexities of a seemingly simple issue. A priest from Soledad Church asked to use the grounds at Brooklyn Avenue School for the culmination of a Corpus Christi procession. The counsel noted that even though the school's support was minimal, the event was still clearly sectarian. Likewise, the Zion Lutheran Church was denied the use of a school building to hold its confirmation ceremonies. But the Paulist Woman's Club might use a school auditorium to perform the play *The Bohemian Girl.* The ensemble, made up of students from St. Paul the Apostle School, offered entertainment free of charge, and the play was not sectarian in nature; the connection with the parochial school was "not fatal," since the "entertainment was not religious." Similarly there seemed to be no constitutional prohibition against allowing the Torrance chapter of the DeMolay, a male youth group sponsored by the Masons, to use a school auditorium for a concert. The concert was presented by the music department of Compton Junior College, with proceeds going to the Torrance group. The counsel ruled that since the DeMolay was nonsectarian, the use of the school for recreation and artistic purposes was well within the provisions of the Civic Center Act.[43]

The Black American Community in the 1930's

The city's nonwhite population grew during the decades between the wars, and so did the number of segregated schools. The Mexican and Japanese communities expanded mainly during the 1920's, the black community mainly during the Depression. According to the board's 1938 *National or Racial Background Survey* 11,485 black students were enrolled in the city's 396 schools. This figure included the 195 students of Los Angeles Junior College, a two-year college then counted as a city school. In comparison, Mexicans, or Spanish as they were designated, numbered 48,748, and Japanese 8,533. Since no differentiation was made in these categories between the native-born and the foreign-born, there is no way to gauge if these students were first- or second-generation Americans.[44]

As we have seen, Los Angeles had segregated black high school students in much the same manner as New York City did, but left it to restrictive covenants and white flight to segregate the elementary schools according to housing patterns. The first step toward official segregation had come in the 1920's, when the board designated Jefferson High as the minority school. Jefferson became known as a minority school or a mixed school, not a Negro or a "colored" school as such schools were called elsewhere.[45] By the mid-1930's, and certainly by the 1940's, de facto segregation had done its work in most elementary schools. By the end of the Second World War, after the heavy migration of southern blacks, Los Angeles had taken on the appearance of a northern city, with separate black and white neighborhoods and schools.[46]

The school board had hired African Americans for many years, but not as secondary teachers. Booker T. Washington, Jr., held the position of supervisor of the Department of Compulsory Education for some time, and the staff included a number of black elementary teachers as well as a number of black custodians.[47] In 1919 Bessie Burke became principal at Holmes Avenue School, the first black teacher to make such a move. Burke, a Los Angeles native, earned a certificate at the State

Normal School and a B.A. and M.A. at the University of Southern California. She stayed at Holmes Avenue until 1939, when she moved to Nevins Avenue, also as principal. Holmes Avenue had become a center for teacher training, and it is not clear why Burke changed schools. Since Nevins had almost twice as many children as Holmes, it is possible that Burke wanted the challenge of a larger school. But demographic changes may have played an equally important role. By 1938 Mexican children slightly outnumbered black children at Holmes, 201 to 170, whereas at Nevins blacks outnumbered Mexicans two to one, 446 to 217. Perhaps in keeping with the board's policy of placing black teachers in black schools, Burke was asked to move to Nevins because it had a majority of black pupils.[48]

Resistance to Jim Crow coalesced during the 1930's. The combination of the black community's growth and the harsh economic climate pushed black leaders to demand more participation in the city's political and economic life, and to have more say in their children's schooling. A small but determined group of middle-class activists tried to push back the barriers of race and to carve a place for themselves in the city schools. Whether this group did more than touch the lives of the city's growing poor black population is a question yet to be answered.

Los Angeles's blacks belonged to a variety of organizations, as did African Americans throughout the nation. Churches, social and civic clubs created a network of support for the community. In 1918 the community had elected former Ohioan Frederick M. Roberts to the California Assembly, the first black man to serve in the state legislature.[49] Roberts, a Republican and a journalist who edited and published the *New Age* newspaper in Los Angeles, represented the 62nd Assembly District for seven consecutive terms.[50]

The Urban League provided one of the most important forums for the black middle class. Its outspoken executive director, Floyd Covington, criticized white society for its treatment of blacks during the Depression and for the "lag of economic competition."[51] Covington was the first black case worker for Los Angeles County's State Emergency Relief Administration (SERA). SERA supervised the distribution of state funds appropriated for unemployment relief, and after 1933, it also distributed the federal funds, which were channeled through Governor Frank Merriman's office. Covington and his co-workers visited the homes of all Americans on relief, no matter what their color. Also, Covington observed, "for the first time in our relief programs, persons of color were permitted to give orders to, supervise, and train young American college students with or without color."[52]

Asserting pressure on the board in 1934, the League for Struggle for Negro Rights requested more "colored teachers" at Jefferson High. Loren Miller, a black attorney, took the lead, urging that teachers be placed in the secondary schools. Miller had had opportunities beyond the reach of most African Americans in the 1930's. Born in a small Nebraska town, he came to the City of the Angels in 1929, then left to serve as foreign correspondent for the Associated Negro Press in Russia, Germany, and France in the early 1930's. In Los Angeles he wrote for and edited several dailies, including the *California Eagle.* As an attorney, Miller considered himself an authority on racial restrictive covenants. In 1953 he served as counsel in *Barrow* v. *Jackson*, the case that struck the final blow against the covenants and earned him a judgeship. As a frequent visitor to the school board meetings, Miller often addressed the board on racial matters.[53]

In 1934 Miller sent a memo to the board questioning the apparent bias in oral examinations.[54] Oral examinations were an important element in job placement. Applicants who scored well on written examinations could be marked down because of the decision of an oral examiner. Apparently qualified blacks had been turned down for teaching positions because of their low oral examination marks often enough for Miller to bring the matter to the board's attention.

It was a practice that easily lent itself to controlling the numbers of nonwhites teaching in the schools. For instance, at a superintendents' conference in 1924, the assembly "discussed at length" the matter of a vacancy for a "colored teacher." They concluded that "there were no vacancies for colored people in either elementary, junior, or senior schools," and decided to "keep their names off [the] eligible lists."[55] A simple way to do this was to be sure that those who would otherwise qualify were ranked low on oral examinations. No visitors attended the superintendents' conferences, and their recommendations of eligibility for "colored teachers" were not written into the minutes of the Board of Education. On most matters concerning faculty eligibility, the board relied on the superintendents' recommendations. Few board members questioned the superintendents' policies on minority hiring.

The question of the placement of "Negro teachers" arose during the 1930's for several reasons. First, blacks, as other groups, perceived teaching as a way to climb the social and economic ladder. Second, they had grown populous enough by now to become more aggressive in their demands for better positions in the schools. Third, they hoped that increasing the number of black teachers would allow the black community to assert more control over the education of its children. The drive to place more blacks on the schools' payroll took two forms, one, through citizens addressing the board, as exemplified by Loren Miller, and the other, through electing blacks to the board itself.[56]

By 1938 black students at Jefferson High accounted for 1,183 of the school's 1,995 students, and most of the other students were Mexicans (417). Other nonwhite minorities found Jefferson High uninviting. According to one account, Chinese students changed their addresses so they could go somewhere else. Their main objections were that blacks "dominate everything in the student body and athletics, and that they are rowdy." Another, more important reason was that just as white students discriminated against the Chinese, so the Chinese students "do not like to associate with Negroes and Mexicans." The Chinese public school population was quite small; only 1,009 attended regular day schools. Thirty-nine Chinese students attended Jefferson in 1938.[57]

The only other high school with a substantial nonwhite student body was Jordan in nearby Watts. Los Angeles annexed this lower-middle-class community in the southeastern part of the county in 1925. Watts had been a settlement of white family farms at the turn of the century, but by the 1920's Mexican and Japanese families had moved into the area. Jordan's emergence as a black school came in stages as more blacks moved south down Central Avenue into Watts. In 1938 Mexicans were still the largest ethnic group, accounting for 804 of the 1,749 students, but blacks now outnumbered English-speaking whites, 533 to 349.*

Other high schools throughout the city continued to have black students but in much smaller proportions. Polytechnic had 183 in a student body of 2,563, one of whom, Boys' League President and school athlete Tom Bradley, was to become Los Angeles's first African American mayor. Manual Arts had 128 blacks among its 3,390 students, Frank Wiggins Trade 103 among its 3,224. Other senior highs had considerably fewer. There were only three blacks at San Pedro and nine at Marshall. Sixteen of the city's forty-two high schools had no black students at all, and fifteen had fewer than ten.[58]

Jefferson High, with its predominantly black student body, became the city's first African American high school. The demographic changes that had accompanied its new status attracted attention in various quarters. A short distance away, students in the University of Southern California's graduate schools of Education and Sociology found Jefferson a rich source for study and produced master's theses on such topics as attendance patterns, school clubs, employment opportunities, and IQ tests.[59] Each study began by noting the shift in the area's demography and in the school's racial mix, although at the time the theses were written the school was not very mixed at all. In 1938, as we have seen, blacks accounted for 1,183 of the 1,995 students.[60]

The segregation of Jefferson allowed a few black teachers to advance their careers and their position within the black com-

*The board assumed that Jordan would become a minority school when the district annexed all-white Bell High School in the adjoining white community of Bell in 1926. Parents of Bell students objected to their children attending schools with blacks and Mexicans. The board, deferring to these objections, drew the boundary at Alameda Street, saying that it was too dangerous for high school children to cross the thoroughfare. Those west of Alameda went to Jordan, and those to the east to Bell. (Hendricks, "Public Policy," pp. 192–93.)

munity. The school also became the focus of the community's attention, a place where it could pursue its goals. The black community's major newspaper, the *California Eagle*, was full of Jefferson High's business. Many of the articles editorialized on the discontent within the school and the community, but many also clearly exhibited pride in the school's accomplishments. There were complaints from "the whispering walls of Jefferson High" when black teachers were transferred or lost particularly attractive positions, moves that the *Eagle* inevitably attributed to racism. But there were many prideful articles as well, in addition to articles of general interest. The *Eagle* dutifully announced all important events, such as a talk by the prominent writer Langston Hughes, sponsored by the Negro History Club; kept its readers informed of the new classes available at the evening school; and noted the dates and times when the school orchestra performed in concert.[61] Yet the *Eagle* never let up in its unequivocal stand against segregation. In 1939 the editorial staff wrote: "Negroes should not invite segregation by seeking establishment of separate educational institutions or separate public conveniences, but in business, politics and all civic affairs we should measure their leadership ability by the American yardstick."[62] This came as part of a campaign the paper mounted in the late 1930's against what it saw as an increasing threat of legalized school segregation in California and the self-interest of certain black educators who favored it. The most striking feature of a new concerted effort to segregate black children, the paper's editor, Charlotte Bass, charged, was that it came from some of the black leaders themselves. Bass noted that segregation was self-serving but did not serve the black community at all. The hypothesis sometimes advanced that it was in the vested interest of some black teachers and administrators to continue segregation in Los Angeles and elsewhere, for fear they would not otherwise move up in the system and might even lose their jobs, is easier to offer than to substantiate.[63]

All the same, segregation may have allowed the Board of Education to make certain advancements without fear of a white backlash and permitted some blacks to secure a foothold within the profession. In 1938 the board received several letters backing Senola Reeves's petition for appointment to the position of counselor at Jefferson High. Reeves had taught at Twentieth Street School and was teaching at McKinley Junior High when she filed her petition.[64] By this time there were a few black teachers at Jefferson, but the only black counselor in the district worked at Jefferson evening school.[65] Reeves wanted to help teenagers. She noted that she had been counseling black students for years without benefit of title, and now she felt it was time to have the official position. In her letter to the board, Reeves cited the interracial conflicts in the city and the power that black community leaders felt was vested in the role of teacher at Jefferson. The next year Reeves was hired to teach the basic course, a combination of English and social studies, at Jefferson. She was not hired as a counselor, although some of her time may have been spent in the counselor's office.

Also in 1939 a local black civic group had succeeded in adding the first course in "Negro History" to the curriculum in Los Angeles schools. The multitalented Hazel Gottschaff Whitaker, whom we met earlier, taught the new course at Jefferson.[66] Jefferson High earned another distinction as well when the evening school offered a course in aeronautics taught by Lieutenant William J. Powell. Powell, one of a handful of black airmen who flew during the First World War, had gotten his flight training at Tuskegee Institute, and in 1934, in Los Angeles, he published a book about black pilots, *Black Wings*. With the introduction of this course, Los Angeles became one of three places in the nation where a black could learn to fly.[67]

It is not clear how many African American secondary teachers the district employed the year Reeves wrote to the board, but in 1935 there were none at all. For that matter, there were not many in the elementary schools, just twenty-eight in a total of 4,829 elementary teachers. By July 1939 forty-five blacks were teaching in the elementary schools and eighteen in the secondary schools; in 1945 there were 101 black teachers in the elementaries and fifty-seven in the senior and junior highs.[68]

As the black community grew in size and influence, it launched a drive to elect a black to city government. When success came, it was not on the city council. The victorious campaign of Fay Allen in 1939 marked the entrance of blacks in school board politics. Allen, an accomplished music teacher and conductor of the Jefferson Evening School Orchestra, made a fine candidate. School board members, like city councilmen, ran at large, and Allen had appealed to enough nonblack voters to win. She had the endorsement of the United Veterans of Los Angeles and the *California Eagle* but not the powerful *Los Angeles Times*. To its credit, though, the *Times* refrained from the kind of slur campaign it waged against several other candidates in the 1939 election, candidates it linked to the Communist Party. Allen served on the board until 1942, when her former campaign manager helped to unseat her by supporting another black woman candidate. The divided black community was not able to elect either woman in 1943. In later years Allen observed that it was not always easy to be a black board member. Many of the board's committee meetings were held at the Jonathan Club, one of the city's most restrictive clubs. Blacks were not admitted, and Allen missed several of the meetings.*

Choosing the Board of Education as a stepping stone to political leadership testifies to the importance black Angelenos, certainly those from the middle class, placed on education. Blacks, like many other Americans, saw the schools as agencies of reform and progress, but their way was often blocked by racism. To be sure their activism in the 1930's, prodding Los Angeles and the nation toward integration and bringing hope for equality during the years between the wars, did not center around the schools alone. But when bigots persuaded the board to maintain Jefferson High as a predominantly black school, and when

*According to the *California Eagle*, April 6, 1939, p. 1, Allen polled 35,000 votes in her first run. Born in Iowa, she accompanied her father to France after the First World War and studied music there. Allen's father was the only black to be elected to the Society of Musicians in Paris. Before her election to the board, Allen had combined her musical talents with her political ability as treasurer of Musicians' Local 767 of Los Angeles. She was also secretary of the Los Angeles chapter of the American Federation of Teachers and vice-president of the Los Angeles Negro Club. The club's president, Gilbert Lindsey, acted as her campaign manager before going on to be elected to office himself. Allen had also served with the Red Cross during the First World War, for which work she had been decorated by President Woodrow Wilson. (Ostrom, "School Board Politics," pp. 55, 99–101, 111–12.)

housing became more restrictive through racial covenants and white flight, and as the black population grew in size, black Angelenos began to fight for local control of schools. Success first came in the state legislature in 1918 and then, finally, twenty-one years later, on the school board. The war and the incredible postwar growth changed the face of Los Angeles. Civil rights sentiments accelerated, ridding the city of restrictive covenants by 1953. Unfortunately, by then the patterns of segregation had already solidified.

By 1941 the Los Angeles city schools were indeed the central tax-supported institution that Pauline Young had pronounced them a few years earlier: truly agencies of social reform and completely run by professionals. The social services were so entrenched that even during the Depression, most of them continued. When the board tried to cut back on some, for example the kindergartens, a rallying cry went out to protect the endangered species. At the same time other services grew stronger. The school cafeterias reorganized and separated themselves from the control of the principals. Even the controversial after-hour foreign-language classes had won their place on the Master Calendar. Superintendent Kersey enumerated the scope of the services beautifully in a letter to Supervisor Ford. Asked to name the extent of the services the Los Angeles schools provided for the Mexican community, Kersey cited ten, but if the list were broken down the services would in fact add up to many more. Also by 1941 many minorities had learned how best to use the schools to meet the needs of their own communities. When the editor of the Japanese-language newspaper felt Japanese American children needed incentives to study their ancestral language, he turned to the most important institution for social services, the public schools.

Yet even as the schools became the premier institutions for assimilation through their policies of services, they also became institutions for racial segregation. Progressives found themselves caught on the horns of a dilemma. Many who worked in the schools and served on the board had fought for years for the inclusion of welfare programs to ease the poverty of immigrants and to speed up the process of Americanization. Many had seen segregation as counterproductive to that process because it isolated ethnic groups, and in so doing, reinforced native cultures and languages, the very trappings they wanted to eliminate. Nevertheless, with seemingly little difficulty, racists persuaded the Board of Education to segregate Hispanic children in the San Fernando Valley and maintain Jefferson High School as a predominantly black school. It is true that the board never committed itself to the total segregation of racial minorities and resisted attempts to segregate Japanese American students during the height of the anti-Asian hysteria following the First World War. But it is also true that the board aided the process by allowing students to transfer schools without too many difficulties.

In the early years of the century, reformers had decided what was best for poor children. Under the rubric of Americanization, school people and volunteers created a whole world of reforms. For the dual purpose of helping and assimilating, they stood their ground to effect policy changes in social welfare and curriculum. And at the same time they allowed ethnic groups limited pluralism. In the case of segregation, however, they caved in. Succumbing to outside pressure, perhaps playing out their own biases, school people agreed to a policy that proved neither helpful nor assimilating.

Conclusion

> Provincialism will find no place in future Los Angeles.... Unhampered by traditions, untrammeled by the conventions which hedge in old and long established communities, she can forge ahead with her eyes on the future and that future one of glorious promise.... In education ... a leader.
>
> —*Louise Ward Watkins, 1932*

The Los Angeles city schools provide an excellent backdrop against which to study the ways reformers and immigrants and African Americans influenced public policy in the years before the Second World War. The city schools also provide a rich environment to analyze professionalization and Progressive reform, forces that worked simultaneously to transform Horace Mann's common school into modern urban schooling. At the end of the last century, Los Angeles beckoned new arrivals by its promise of a better life. Newcomers flocked to the "land of fair promise,"[1] armed with fresh ideas and plans that soon changed the nineteenth-century Western pueblo into the quintessential twentieth-century city.

The public schools reflected the city's Progressive spirit. White Americans carried the banner for school reform, but immigrants and black Americans took vital positions in this parade. Reformers developed programs for a wide spectrum of students, directing many at nonwhite and non–English-speaking children in the hope of bringing them into the mainstream of American life. The success of their programs depended on the support of minority communities, and within the shifting boundaries of majority culture, ethnic groups shaped policies to protect their interests.

Compulsory school laws had made it necessary to broaden their ideas of community and reform to include newcomers—multiracial, multicultural immigrants—whose children were required to attend schools. Reformers recognized that by their very nature schools and other American institutions intimidated immigrants; therefore, they worked to make schools responsive, so that immigrant parents would look upon them with favor. If reformers accomplished that, newcomers would be more likely to send their children regularly, vote for school bonds, and be more receptive to Americanization programs dear to reformers' hearts. In the process of making schooling inclusive, reformers turned neighborhood schools into community centers.

At the time this study begins, in 1885, modernization had begun to transform the lives of most Americans. The shift from rural to urban and from household industry to factory had placed in the hands of professionals many of the functions routinely performed by the family and church. These changes led to a restructuring of society that was most evident in education.

The core belief of these early reformers was that institutions could and must be molded for society's betterment. Late-nineteenth-century Progressives had found themselves caught in the turmoil of modernization: industrialization, mass immigration, and urbanization. Everywhere they looked they saw disorder and corruption. They made it their duty to re-establish order, and in the process to purify society through reform.[2] They passed laws to take control away from the corrupt and put it in the hands of law-abiding citizens like themselves. City governments were reorganized from top to bottom; included in the reorganization came new, efficient means of running public schools. Reformers had unrealistic expectations that schooling, like city government, could be separated from politics. In fact, their efforts at reform not only embroiled them in politics but frequently led to conflicts that turned on their own self-interest rather than legitimate reform.

The stakes were high. The role of public schooling in American society had grown significantly during the nineteenth century, and for the first time great numbers of common people began to look to education as a means of fulfilling their rising expectations.[3] A prime factor in that growth, particularly by the end of the century, was the cultural transformation that social service programs brought to the schoolhouse. Long before school boards schematized Americanization projects, reformers had devised ways to uplift, socialize, and Americanize along middle-class lines those they categorized as less fortunate. The local interest groups who helped shape educational policy allied themselves with school people; settlement workers, clubwomen, and ethnic communities often tailored the services to increase their own power. Together, between 1885 and 1941, they created a modern, urban school system.

Many Americans even now hold the view that public education provides social mobility and participation in a democratic society. That belief has become so powerful in American culture that it has been woven into the fabric of the American Dream.[4] Not everyone has agreed. Some have insisted that the schools merely reflect the values imposed upon them by an elite class whose main purpose is social control.[5] These conflicting interpretations have made it difficult for historians in either camp to treat Americanization separately from questions of social control. Recent studies have made it possible to move away from those questions and begin to look at other issues that motivated reformers, such as self-interest and professionalization, and the role each played in the politics of reform.[6]

Historians found it equally difficult to separate Americanization from questions of social welfare services, the major vehicle of the Americanization movement. John Higham's description of the two currents in the movement, impulses of fear and of love, aptly apply to the experiences in Los Angeles.[7]

This history of the Los Angeles city schools demonstrates that "Americanization" can be interpreted in a much broader context than it has been given in the past. Beginning in 1885 with kindergartens and moving through the Depression, Americanization can be seen as a continuing form of social service that both uplifted and assimilated immigrants into American society. On some levels it worked very much as the reformers intended because educators had incorporated the reformers' attitudes into their policies and also because their charges' ties to their parents' homeland had weakened. On other levels Americanization failed. Even if it was possible to make foreign-born or native-born children model citizens, Progressives never committed enough financial support to give their theories a fair trial, and in many cases racial biases worked against assimilation.

In the beginning the reformers set up many programs, such as penny lunches and tub and shower baths, as temporary measures to rescue children from conditions of poverty. They established other, more enduring services such as tuition-free kindergartens to make up for inadequate homes. At the start the kindergartens were meant to Americanize immigrants, but with this as with other programs, it soon became difficult to distinguish between services intended to help the immigrants and those designed to assimilate them. This was especially true after middle-class parents demanded many of the same services for their children. As soon as the board established services outside the immigrant districts, the programs were no longer identified with Americanization, but were thought of as part and parcel of public schooling. Americanization as such did not end in a specific year; it was a matter, rather, of those programs once identified exclusively with Americanizing gradually becoming institutionalized into the public schools.

At the same time that reformers introduced social services and the schools responded by incorporating them, the educational establishment made important changes in the school curriculum. In part the changes were made to accommodate industrialized society and compensate for the growing differences among its school population. But an equally important factor was the influence of a different pedagogy emanating from newly established university schools of education. Educators had become certified experts, professionals who claimed to know better than their predecessors ways to manage efficient programs that best suited different children. Yet not all educators were of the same mind. Although many greeted the diversification of curriculum, the availability of commercial and vocational training, and the early introduction of foreign languages with enthusiasm, for some these changes came too fast. Moreover, at times pedagogical reform became entangled in conflicts of interest, as most clearly demonstrated in the case of General Otis, Superintendent Francis, and members of the 1914 school board.

Progressive reformers from the settlement houses, women's clubs, and civic organizations, along with teachers and clergymen, devoted themselves to helping the poor in the "foreign district." Yet the altruism of the reformers was rooted in the expectation that the immigrants would conform to their methods and ideals. The reformers believed that they could succeed with their clients if they provided essential services such as food, clothing, and English instruction. As the city's population ballooned, the reformers could no longer manage the services themselves and turned to the schools for help. The schools, at first reluctantly but eventually willingly, accepted the responsibility and became the premier institution for social reform and assimilation.

As the services expanded official policy changed. No longer would outside groups have as much access to the schools. After the First World War, educators began to orchestrate their own programs for two reasons: first, the widespread fear in the country of new foreign entanglements and of socialism in particular; and second, the fear that too many unassimilated immigrants would alter the texture of American life. Until this time the majority of Americans felt secure in American cultural hegemony and only isolated nativists raised fears that the United States could not absorb the multitude of newcomers arriving at its shores. But after the war many Americans recognized that the melting pot was only a term, and that assimilation was not universal. That recognition soon brought restrictionists to initiate immigration quotas and concerned citizens to formulate a semiofficial doctrine of Americanization.

In the postwar years the expanded Americanization movement emphasized better programs for teaching both English language and American traditions, and had little tolerance for linguistic or cultural pluralism. Yet the Americanization movement lacked a core. There was no central administering organization, and even though there were some general guidelines, each agency proceeded independently. In Los Angeles the Americanizers reflected the traditions of the reformers. Teachers continued to visit immigrant homes, draw up legal documents, and preach understanding and even limited pluralism well into the 1930's. The real change during the period was in the immigrants' view of the schools and their services.

Initiated by reformers to meet the needs of the poor, the services grew to include the entire school population. Services like the penny-lunch program, which had begun slowly in the foreign district, now served middle-class schools as well. Within a short period most parents welcomed the opportunity of inexpensive, hot meals for their children. It is nearsighted, however, to think that the schools initiated the programs with no regard for the community's desires. Many immigrants defended their own interests. Often they worked directly with the schools to add programs to benefit their group, as the Molokan Russians did in 1924 when they petitioned the city council to add an after-school playground at their local junior high. Groups petitioned the Board of Education to use classrooms to teach their native languages, just as they petitioned to use school facilities for their native holiday celebrations. In this way the immigrants used schools to reinforce many of their values and in some sense became agents of their own social change.

Sometimes the two worked together. When teachers worried that the Chinese community clung to its native customs and resisted assimilation in the 1920's, they couched their worries in terms of the children's well-being: their students' health was at risk because they spent too much time studying Chinese language and culture during periods when they should have been relaxing and playing. An elementary teacher arranged for the city to purchase a run-down property in Chinatown and with the help of school children it became a neighborhood playground—and a temptation to assimilation. During the same period, some American-born Chinese boys lacked a home field for their baseball team to compete with other city teams. Their elders were not sympathetic, but the playground gave them a home base. These Chinese American baseball players represent the essence of an Americanizer's dream.[8]

Los Angeles school people wanted to bridge the gap between

the city's alien poor and the native middle class. They expected that the reforms would serve as controls as well. Many of their methods were innovative, and in many ways they successfully met the educational challenge posed by immigrants. Inexpensive hot meals at lunch served a sound purpose, but it also allowed school people to impose middle-class American tastes on children of immigrants. Americanization left little room for variation. Moreover, the schools had grown too large. Rapid growth and increased cultural diversity pushed educators toward greater dependence on standardized scientific methods of mental testing.

Many of the reformers and educators were women. Before they attained federal suffrage, elite women like Caroline Severance and Mary Gibson moved from the private world of women's clubs to affect public policy. Later, enfranchised teachers, white and black women like Fay Allen, Ruby Baughman, and Anne Reynolds, worked as professionals in the public sphere to create a school system more responsive to the children of Los Angeles.

Much of the criticism of public education in the twentieth century cites its failure to provide the poorer classes, particularly immigrant and black children, with alternatives to vocational training.[9] In many cases the criticism is justified: how can someone break into the professions with only vocational training? On the other hand most immigrants, like most native-born Americans until after the Second World War, had modest expectations and did not consider sending their children to college. There were exceptions of course. There were families that would have liked their children to attend university but could not spare the children from contributing to the family income; and others that scrimped and pooled their resources so that one child at least could go to college.[10] Generally, however, it was children of the second and third generation, the children and grandchildren of Nora Sterry's and Grace Briggs's former students, who used education as a stepping stone to success.

The irony of Americanization and public policy comes full circle in a 1986 *Los Angeles Times* article headlined PLAN TO AID IMMIGRANT STUDENTS UNVEILED. School board members proposed a network of centers where newly enrolled immigrant students would be "introduced to the ways of American public education." * Newcomer Assistance Centers, staffed by teachers and aides who spoke foreign languages, would administer diagnostic tests to determine grade level and orient students on what to expect at an American school. At some schools classrooms would be set aside, but in neighborhoods where there was a continuous stream of immigrants, a separate district-financed center would be established. Children would remain segregated until instructors believed they were ready to enter regular classes—perhaps for two weeks or two months, according to board member Jackie Goldberg.

Alan Gershman, another board member, hoped to get the plan under way by the fall of that year. He expressed concern because many of the newly arrived from overcrowded schools on the east side and the central city were bussed to the San Fernando Valley, where there were few bilingual teachers. He was quoted as saying, "The saddest thing in the world is to see some youngster sitting in a classroom with a glazed look on his face because he just doesn't understand what's going on."[11]

What board members Goldberg and Gershman had in mind would come as no surprise to Sterry or Briggs. The Newcomer Assistance Centers would fit in nicely with what those educators had promoted a half century earlier.

*Federal regulations discourage the district from keeping track of the number of immigrants enrolled in the schools to prevent discrimination against illegal aliens. Nevertheless, some principals reported in 1986 that foreign-born children made up a third to a half of their student bodies (*Los Angeles Times*, June 20, 1986, sec. 2, p. 4).

Reference Materials

APPENDIX A

Statistical Data

The source for the data in Table A.1 is the Los Angeles Board of Education's *Annual Report, 1904*, pp. 24–25. Tables A.2 and A.3 are based on U.S. Commerce Department, *Fourteenth Census of the United States* (1920), *School Attendance in the U.S.*, 5: 256, 257, 259.

TABLE A.1

Nativity of the 30,909 Schoolchildren of Los Angeles City, 1903–1904

U.S. and U.S. territories		U.S. and U.S. territories	
Area	Number of children	Area	Number of children
California	16,028	Montana	158
Alabama	68	Nebraska	546
Alaska	5	Nevada	45
Arizona	445	New Hampshire	29
Arkansas	127	New Jersey	129
Colorado	766	New Mexico	152
Connecticut	81	New York	791
Delaware	5	North Carolina	11
D. of Columbia	44	North Dakota	123
Florida	33	Ohio	604
Georgia	152	Oklahoma	46
Hawaii	5	Oregon	300
Idaho	55	Pennsylvania	505
Illinois	1,474	Rhode Island	27
Indiana	440	South Carolina	9
Indian Terr.	35	South Dakota	134
Iowa	743	Tennessee	184
Kansas	916	Texas	693
Kentucky	160	Utah	208
Louisiana	146	Vermont	32
Maine	41	Virginia	27
Maryland	38	Washington	361
Massachusetts	293	West Virginia	36
Michigan	460	Wisconsin	261
Minnesota	475	Wyoming	31
Mississippi	64	SUBTOTAL	29,422
Missouri	881		
Foreign		**Foreign**	
Area	Number of children	Area	Number of children
Africa[a]	4	Cuba	4
Armenia	5	Denmark	11
Asia[a]	1	England	106
Assyria	2	Finland	2
Australia	16	France	35
Austria	28	Germany	80
Belgium	9	Greece	7
Bohemia	1	Holland	3
Br. Columbia	5	Honduras	2
Bulgaria	1	Hungary	1
Canada	354	India	1
Chile	2	Ireland	5
China	7	Italy	113

TABLE A.1 (cont'd.)

Foreign		Foreign	
Area	Number of children	Area	Number of children
Japan	93	Serbia	2
Mexico	364	South America[a]	2
New Zealand	5	Spain	16
Norway	9	Sweden	18
Nova Scotia	1	Switzerland	9
Poland	2	West Indies	5
Portugal	1	SUBTOTAL	1,394
Roumania	8		
Russia	41	Uncertain	93
Scotland	13		

[a] Not further specified.

TABLE A.2

Grade School Attendance in Los Angeles (Children Ages 7–13) by Color, Nativity, and Parentage, 1920

Category	Total number of children	Attendance	
		Number	Percent of total
Native white	29,686	28,306	95.4%
Native white, with at least one foreign-born parent	17,508	16,728	95.5
Foreign-born	4,396	4,000	91.0
Black	1,497	1,411	94.3

TABLE A.3

School Attendance by Percentage in Los Angeles, San Francisco, and New York, 1910 and 1920

Category	Los Angeles		San Francisco		New York	
	1910	1920	1910	1920	1910	1920
Native white	93.7%	95.3%	91.2%	92.5%	94.2%	93.3%
Native white, with at least one foreign-born parent	93.3	95.5	92.4	93.1	95.2	94.5
Foreign-born	90.3	91.0	88.9	88.4	92.6	88.2
Black	95.4	94.3	—	91.8	91.9	92.9

APPENDIX B

Examples of Nonverbal IQ Tests

The Haggerty Intelligence Test is reproduced from Frank N. Freeman, *Mental Tests: Their History, Principles, and Applications* (Boston: Houghton Mifflin, 1926), p. 166. The source of the Kohs Block-Design Test is S. C. Kohs, *Intelligence Measurement* (New York: Macmillan, 1923), p. 66.

Part of a nonlanguage test for primary grades, from the Haggarty Intelligence Examination, Delta 1

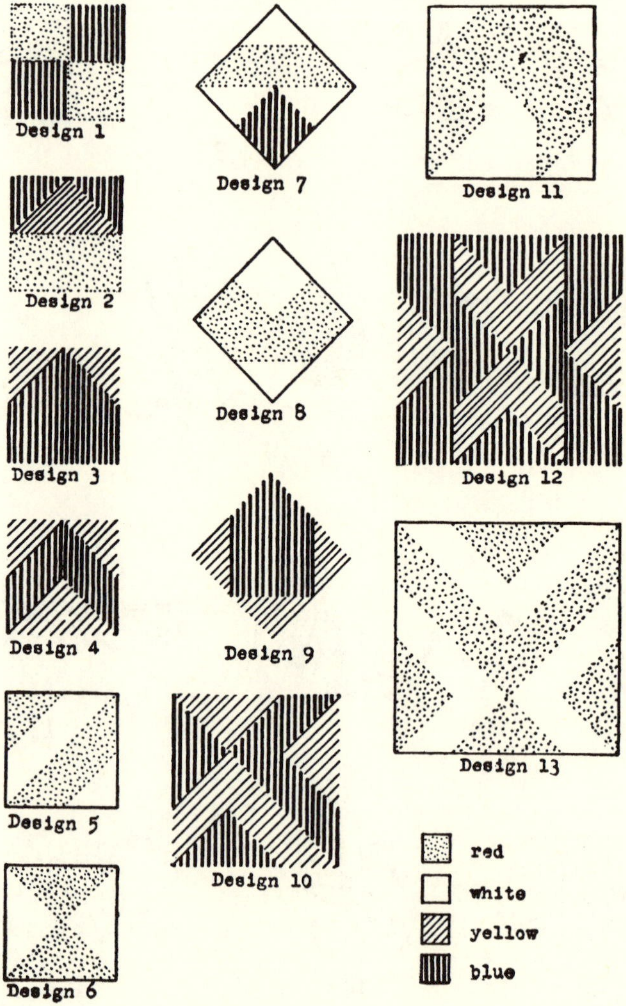

Part of the Kohs Block-Design Test

Notes

For complete authors' names, titles, and publication data on works cited in short form, see the Bibliography, pp. 247–62. The following abbreviations are used in the Notes:

Board	Los Angeles City Board of Education
Bulletin	*Educational Research Bulletin*, published by the Los Angeles Board of Education (originally, titled *High School Research Bulletin*)
CCIH	California Commission of Immigration and Housing
HL	Huntington Library, San Marino, California
LAT	Los Angeles Times
Minutes	Minutes of the Los Angeles Board of Education
School District	Los Angeles City School District
SJ	*School Journal*, published by the Los Angeles Board of Education

Introduction

EPIGRAPH: Shippey, "Los Angeles," p. 135. Los Angeles had been described as a city composed of white Midwesterners, yet this poem, selected with others to represent Los Angeles in a 1927 contest, emphasized the diversity of the population rather than its homogeneity.

1. McDonald, *Urban Fiscal Policy*, p. 12, reminds us that 19th-century Americans were regularly taxed by state and local governments, not by the federal government, and that their dependence on local government for "streets, education, sewers, and policing" thus intensified their interest in local politics and took precedence over what went on in Washington. McDonald put this in a different context, but that interest seemed to reinforce the sense of community many citizens felt in the 19th century, something that ought to be preserved, as they saw it, especially in the face of the influx of newcomers.

2. Bernard C. Watson, "The Principal Against the System," in Erickson and Reller, *Principals*, pp. 40–54. On p. 48 Watson writes, "the notion . . . that schools should and could exist uncontaminated by politics is a relatively recent aberration."

3. See Katz, *Irony of Early School Reform*; Cremin, *Transformation of the School*; Tyack, *One Best System*; Maris Vinovskis, *The Origins of Public High School: A Reexamination of the Beverly High School Controversy* (Madison: Univ. of Wisconsin Press, 1986); Peterson, *School Reform*; Urban, *Why Teachers Organize*; William J. Reese, *Power and Promise of School Reform: Grass Roots Movements During the Progressive Era* (Boston: Routledge, Chapman & Hall, 1986); Carl Kaestle, *Pillars of the Republic*; Katznelson and Weir, *Schooling for All*; Wrigley, *Class, Politics, and Public Schools*; Hogan, *Class and Reform*; Fass, *Outside In*; and Cohen, *Children of the Mill*. Katz's influence has been so pervasive that most historians writing after the publication of *The Irony of Early School Reform* have tended to interpret the goals and responses of school reformers as purely self-serving and have imputed xenophobic motives to their actions. Rarely have they found humanitarianism active in this period. Instead, their writings create a picture of zealots whose regard for the people they hoped to reform borders on contempt, if not downright disdain. Indeed, these historians have argued the point so convincingly that Progressive reform has become synonymous with "social control," a term replete with conspiratorial connotations. While I distance myself from their interpretations by posing a new set of questions related to the interaction of reformers and ethnic communities and their effect on public policy, I owe a considerable debt to these historians. Their writings have caused me to rethink much of what I had taken for granted about public education. See also Shultz, *Culture Factory*; Bowles and Gintis, *Schooling in Capitalistic America*; and Greer, *Great School Legend*. See also Cohen and Mohl, *Paradox of Progressive Education*. For other views not already mentioned, see Kaestle, *Pillars of the Republic*; Troen, *Public and Schools*; Gordon, "Patriots and Christians"; and D. Moore, *At Home in America*.

Chapter One

EPIGRAPH: Louise Ward to Charles Thompson, Jan. 5, 1906, Louise Ward Watkins Collection, box 1, HL.

1. Ibid. Ward's father, the engineer George Clinton Ward, brought his family to Los Angeles in 1905 in order to work more closely with Henry E. Huntington on Huntington's vast hydroelectric projects. Louise wrote that her father never tired of "extolling the merits of wonderful Southern California."

2. Louise Ward to Aunt Harriet, June 4, 1905, in ibid.

3. Board, *Annual Report, 1884–85*, p. 13.

4. Warner et al., *Historical Sketch*, pp. 142–43.

5. For a detailed examination of the Chinese community, see Lou, "Chinese American Community." Another source on California's Chinese population, Chan, *This Bittersweet Soil*, although spotty on Los

Angeles, tells a fascinating story of the Chinese contribution to 19th-century California agriculture.

6. Dumke, *Boom of the Eighties*, pp. 24–25. Dumke has the lowest rate occurring on March 6, 1887, but either he or another scholar corrected it in pencil in one of the Huntington Library's copies to read 1886. The normal rates from the Mississippi Valley to Southern California were in the neighborhood of $125.

7. *Thirteenth Census: Abstract with Supplement for California*, p. 568.

8. Nordhoff and Warner, quoted in Dumke, *Boom of the Eighties*, pp. 30–31.

9. Edwards Roberts, "In the City of Angels," *Chicago Daily News* (morning ed.), June 26, 1884, p. 3. Roberts published his essays in 1885 (*With the Invaders: Glimpses of the Southwest*).

10. Dumke, *Boom of the Eighties*, remains the best account of this period.

11. Ibid., p. 267; Cleland and Putnam, *Hellman*, pp. 52–53.

12. Dumke, *Boom of the Eighties*, pp. 268–69; Midge Sherwood, "Eliza Ann Otis, Co-founder of the *Los Angeles Times*," *Pacific Historian*, 28 (Fall 1984): 45–53.

13. Dumke, *Boom of the Eighties*, p. 70.

14. Rolle, *California*, pp. 411–12. Deverell, "Los Angeles Free Harbor Fight," offers a fresh analysis of this episode.

15. Dumke, *Boom of the Eighties*, pp. 244–55.

16. Board, *Annual Report, 1884*, pp. 13–14; *1885*, p. 25.

17. Ibid., *1884*, pp. 50–51. Reller, *Development of City Superintendency*, p. 188, describes the changing role of the superintendent.

18. *Los Angeles Express*, Jan. 2, 1906, p. 6.

19. *Minutes*, 14: 253–54, 17: 361. A decade earlier, in 1905, the figure was some 20,000 lower—34,326.

20. Camarillo, *Chicanos*, pp. 200–201.

21. *Twelfth Census* (1900), 1 (*Population*): part 1, pp. 798–99. Western Europe here embraces only the northern states: Belgium, British Isles, France, Germany, Holland, Luxembourg, Scandinavia (including Finland), and Switzerland. Greece supplied the largest group of Southern Europeans, with 1,203, Italy the next largest, with 763.

22. *Thirteenth Census* (1910), 1 (*Population*): 854–55; *Fourteenth Census*, (1920), 2 (*Population*): 47, 854–55. The Mexican population figures are misleading, as I have noted. The 13th census tallied 5,632 Mexicans, but American-born people of Mexican descent were typically counted as whites. See Camarillo, *Chicanos*; and Fogelson, *Fragmented Metropolis*, p. 76. According to Fogelson, there were 14,218 Mexicans in Los Angeles in 1910 and 36,177 in 1920.

23. *Thirteenth Census* (1910), 1 (*Population*): 207–13; *Fourteenth Census* (1920), 3 (*Population*): 40–45.

24. *Minutes*, 14: 1–19. Petitions to the *Minutes* provide a sense of where various ethnic and racial groups lived in the city.

25. Revisionist historians have treated these reformers rather contemptuously. Robert Wiebe, for example, finds the Progressives motivated by the fear of losing political or social status, and Gabriel Kolko accuses them of cloaking their own greedy desires for economic betterment behind their reforming spirit. Progressives generally wanted to bring newer business techniques for efficiency to government. Often, as Samuel Hays, Joseph Huthmacher, and Wiebe have pointed out, many of the reforms centered around social classes fighting for control of the cities (Hays, "Politics of Reform"; Huthmacher, "Urban Liberalism"; Kolko, *Triumph of Conservatism*; Wiebe, *Search for Order*).

Chapter Two

EPIGRAPH: *Los Angeles Examiner*, Jan. 13, 1912, in Friday Morning Club, Scrapbook 1911–12.

1. Wiebe, *Search for Order*. The accepted periodization for the Progressive Era is from 1890 to 1919 or 1920. For Los Angeles schools, this standard periodization must be extended, because reformers continued many of their innovations well into the 1920's.

2. Tyack, *One Best System*, p. 127. Tyack uses the term "administrative progressives."

3. R. Williams, *Democratic Party*, pp. 206, 228.

4. Schiesl, "Progressive Reform" (Schiesl provides detailed material on the reform movement in Los Angeles, as does Mowry, *California Progressives*); Freeman, "Board-Superintendent Relationships," pp. 625–34; Fogelson, *Fragmented Metropolis*, pp. 205–29.

5. Bettinger, "Twenty-Five Years," p. 70.

6. Freeman, "Board-Superintendent Relationships," p. 258.

7. Ibid., p. 259.

8. Ibid.

9. Bettinger, "Twenty-Five Years," p. 71.

10. Ibid.; Tyack, *One Best System*, p. 127.

11. Freeman, "Board-Superintendent Relationships," pp. 265–69, 278.

12. Urban, *Why Teachers Organize*, pp. 31–43; McCoy and Tanner, *Report*, tabulation sheets 1, 2; NEA, *Report*, p. 181.

13. Freeman, "Board-Superintendent Relationships," pp. 318, 325. California's first compulsory school statute, enacted in 1874, linked compulsory attendance to prohibiting the use of public money for religious schools. The issue divided educators along religious and political lines. Republicans favored it; Democrats opposed it. The mechanism to enforce the law was weak and ineffective, and rendered the act unsatisfactory to almost everyone. (Katznelson and Weir, *Schooling for All*, pp. 70–71.)

14. P. Young, *Pilgrims*, p. 147. See also *Minutes*, 10: 28.
15. Peterson, *School Reform*, pp. 9–10.
16. Schlossman, *Love and the American Delinquent*, p. 134, pronounces them neither ladies bountiful nor ladies vindictive. These themes are elaborated throughout Pascoe, *Relations of Rescue*. Pascoe finds that the women's commitment to orthodox Protestantism gave rescue missionaries the moral authority to challenge men's position to a greater extent than most Progressive women in school reform.
17. Since the 1980's there has been an outpouring of scholarship on the importance of a literal "separate sphere" for women. For an excellent overview of the historiography, see Kerber's article by that title. For a complete account of the development of women's clubs and their importance in the movement of middle-class women into the public sphere, see Blair, *Clubwoman as Feminist*.
18. Sklar, "Hull House," p. 670.
19. J. Jensen, "After Slavery"; Blair, *Clubwoman as Feminist*, pp. 31–32; Ruddy, *Mother of Clubs*. The Severances had five children, two of whom preceded them to California. Jane Cunningham Croly founded Sorosis in 1868, in New York, and along with Severance shares the honor of being founding mother of women's clubs.
20. Hanson, "Kindergarten Movement," pp. 5–25. Mrs. Carl Schurz opened the first kindergarten in her home in Watertown (Wis.), in 1856, where she taught her own children and children of friends in the German language. By 1873 ten cities had training schools for kindergarten teachers, and in that same year Saint Louis incorporated kindergartens into its public school system (Troen, *Public and Schools*).
21. Swift, *Marwedel*, pp. 153–55, 161, 167. Kate Douglas Smith Wiggin, later to gain fame as an author of children's stories, recorded her experiences in kindergarten activities in Los Angeles and later in San Francisco in *My Garden of Memory*, pp. 89–139. Severance had visited Wiggin in Santa Barbara, and it was at her behest that Wiggin first came to Los Angeles to enroll in Marwedel's class. The Los Angeles Normal School reported a Kindergarten Department offering a two-year course in 1896 (*History of the Los Angeles State Normal School, Quarter Centennial, 1882–1907*, p. 9, HL, UCLA).
22. Caroline Severance to Jane E. Collier, June 26, Oct. 12, 1895, Graham Collection, box 24, HL. The folder containing the October letter has a question mark indicating that there was some question about the year. From all indications, both letters were written in 1885. The "public interest" quote is from the October letter. Dr. Stebbins had replaced the much-admired and beloved Thomas Starr King after King's untimely death in 1864 (H. E. Starr, *Dictionary of American Biography*).
23. A. Allen, "Let Us Live with Our Children."
24. Felix Adler, the well-known philanthropist and leader of the

New York Society for Ethical Culture, came to San Francisco in 1878, and with some wealthy San Franciscans, raised enough money to open the Silver Street Kindergarten in the poverty-stricken Tar Flats. Wiggin, then known as Kate Douglas Smith, had been recruited to help organize the new kindergarten (Wiggin, *My Garden of Memory*, p. 107).

25. Board, *Annual Report*, 1914, p. 57.

26. A. Allen, "Let Us Live with Our Children," p. 40. Calvin Stowe's 1837 "Report on Elementary Public Instruction in Europe to the State of Ohio" was heavily influenced by the ideas of the Swiss educator Johann Pestalozzi about the importance of females as nurturers for small children (Spring, *American School*, pp. 118–19, 130–31).

27. *Minutes*, 11: 172, 176.

28. Ibid., 10: 306.

29. Ibid., 12: 172, 321.

30. Bettinger, "Twenty-Five Years," pp. 71, 72. Sloyd, a Swedish term for a particular form of manual training using hand tools, had been incorporated in some schools in Russia and Prussia, as well as Sweden, and soon after American educators saw demonstrations of it at the 1876 Philadelphia Exhibition, they introduced it into certain public school systems.

31. There are several interesting studies that cover the play movement, including Lazerson, *Urban School*; and Violas, *Urban Working Class*. Spring, *American School*, pp. 162–64, presents an overview of the literature. Glassberg, "Forgotten Childhood," presents a different view from the others; the Addams quote is from p. 358 of his article.

32. Bettinger, "Twenty-Five Years," p. 74.

33. Kerber, "Separate Spheres"; Sklar, "Hull House"; Freedman, "Separatism." Settlements had become common in most major cities by 1910: Philadelphia, with a population of 1,549,000, had 23; Saint Louis, with a population of 689,000, had 8 (Woods and Kennedy, *Handbook*, pp. 153–57, 262–81; Fogelson, *Fragmented Metropolis*, p. 78).

34. Woods and Kennedy, *Handbook*, pp. 9–13.

35. Ibid., pp. 11–12; Stoddart, "Recreative Centers"; *History of the Los Angeles State Normal School, Quarter Centennial, 1882–1907*, p. 45, HL, UCLA. I thank Lewis O. Saum for consulting the *Los Angeles City Directories* from 1895 to 1920 to learn how long Bessie lived at the settlement. The evidence was not conclusive; some years the Directories did not list her. The years when she is listed and not living in the settlement, Bessie and sister Evelyn, who was active in the development of a juvenile court in Los Angeles, lived with their widowed mother and two sisters in what appears to have been modest circumstances.

36. *Los Angeles Settlement Association*. Although there is no date of publication, the pamphlet describes the functions of the settlement in 1904–5. At that time the city district nurse lived at the settlement. One of the residents was male.

37. *Minutes*, 10: 31, 365; Bartlett, *Better City*, p. 90.

38. *Minutes*, 14: 359. For a description of the conflict caused by the new mass culture, and of the reformers' efforts to thwart what they considered its unwholesomeness, see Kasson, *Amusing the Millions*.

39. Board, *Annual Report, 1914*, p. 57. The *Los Angeles Times* of Nov. 16, 1918 (sec. 1, p. 8) reported that nine additional after-hours playgrounds had opened in the city. Some years later the playgrounds' role in combating delinquency came under suspicion. A report published during the 1932 Olympic events in Los Angeles disclaimed their merits as deterrents of juvenile crime. "As for playgrounds, Los Angeles has no lack"; nevertheless it had "youthful crimes, mostly from immigrants" (*LAT*, Aug. 3, 1932, sec. 2, p. 4).

40. P. Young, *Pilgrims*, pp. 229, 230.

41. Ibid., pp. 141–42, 144.

42. *Minutes*, 16: 262.

43. Ibid., 7: 210, 8: 125.

44. City public health departments developed throughout urban America during the Progressive Era. Schools then followed suit to augment services for the children in their care. On the trend in Los Angeles, see ibid., 8: 149, 151–52.

45. Ibid., 9: 284.

46. Ibid., 11: 50, 340. Sex hygiene classes grew out of the social hygiene movement that insisted on open discussions of the sexual process as a way to eliminate the double standard and male patronage of prostitution. As in other areas, Los Angeles schools were ahead of the National Education Association, which did not endorse sex education until 1912 (D'Emilio and Freedman, *Intimate Matters*, pp. 205–8).

47. *Minutes*, 12: 5.

48. Ibid.

49. Board, *Annual Report, 1914*, pp. 90–91.

50. *Minutes*, 12: 46, 14: 86. Public baths became a part of urban reform during this period. By the 1890's American physicians and the general public recognized that germs, not just simple filth, were the real cause of disease. An earlier hypothesis on the interrelationship between disease, poverty, physical environment, and crime was now replaced by the "germ theory." According to Marilyn Williams, "Focus on the germ theory rather than the filth theory of disease transferred attention from the environment to the individual as a source of contagion while emphasizing the importance of personal cleanliness." Public baths and shower baths, installed by reformers to augment inadequate home facilities, were attempts by these progressive-minded citizens to prevent the spread of disease ("New York City's Public Baths," p. 50).

51. *Minutes*, 16: 155.

52. Morantz-Sanchez, *Sympathy*, pp. 282–83.

53. Board, *Annual Report, 1914*, pp. 154–56. The GFWC encouraged local clubs to create watchdog committees and proposed that each

committee lobby for a specific cause. In the West, committees worked for such conservation measures as preserving the redwoods, the Palisades, and Mesa Verde. Other offshoots looked after matters closer to home, requesting more professional women to administer to women in such functions as doctors, prison guards, and wardens. The civil service commission in Los Angeles may have seen its role in this way as it called for female physicians to examine female employees. (Blair, *Clubwoman as Feminist*, pp. 102–4; see also *Minutes*, 18: 334.) Nurses' salaries were comparable to the mid-range of elementary classroom teachers' salaries.

54. Bancroft, "Health Supervision," p. 14; Board, *Annual Report, 1914*, p. 89. See Rothman, *Conscience*, p. 381, on institutions assuming specific characteristics.

55. Bryan, *School Cafeteria*, pp. 1–14; Matthews, *Just a Housewife*, p. 149.

56. Levenstein, "New England Kitchen," pp. 384–86; Rossiter, *Women Scientists*, p. 65; *Minutes*, 9: 87. Los Angeles reformers may have seen examples of the new nutrition and new cooking methods at the 1893 Chicago Exposition, where a model workingman's cottage had been set up in the Massachusetts pavilion. For a lively discussion of the culture surrounding the Boston Cooking School, see L. Shapiro, *Perfection Salad*; the boiling times in the text are from p. 96 of this work.

57. Carrie Bryant, secretary of the School Lunch Committee of the Civic Association, requested the lunch programs (*Minutes*, 10: 161, 10: 275, 11: 44).

58. Flagg felt the founders of the program had not received the recognition they deserved, and in 1936 she demanded that the board set up a special file on all references to the penny lunches. Finally, in 1949, 40 years after the start of the program that resulted in the school cafeterias, the board dedicated a commemorative plaque at Ann Street School. (The penny-lunch folder is available in the File Unit of the Secretariat Office of the Los Angeles Unified Schools District.)

59. Bancroft, "Health Supervision," p. 25.

60. *Minutes*, 18: 336.

61. Maidenberg, *Do You Remember?*, pp. 3–4.

62. Covello and D'Agostino, *Heart Is the Teacher*.

63. Tyack, *One Best System*, p. 242.

64. For most of the Molokan material, I have relied on P. Young, *Pilgrims*; and W. Moore, *Molokan Oral Tradition*. Two Molokan elders, Peter Shubin and Ivan Samarin, came to Los Angeles in 1900. Apparently pleased with what they saw, they arranged for their co-religionists to migrate. Some Molokans tried farming in Utah and Mexico.

65. W. Moore, *Molokan Oral Tradition*, p. 9.

66. P. Young, *Pilgrims*, p. 153.

67. Sokaloff, "Russians," p. 10.

68. P. Young, *Pilgrims*, p. 150.

69. *Minutes*, 10: 80, 84, 11: 355. The *Los Angeles Express* of Feb. 9, 1912, noted that the Board of Education paid to bring in a Russian-language teacher for the colony, but there is no evidence to support that statement in the board minutes.

70. *Minutes*, 11: 50, 9: 149, 17: 19.

71. Ibid., 7: 196–97, 198.

72. Ibid., 13: 259.

73. Ibid., 12: 311, 13: 103, 376, 15: 345, 362.

74. Ibid., 13: 367, 18: 126.

75. Ibid., 10: 216.

76. Ibid., 13: 31.

77. Tyack, *One Best System*, pp. 160–67. Ethnic groups in San Francisco, allied with the Union Labor Party, also founded a "cosmopolitan" school. In 1916, during an extensive school survey conducted by the U.S. Commissioner of Education, Philander Claxton, that school came under fire (Herman, "Neighbors," pp. 433–35).

78. Jessup and Shiels, "Report," pp. 131–32.

79. *Minutes*, 14: 48; 19: 257.

80. Ibid., 17: 18, 265, 343; 15: 42.

81. Ibid., 14: 49.

82. Board, *Annual Report, 1914*, p. 127.

83. *Minutes*, 18: 301–2.

84. Ibid., 19: 235.

85. Jessup and Shiels, "Report," p. 130.

86. Board, *Annual Report, 1914*, p. 128.

87. Tyack, *One Best System*, pp. 241–42.

Chapter Three

EPIGRAPH: E. Moore, "Fundamental Concepts," p. 11.

1. Kirschner, *Paradox of Professionalism*, discusses the changes in reform and the demands of professionalism. Matthews, *Just a Housewife*, pp. 145–71, shows how professionalization changed homemaking from a respected, traditional occupation for women to a job with little respect.

2. *Who Was Who in America, 1897–1942*, p. 421. Francis received an M.A. at San Joaquin Valley College in Woodbridge in 1892 and taught in Woodbridge and Stockton before moving to Los Angeles (Guinn, *History of California*, 3: 895–96).

3. Guinn, "School System of Los Angeles," p. 206.

4. Bettinger, "Twenty-Five Years," pp. 71, 73.

5. The California legislature approved the term junior high school in 1920, and Los Angeles adopted the name shortly after (Eales, "Los Angeles School System," p. 145).

6. Bunker, *Junior High School Movement*, p. 39. G. Stanley Hall's

Adolescence: Its Psychology and Its Relations to Physiology, Anthropology, Sociology, Sex, Crime, Religion, and Education appeared in 1904. In 1892 the NEA set up a commission to study high school curriculum. Led by the president of Harvard University, Charles Eliot, the Committee of Ten decided against a differentiated curriculum. Shortly after the committee released its results in 1894, its recommendations came under fire (Addresses and Proceedings of the National Education Association, "Committee of Ten on Secondary Schools," 1895). Doubts lingered on both fronts. See Briggs, "Some Old-Fashioned Doubts." Le Baron Russell Briggs was a Harvard professor and dean before becoming president of Radcliffe College in 1903.

7. Spring, *American School*, pp. 202–16; Lazerson and Grubb, *American Education*. The Committee on Industrial Education of the National Association of Manufacturers praised the German technical schools in its 1905 report. In 1912 the NEA's Committee on Industrial Education came out with a report of its own, endorsing vocational training.

8. Spring, *American School*, p. 209.

9. Freeman, "Board-Superintendent Relationships," p. 394. In 1905 the California Teachers' Association discussed reorganizing the school system and concluded that the 7th and 8th grades belonged in secondary education (Eales, "Los Angeles School System," p. 141). Moore credited Francis with originating the junior high school idea and contended that both junior highs and junior colleges originated in California. He took some umbrage at the remark of Professor Charles Judd of the University of Chicago that junior highs were not the product of one individual (E. Moore, "Fundamental Concepts," pp. 9–10; E. Moore, "John H. Francis").

10. *Minutes*, 9: 224–25. Francis appears to have brought back the idea of a three-year junior high from a fact-finding trip to Europe in 1908–9 (Eales, "Los Angeles School System," p. 142).

11. Bettinger, "Twenty-Five Years," p. 73; Eales, "Los Angeles School System," p. 141. Bettinger may have been premature in his assessment of Bunker's ability to wait for his followers before moving too far ahead. S. D. Waterman, a former Berkeley superintendent, noted that three years after Bunker arrived in Berkeley his contract as superintendent was not renewed. Waterman also accused Bunker of trying partisan methods to hang on to his job (*History of Berkeley Schools*, pp. 46, 64). Spring, *American School*, p. 215, notes that the first intermediate school may have opened in Columbus, Ohio, in September 1909. Bunker took most of the credit for junior high schools, refuting Moore's statement that the idea of intermediate schools originated with Francis (*Junior High School Movement*, pp. 49–50).

12. Board, comp., *Chronology of Los Angeles City Schools* (1961), part 2, pp. 1–8.

13. Board, *Annual Report, 1914,* pp. 11–13.
14. Freeman, "Board-Superintendent Relationships," pp. 439–40.
15. Ibid., pp. 438–39.
16. Ibid., pp. 457–58.
17. Ibid., p. 423.
18. Ibid., p. 458.
19. Guinn, *History of California,* 3: 895–96. Joseph Scott and Mrs. R. L. Craig were the two members who were absent when Francis rammed his Schedule B through the board in 1912. An interesting aside to this story comes in the form of a biographical sketch in a multivolume history of California compiled and perhaps written by Guinn. Even as Guinn criticized Francis publicly, the supervisor appears in vol. 3 of that work in the most elevated terms. First noting publicly Francis's accomplishments, the *History,* published in 1915, goes on to say: "If his policies are carried out for the next ten years Los Angeles will easily become one of the foremost educational centers in the land" (p. 896). Earlier, on pp. 886–87, in a section on the YMCA, a letter by Francis extolling that organization's virtues is the featured item. This genre of publication, combining history with many biographical sketches of living contemporaries, would not have provided the author with a likely place for airing his genuine feelings about the subjects of the sketches. If, in fact, Guinn wrote the individual sketches, he would have felt constrained to avoid making disparaging remarks about people who may well have financially subscribed to the multivolume set before publication.
20. Susan Dorsey taught at Los Angeles High School and served as vice-principal before being promoted to assistant superintendent in 1913.
21. Freeman, "Board-Superintendent Relationships," pp. 448–50.
22. *Minutes,* 14: 5.
23. Freeman, "Board-Superintendent Relationships," pp. 454–55; *Minutes,* 14: 49.
24. Ibid., 2: 455.
25. *LAT,* June 18, 1914, sec. 2, p. 1.
26. *LAT,* June 23, 1914, sec. 1, p. 7.
27. *LAT,* June 20, 1914, sec. 2, p. 5.
28. Guinn, *History of California,* 2: 77–79. The question of the intermediate schools' legality was placed before County Superintendent Mark Keppel in 1914. He upheld their legality (Eales, "Los Angeles School System," p. 143).
29. Freeman, "Board-Superintendent Relationships," p. 471; *LAT,* June 22, 1914, sec. 2, p. 1. The *Times* suggested that teachers would demonstrate in support of Francis, and that Polytechnic High School would be one of the demonstration sites.
30. *LAT,* May 25, 1915, sec. 2, p. 3.

31. *LAT*, May 28, 1915, sec. 2, p. 5.
32. *LAT*, May 30, 1915, sec. 2, p. 4.
33. *LAT*, May 27, 1915, sec. 2, p. 5.
34. *LAT*, June 22, 1914, sec. 2, p. 1. In 1914 Los Angeles had eight senior high schools, according to "Chronology of Los Angeles City Schools," April 3, 1961.
35. Urban, *Why Teachers Organize*, pp. 41–43. Urban finds that most teachers tried to keep the status quo. They wanted their promotions based on the old system of seniority, not on examinations and educational attainment.
36. The NEA met in Los Angeles in 1899. Superintendent Foshay, with board approval and at taxpayers' expense, had traveled to Washington, D.C., in June 1898 to make the appropriate arrangements. It was understood by all that in bringing the prestigious group to Los Angeles, Foshay had shown the growing professionalization among city educators (*Minutes*, 3: 2).
37. Tyack, *One Best System*, p. 254. The National Federation of Teachers was reorganized in 1901 to fight discrimination by the male-dominated NEA and to gain better wages and working conditions for female teachers.
38. Freeman, "Board-Superintendent Relationships," pp. 406–9. The Education School at UCLA bears his name. Moore married Dorothea Lummis, the first wife of Charles Lummis and one of the first female physicians to settle in Los Angeles. Sharing many of her future husband's progressive instincts, Dr. Lummis lent her support to Severance and the kindergarten movement in 1886 by offering her own office as a meeting place (Carolyn Severance to M. C. Graham, June 22, 1886, Graham Collection, box 24, HL).
39. Stimson, *Labor Movement*, pp. 391–406. The Socialist Job Harriman, working with the McNamaras' defense team, was thought to have a good chance to win the upcoming mayoral election in Los Angeles. Most observers tie his loss to the McNamaras' confession.
40. *LAT*, June 21, 1914, sec. 2, pp. 1, 6, June 23, 1914, sec. 2, p. 4.
41. Weyer, "Scott," p. 247. According to two Scott sons, it was not chief defense counsel Darrow who persuaded James McNamara to confess, but Scott. On hearing that Scott won his libel case, Governor Hiram Johnson wired him a congratulatory note.
42. *LAT*, June 2, 1915, sec. 1, p. 1; Freeman, "Board-Superintendent Relationships," pp. 681-82. With most of the precincts complete, the *Times* reported that Bordwell had 24,888 votes, against 19,017 for his nearest opponent.
43. Stimson, *Labor Movement*, pp. 391–406.
44. *Minutes*, 15: 11.
45. Carstensen, "Jessup." Shiels had co-authored *City Arithmetic, Grades 1 Through 8* (1916) with George Wentworth and David Eugene Smith.

46. *LAT*, June 2, 1916, sec. 2, p. 1; Freeman, "Board-Superintendent Relationships," p. 489.

47. *LAT*, Sept. 10, 1916, sec. 2, p. 12. On March 14, 1916, the *Los Angeles Express* reported that the former Chicago superintendent Ella Flagg Young had been named as a possible successor of Francis (Cole Collection 217, box 18, Francis Folder).

48. Albert Shiels, ed., *The School and the Immigrant: A Series of Articles on the Education of Immigrants* (1915), prepared by direction of Thomas W. Churchill, president of the Board of Education.

49. Board, *Directory of Personnel, 1915–1916*, p. 139.

50. Spalding, *History*, 1: 383; *LAT*, June 11, 1916, sec. 1, p. 1, June 15, 1916, sec. 2, p. 1; Bean, *California*, pp. 363–65. For a full description of the Mooney case, see Frost. Los Angeles's involvement in the war effort touched all segments of society. As part of the fight against venereal disease, and influenced by the social hygiene movement, the government asked community volunteers to create homelike atmospheres for servicemen, replete with hometown activities. The War Camp Community Services provided facilities for good wholesome fun away from the temptations of saloons and red-light districts. In nearby Arcadia the committee constructed a showcase recreation center that included a clubhouse, library, study room, canteen, and swimming pool. The soldiers from the Balloon Camp benefited from the generosity of Anita Baldwin, who donated the land and money for landscaping, the talents of the renowned architect Myron Hunt, who designed the center, and the energy of Mrs. Myron Hunt, who presided over the local War Camp Community Services Committee. (*California Southland*, no. 2, 1918–19, p. 7; D'Emilio and Freedman, *Intimate Matters*, pp. 203–15.)

51. See Spalding, *History*, 1: 383; and for a full account of the affair, see Tuchman, *Zimmermann Telegram*. In nearby Pasadena the city's Food Conservation Center urged women to use less wheat because of the national shortage and published recipes for bread made with corn flour and potato flour. One day a week the center directed its attention specifically to the city's Mexican population. Mexican women had begun using wheat for their tortillas because they found the local ground corn unsuitable, or at least not to their taste. Attempts were now made to lure them back to corn. A new type of ground corn appeared on the market, "Maizarina," packaged by Bloke Milling Company, and the center undertook to educate the Mexican population into using this product. (*California Southland*, no. 1, 1918, p. 22.)

52. The Germans met first at Frau Wiebecke's Gardens and then moved to larger quarters, a barn on Alameda Street between Ducommon and First streets, to provide space for gymnastics. In the barn groups of boys enjoyed thrilling onlookers with their human pyramid. Around the middle of the 1870's, the society merged with the Teutonia-Concordia to form Turnverein-Germania. (Newmark, *Sixty Years*.) As in many Western towns, Jews actively participated in German organi-

zations. For an account of the Jewish community of Portland, Ore., see Cline, "Creation of an Ethnic Community."

53. Saum, "Astonishing the Natives." Jack Crawford tried to enlist the young Kate Douglas Smith Wiggin in his troupe during his Los Angeles tour. While attending the kindergarten training school, she aided many worthy causes with her theatrical talents. When Crawford saw her, she was working on behalf of the Unitarian Church. Mary Simons Gibson and Caroline Severance also worked for those causes but strictly from the financial end.

54. Spaulding, *History*, 1: 237, 260; U.S. Congress, *Reports* of the Commission, 29: 21, 31: 554. According to Geltner, "Common Schools," p. 203, the city gave the Turnverein Society a lot on which to build its school. In a pamphlet of ca. 1910, the society advertised its program of physical activities as the "German system" and offered membership to anyone, German or not, over the age of 18; Turnverein offered members several benefits, including access to its library, entertainment, and sick care (Turnverein, Germania, School for Physical Training, "Class Hours, Rules and General Information," Ephemera Collection, Educational File, HL). In 1919, reestablishing themselves as good citizens, the society members petitioned the City Council for permission to provide space for returning soldiers and sailors (Los Angeles City Council, *Petitions to the City Council*, 1919, no. 39; *Minutes*, book B, p. 11; *Minutes*, 13: 31.)

55. *Minutes*, 21: 168, 30: 442. In 1921 teachers petitioned the board to have German music reinstated but were told such a decision had to await confirmation from Sacramento. The city schools' publication *Courses of Study for the High and Intermediate Schools*, 30 (Jan. 1920): 73, suggests that the edict against German music was already being ignored. It recommended that the 8th and 9th grades begin their study of the lives and works of the great composers with Bach.

56. *Minutes*, 21: 20, 22: 22, 23: 29, 250; Shiels, *Los Angeles City Schools*. Shiels prepared a letter for all principals to post on the subject of loyalty. One city teacher, Mary Buerger, the daughter of a Civil War veteran, lost her job because her husband was an unnaturalized German (Beale, *Are Teachers Free?*, p. 26).

57. Dewey, *Enlistment*, pp. 1–10; Bullert, *Politics of John Dewey*, p. 41.

58. *LAT*, Sept. 14, 1916, sec. 1, pp. 1, 3.

59. Shiels, *Los Angeles City Schools*; John S. McGroaty, *Los Angeles from the Mountains to the Sea* (Chicago: American Historical Society, 1921), 1: 255–58.

60. Spalding, *History*, 1: 383.

61. *Fourteenth Census* (1920); Frank Alexander Ross, *School Attendance in the United States*, Census Monographs 5 (124): 256–57.

62. U.S. Congress, *Reports* of the Commission, 31: 559. The total 1908 enrollment was only 33,422. In part the jump in the proportion of immigrant children may be due to the incorporation of county areas with large concentrations of the foreign-born since 1908.

63. *LAT*, May 1, 1921, sec. 2, p. 7.

64. *Minutes*, 18: 399.

65. *Los Angeles Examiner*, Nov. 6, 1912. I thank Abraham Hoffmann for sharing this item.

66. Bartlett, *Better City*, p. 27.

67. Ibid., pp. 123–24.

68. Freeman, "Board-Superintendent Relationships," p. 555; *Fourteenth Census* (1920) 1 (*Increase of Population in the U.S., 1910–1920*): 79; *Fifteenth Census* (1930), 1 (*Population*): 18.

69. *LAT*, May 28, 1915, sec. 2, p. 5. In 1915 there was one automobile for every 43.1 residents in the United States, one for every 8.2 in Los Angeles. The rates in 1920 were 13.1 and 3.6, respectively, and in 1925, 6.6 and 1.8 (Bottles, *Los Angeles*, p. 93). Bottles's study shows the many factors that contributed to the popularity of the automobile in Los Angeles, not least the failure of public transportation to keep up with the area's needs.

70. Bean, *California*, p. 337. Bean's quote of Johnson comes from a 1910 Los Angeles speech.

71. *LAT*, Oct. 10, 1914, sec. 6, p. 14.

72. Braitman, "California Stateswoman," p. 87.

73. CCIH, *Report*, p. 100; Bary and Cahn, *Welfare Activities*, p. 351.

74. *The Survey* (Charity Organization Society) 28 (1912): 785; CCIH, *Report*; Charles W. Blanpied, comp., *A Humanitarian Study of the Coming Immigration Problem on the Pacific Coast* (San Francisco: Young Men's Christian Association, 1913).

75. Katherine Philips Edson to Harriet Vittum, Sept. 6, 1916, Edson Collection, box 1, UCLA. See also Friday Morning Club, "Gibson, Pioneer." Gibson's tireless campaigning throughout the state in 1911 worried her son. Writing from his diplomatic post in Havana, Hugh reminded his mother that their family needed no martyrs and begged her to slow down (Hugh Gibson to Mary Simons Gibson, Sept. 23, 1911, Hugh Gibson Collection, box 25, Hoover Institution Archives, Stanford, Calif.) Mary and Frank A. Gibson shared many of the same reform ideas. Mary retired from teaching to raise a family and take an active role in civic affairs. Of her four children, only Hugh survived to adulthood. Widowed in 1902, Mary drew support from women's organizations. She helped establish the first home for orphaned children and raised money for the public library by staging amateur theatrical productions with her friends Caroline Severance and Kate Douglas Smith Wiggin. She championed birth control, a single moral standard,

Indian policy reform, and world peace. Her dedication to peace was so strong that in 1920 she broke with the Republican Party over its stand against the League of Nations.

76. CCIH, *Report*, p. 99.

77. Gibson, "Schools," p. 301.

78. Gibson, *Program for Americanization*, pp. 12, 14, 35. See Schlossman, *Love and the American Delinquent*, for more details on the juvenile courts and immigrants. See also Bodnar, "Schooling and the Slavic American Family." For two excellent accounts of strong immigrant mothers by writers from the San Francisco Bay area, see McLean, *Mama's Bank Account* on Norwegian mothers; and Tan, *Joy Luck Club*, on Chinese mothers. Other sources paint a very different portrait of immigrant mothers of Slavic, Southern Italian, and Russian Jewish extraction. See, for example, Ewen, *Immigrant Women*.

79. Lillian M. Warner, "Minutes of Executive Board," March 26, 1921, California Federation of Women's Clubs, Clara Bradley Burdette Collection, HL.

80. *California Southland*, 6 (March 1923): 39.

81. Gibson, *Program for Americanization*, p. 10; California Home Teachers Act of 1915, reprinted in Gibson, "Schools," p. 301. Not wishing to alienate the club members, Gibson urged that they make use of their considerable talents by endorsing "proper social and industrial conditions"—but leave teaching to professionals.

82. Tyack, *One Best System*, pp. 59–64. Nationally, 86 percent of the teachers were women in 1920, and the percentage was still higher in urban areas, and certainly higher in elementary schools. In 1905 only 2 percent of the elementary teachers were men, but men accounted for 38 percent of the elementary principals. For a complete breakdown, see NEA, *Report, 1905*. Two of Los Angeles's eight intermediate schools in 1915 had female principals, compared with 11 of 18 in 1939; all but one of the high school principals at the time were men (and the exception was probationary); as late as 1939 32 of the 35 high schools were still administered by men. (Board, *Directory of Personnel, 1915–16, 1939–40*.) Edson's study *Pushing the Limits* shows that nationwide men continued to hold most high school principalships in the late 1980's. Ella Flagg Young of Chicago was the only woman in the early 20th century to hold a large city superintendentship until Susan Dorsey's appointment in Los Angeles in 1919.

83. For a discussion of teacher organization in Chicago, see Wrigley, *Class Politics*, particularly chap. 4; and W. Urban, *Why Teachers Organize*, pp. 113–14.

84. Gibson, "Schools"; Gibson, *Record of Twenty-Five Years*, pp. 204–6. Gibson spent six weeks lobbying the California Legislature for the passage of the act.

85. The DAR established a Patriotic Education Committee in 1915,

and Chase's salary was paid out of this fund for a year and a half (Herman, "Neighbors," 2: 381, 383).

86. Gibson, "Schools," p. 302.

87. Ibid.; Mary Cunliffe Trautwein, "A History of the Development of Schools for Foreign-born Adults in Los Angeles," M.A. thesis (University of Southern California, 1928), p. 64; Board, *Annual Report, 1886–87*, p. 74. *Los Angeles Settlement Association* lists Amanda Mathews as resident in 1904–5. See Chase, "Explosions of Tommaso," *OutWest Magazine*, for an example of her short stories. Herman, "Neighbors," p. 383, reports that Chase taught for 12 years in a private girls school in Mexico City. Chase had lobbied the legislature, along with Gibson, for the passage of the Home Teacher Act.

88. University of Minnesota, "Faculty Record," 1921; Montana State Board of Education, "Annual Report of Helena High School," 1906–7; *City Directory*, Helena, Mont., 1907, p. 94; personal communication from Peter L. Carparelli, Superintendent of Schools, Butte, Mont., Jan. 29, 1988. Baughman published several short stories and poems in *OutWest* and *Sunset* magazines between 1907 and 1912.

89. Board, *Annual Report, 1914*, p. 126; CCIH, *Report*, p. 100; G. Jackson, "History of Adult Education," p. 92.

90. Herman, "Neighbors," p. 380. In 1921 the Los Angeles District of the California Federation of Women's Clubs had another map made. It can be found in the Huntington Library.

91. *Minutes*, 18: 399.

92. University of Minnesota, "Faculty Record," May 1922.

93. Baughman, *Elementary Adult Education*, p. 47; Baughman, "Elementary Education."

94. *Fourteenth Census* (1920), 3: 110, 123–25; Gibson, "Schools," p. 302. The historian George J. Sánchez observes that because many immigrants must make frequent family moves for job purposes, wives necessarily have difficulty finishing a course ("Historic Roots of 'English Only' ").

95. CCIH, *Home Teacher*, pp. 49–50.

96. *The Woman Citizen*, Oct. 20, 1917, p. 396.

97. Friday Morning Club, "Gibson, Pioneer," p. 10.

98. G. Jackson, "History of Adult Education," p. 92.

99. Baughman, *Elementary Adult Education*, p. 81 (for photo showing a Chinese-American teacher conducting a class); L. A. City Teachers *Directory, 1922, 1945*; L.A. City *Directory, 1922, 1929, 1945*.

100. D. Moore, *At Home*, p. 95.

101. *Minutes*, 25: 327.

102. G. Jackson, "History of Adult Education," pp. 81–82.

103. Baughman, *Elementary Adult Education*, pp. 85–86.

104. Baughman, "Elementary Education."

105. Ibid. The 1930 census's estimate of 53,648 Mexicans was probably much too low (*Fifteenth Census*, 2 [Population]: 248–50).

106. Baughman, *Elementary Adult Education*, pp. 47–48, 72, 84.

107. *San Francisco Chronicle*, Aug. 17, 1918, p. 9; *The Minnesotan* (Univ. of Minnesota Alumni Weekly), 28 (Jan. 27, 1919): 6–7; "The Americanization Training Course of the University of Minnesota," 24 (Oct. 24, 1921): 4–13.

108. Baughman, *Elementary Adult Education*, p. 84.

109. P. Young, *Pilgrims*, p. 129; Baughman, *Elementary Education*, p. 84. Recent studies like Acuña, *Occupied America*, and Camarillo, *Chicanos*, have shown that for a variety of reasons, few Mexicans became naturalized. According to Camarillo, only 77 Mexicans filed for naturalization in Santa Barbara from 1910 to 1927, out of a total of 849 petitions for citizenship. That trend continued through the end of his study, 1930.

110. Gibson, *Program for Americanization*, p. 10.

111. Ibid., pp. 2–13, 20–22.

112. Ibid., p. 10. The NEA supported her. See Tyack, *One Best System*, pp. 126–216, for a discussion of the professionalization of education and the growing importance of university schools of education.

113. Dumenil, "Antistatism and Education Reform," *Journal of American History*, 77 (Sept. 1990): 499–524.

114. Gibson, "Schools," p. 303.

115. G. Jackson, "History of Adult Education," p. 92.

116. Cott, *Modern Feminism*, pp. 215–39.

117. *Los Angeles Express*, June 26, 1916, Cole Collection 217, box 18.

118. *LAT*, Sept. 10, 1916, sec. 2, p. 2.

Chapter Four

EPIGRAPH: Gibson, *Program for Americanization*, p. 11.

1. McGregor, "Dorsey," pp. 15–35; Board, *Annual Report, 1904*, p. 175.

2. Freeman, "Board-Superintendent Relationships," 2: 661; Cloud, *Education*, p. 129. Dorsey is still one of the few women to become school superintendent in a large city. Ella Flagg Young held the position in Chicago from 1909 to 1915, and Helen Ira Jarrell was superintendent in Atlanta from 1944 to 1960 (Hundley, "Dorsey"; Tyack and Hansot, *Managers of Virtue*, pp. 180–201).

3. Sinclair, *Goslings*, pp. 23–59. Sinclair wrote a scathing indictment of the school board and the *Los Angeles Times*, and their supporters, referring to them as "the Black Hand." The best he could say about Dorsey was "this elderly lady superintendent . . . has a formula of subservience which she is accustomed to repeat to her teachers and subordinates: 'We must please the businessmen, otherwise they will not vote the bonds to keep our schools going'" (pp. 45–46). One has

to be careful when reading Sinclair, but from Dorsey's unusual rise to the position of superintendent, one has to think she did indeed make concessions to the business community in her own interest.

4. Smith, *Ella Flagg Young*; Reid, *Battleground* (which has important passages on Young throughout); Wrigley, *Class Politics*, pp. 120–37; Hogan, *Class and Reform*, pp. 207–14. Margaret Haley, the most renowned teacher-advocate of the Progressive Era, led the Chicago Teachers' Federation in a demand for teacher security, higher wages, and decentralization. Peterson, *School Reform*, pp. 155–72, and Katznelson and Weir, *Schooling for All*, pp. 108–17, discuss the complexities of reform and politics. See also Urban, *Why Teachers Organize*, especially pp. 66–88.

5. Friday Morning Club, "Gibson, Pioneer," p. 9. Dorsey became an honorary member of the Friday Morning Club in 1928 (Friday Morning Club, *Directory*).

6. Friday Morning Club, "Severance, Pioneer"; Kennedy, *California Congress of Mothers*, p. 31.

7. Gibson, *Program for Americanization*, pp. 1–4.

8. *Los Angeles Herald*, May 1, 1902; J. Jensen, "After Slavery," p. 182; Blair, *Clubwoman as Feminist*, pp. 108–11; Davis, *Black Woman*, p. 112.

9. Gibson, *Program for Americanization*, pp. 20–21. In its hodgepodge of suggestions, references, and anecdotes, this pamphlet provides some considerable insight into the complexities of the Americanization program.

10. Kelley, *Assault on Assimilation*, pp. 104–7. Frank Gibson had taken an early interest in the treatment of Indians when he worked as a clerk on a reservation in Mendocino County, where his father, a Methodist minister, served as the Indian agent in the early 1870's. Mary herself became active in Indian reform in the 1920's, working with John R. Haynes. (Miscellaneous California Dictations, box 2, Bancroft Library, University of California, Berkeley.)

11. *LAT*, May 1, 1921, sec. 2, p. 7. The *Times* printed the General Federation's survey of immigrant population in the city.

12. *Minutes*, 26: 453, 34: 256.

13. *Educational Journal*, 1917–18, n.p.

14. Daniels, *Politics of Prejudice*, pp. 84–86.

15. *SJ*, Dec. 1921: 3–5.

16. Ibid., p. 4.

17. Kingston, *Woman Warrior*, pp. 163–209. Galarza, *Barrio Boy*, pp. 208–14, paints a very human picture of an immigrant's first encounter with Americanization in the Sacramento public schools. Rolvaag, *Giants in the Earth*, describes how Norwegian immigrants renamed themselves to accommodate Americans as well as to accommodate other European immigrants. Eric Monkkonen, in a conversation he

had in 1982, recalls stories of Finnish camps in Minnesota where children were all given new names.

18. Clymer, "Federal Government."

19. *SJ*, Oct. 1921: 3–6.

20. *SJ*, Nov. 1921: 9–10. The *Los Angeles Daily News*, Jan. 1, 1920, p. 8, reported that seven Los Angeles chapters of the DAR had joined forces to pay the salary of a teacher to teach foreign mothers "American ways." The Board of Education finally cooperated, using Albion School as a model.

21. For similar views, see Byington, *Homestead*; Monkkonen, *Dangerous Class*; and Schlossman, *Love and the American Delinquent*.

22. *SJ*, Nov. 1921: 23.

23. Sterry was a member of the General Federation of Women's Clubs ("Speakers List," Clara Bradley Burdette Collection, box 29, HL).

24. Sterry, "Neighborhood School"; *Minutes*, 4: 7.

25. *SJ*, Oct. 1921: 9–11.

26. The total Chinese population was still not all that large—2,062 in 1920 and 3,009 in 1930 (*Fourteenth Census*, 3: 110; *Fifteenth Census*, 8: 266). Between 1900 and 1910 the population in fact declined, from 2,111 to 1,954.

27. Sterry, "Social Attitudes," p. 331. See also Tom, pp. 107–8. Tom wrote that the second-generation Chinese might want to return to China and therefore needed to study Chinese language and customs.

28. Sterry, "Housing Conditions."

29. *Minutes*, 31: 461.

30. Yee and Yee, "Chinese Baseball Team." An interesting footnote to the 1927 baseball team is that one of the members, George Tong, designed the Los Angeles Sports Arena, a fact that pleased the Yees. The Japanese were avid baseball players even at this early date. The appendix in Ryoichi Shibazaki, "Seattle and the Japanese–United States Baseball Connection, 1905–1926," M.S. thesis (Univ. of Washington, 1981), shows the itinerary of a Japanese university team's visit to the West Coast in 1905. The team started at Stanford, and after several games in the Bay Area, went to Southern California, where it played Occidental College, Sherman Indian Institute in Riverside, a Santa Monica club, St. Vincent College, Pomona College, USC, and a high school, all in one week between April 17 and April 24. The team then went north to the Seattle area.

31. Sterry, "Social Attitudes," p. 333.

32. *SJ*, March 1923: 7–9, 58–61.

33. "Mrs. Pierce and Mrs. Dorsey Discuss Matters Before the Principals' Club, February 12, 1923," *SJ*, March 1923: 59, 61; Los Angeles *City Directory, 1923*, p. 940.

34. *SJ*, March 1923: 61.

35. *Fourteenth Census* (1920), 3: 110, 123–25.

36. Tyack, *One Best System*, pp. 104–5.
37. Peterson, *Politics of School Reform*, pp. 166–67.
38. McCoy and Tanner, *Report*, p. 20, and tabulation table 1; Sinclair, *Goslings*, pp. 25–59. Sinclair did not mince words retelling the incidents involved in the 1923 election, and he found great fault with Dorsey. He felt she went along with the *Times* in order to increase her own salary. He charged that while the actual salaries of teachers went down between 1916 and 1923, Dorsey's salary rose, and after her support for the paper's candidates, she was given a raise of $2,000 (pp. 26–27). Norman Hapgood calls Dorsey courageous for thwarting the deep-dyed conservatives' attempts to silence all avenues of discussion (*Professional Patriots*, p. 146). For Dorsey to keep her job, she clearly had to walk a fine line between them and the teachers.
39. *LAT* (all 1923), May 29, sec. 1, pp. 5, 13, June 1, sec. 2, pp. 1, 12, June 2, sec. 2, pp. 1, 18, June 3, sec. 2, pp. 1, 2; Ostrom, "School Board Politics," pp. 23–24. For accounts of the Klan in Los Angeles, see K. Jackson, *Ku Klux Klan*; and Von Brauchitsch, "Ku Klux Klan," pp. 9–66.
40. Reller, *Development of City Superintendency*, pp. 48, 291. Reller points out that politics and education are tightly tied together, and that no amount of crying for nonpartisan school boards will break that bond. He also notes that pressure groups are ruthless in their attempts to influence school board politics.
41. Louise Ward Watkins agreed to become president of the Friday Morning Club in 1931 because of her fear of communism. As president of the prestigious organization, she felt, she could raise a more effective voice against the Communists (Louise Ward Watkins Collection, "Autobiography," box 13, HL).
42. *SJ*, May 28, 1923: 18. See also p. 21, where the Executive Committee of the Better Schools Committee of Citizens and Teachers (the official name of the Teachers' Ticket) expressed its fear that the PTA was under the influence of the Better America Federation. It believed the Los Angeles group was the only large-city PTA so affected.
43. School District, *Auditor's Annual Financial Report, 1929*, pp. 34–37. The base pay of high school teachers increased from $1,200 in 1916 to $1,800 in 1919 and stayed there until 1930. Elementary teachers had a base salary of $768 in 1916; their pay rose to $1,400 in the years 1917–29.
44. *Minutes*, 36: 504. In the next several months teachers and librarians petitioned the board at least 10 times to reinstate the two magazines, but to no avail. The *Times* accused Bettinger of leading the campaign to reinstate the "radical publications" (June 3, 1923, sec. 2, pp. 1–2).
45. Hapgood, *Professional Patriots*, pp. 147–48. The contest proved so successful that other "professional" patriotic groups introduced it

nationally. But it is doubtful that these contests had much effect, since they tended to draw relatively few participants.

46. *Fifteenth Census* (1930), 18: 266, 267, 270. This census for the first time designated Mexicans as nonwhite. According to p. 110, 97,116 Mexicans lived in Los Angeles, but in the list of nativity on p. 269, 2,803 Mexicans are categorized as white foreign-born. In the third volume of *Population* (part 1, p. 266), Japanese (21,081), Chinese (3,009), and Indian (616) are given separate designations. In the second *Population* volume (p. 80), Filipino (3,245), Hindu (77), Korean (345), Hawaiian (78), and Malay (3) are listed in separate categories.

47. G. Jackson, "History of Adult Education," p. 92.

48. Yee and Yee, "Chinese Baseball Team." A few years earlier the Molokans had petitioned the city for a playground for their children because they believed a suitable play area would keep their children out of mischief (P. Young, *Pilgrims*, p. 230).

49. *SJ*, March 21, 1927: 12–16. See also Sterry, "Neighborhood School."

50. *SJ*, March 21, 1927: 17, 18, 62. Schools had been involved in teaching the relationship between body cleanliness and good health for many years. For specific instances of some of the school's concerns, see *Minutes*, 21: 339, 363, 24: 4, 5, 23, 197, and 26: 201, 438.

51. *SJ*, March 21, 1927: 22–23, 64.

52. Ibid., pp. 24–25, 66. The first model cottage was established in 1913 at Utah Street School to train immigrant girls in American housekeeping techniques; see the Board, *Report, 1914*, p. 73.

53. *SJ*, March 21, 1927: 68.

54. Putnam, *California Politics*, pp. 7–8.

55. *SJ*, March 1923: 58–61.

56. Beck, "Other Children," pp. 79–81; California Dept. of Public Instruction, State Superintendent of Public Instruction, *Biennial Reports, 1866–90*; Board, *Annual Report, 1900–1901*, p. 25. Most Americans lumped all Asians together and referred to them as Mongolians.

57. Board, "Report of the Nativity of the School Children of Los Angeles City," 1904–5, pp. 24–25. The Chinese school population was seven that year.

58. Hendricks, "Public Policy," p. 85.

59. Kawasaki, "Japanese Community," p. 27; Board, *Educational Research Bulletin*, 6 (3): 10–15; Romo, *East Los Angeles*, p. 139. Romo quotes a 1920's study of Joseph Santos suggesting that school districts built schools within a Mexican colony to achieve segregation. That is one explanation. Another may be that Mexican children, like other children, needed schools near their homes.

60. These numbers are not as precise as one would wish because people were often counted as Mexican-born when they and their parents and grandparents were in fact native-born. At times the school

tally contradicts the city census figures because the city schools included districts outside the city, such as Gardena. (*Fourteenth Census, 1920*, 3 [*Population*]: 125, 128).

61. *Minutes*, 19: 395–97. Adamic, *Laughing*, pp. 205–20, provides a good description of a workers' "camp," though his was a construction camp, not a camp exclusively for interurban railroad workers.

62. Board, "Sherman School Register," 1911–27, Microfilm Department.

63. *Minutes*, 24: 432; Los Angeles City Schools, *Nationality or Racial Background Survey*.

64. *Minutes*, 23: 255, 263.

65. Ibid., 32: 158–59.

66. In 1931 Assemblyman George Bliss of Carpenteria introduced legislation that would have allowed the segregation of nonwhite children. The bill failed. (Balderrama, *In Defense of La Raza*, pp. 61–64.)

67. *Minutes*, 33: 292; G. Jackson, "History of Adult Education," p. 87.

68. Whites in Chicago used portable buildings to move unwanted black students out of elementary schools in the early 1930's (Homel, *Down from Equality*, pp. 48–49).

69. Acuña, *Occupied America*, pp. 191–92, 212, 303; Taylor, *American-Mexican Frontier*, p. 173. According to Taylor, mutualistas could be found wherever Mexicans settled. The Sociedad Mutualista Benito Juárez was founded in Corpus Christi, Texas, as early as 1879 for skilled workmen and mechanics. Some mutualistas took up collections for the sick, prepaid funerals, paid doctor bills, and owned property. Many of them were sponsored from Mexico, and these would have had a different attitude toward assimilation than the organizations sponsored by Mexicans living in the United States. For a view of Mexican Americans in Texas, see San Miguel, *Let Them Take Heed*.

70. García, *Mexican Americans*, pp. 12, 264. Ridge, "Bilingualism," raises interesting questions about Los Angeles's Mexican community and its attitudes toward assimilation. Ridge notes the ambiguous position of the community's Spanish-language press, particularly *La Opinion*, its most influential newspaper. During the 1920's, *La Opinion* viewed its readers as potential repatriates and welcomed its self-imposed task of preserving their Mexican culture until their return. It steadfastly opposed Americanization, especially in the schools, and emphasized the necessity of rearing children of Mexican extraction to be Mexican patriots. *La Opinion* sponsored Cinco de Mayo celebrations, encouraged Mexican-American athletic leagues, and donated Spanish-language books to the Los Angeles County Library. The editors, however, faced a stern reality: the United States, not Mexico, would be the native land of their constituency. The economics and politics of both countries dictated that decision.

71. Cremin, *American Education*, p. 533.
72. *Minutes*, 30: 43.
73. Ibid., 36: 462.
74. *SJ*, Jan. 1923: 23.
75. Balderrama, *In Defense of La Raza*, p. 62.
76. Cremin, *American Education*, p. 592.
77. See Lynd and Lynd, *Middletown*, for discussions of parents' expectations for their children.
78. *SJ*, Feb. 1922: 3–5.
79. *Minutes*, 26: 54, 156.
80. Ibid., 22: 40, 72, 33: 263. Japanese children were also active in the schools; in 1908 16 students formed the Japanese Association at Los Angeles High School (Sargent, "History of Secondary Education"). The East San Pedro Japanese community formed the Fu Kei Kai, the Japanese equivalent of the PTA in 1924, and that year the organization donated playground equipment and built a yard at East San Pedro School (Kawasaki, "Japanese Community"). Opposition to the Japanese had earlier come directly to the City Council; in September 1919 property owners and residents petitioned to stop the building of a Japanese Children's Home at Redcliff Street, in the Silver Lake district, but they were told that "such an ordinance could not be sustained in the courts" (Los Angeles City Council, *Petitions, 1919*, no. 2263). The 1921 nationality survey map of the Los Angeles District of the California Federation of Women's Clubs, part of the group's Americanization program, found approximately 200 Japanese living in Gardena. A special school for so few children would have been a terrible expense for the board.
81. *Minutes*, 31: 433; DeGraaf, "City of Black Angels." Black high school students were deliberately segregated in several northern cities in the 1930's.
82. McClenahan, *Urban Neighborhood*. Not only blacks were moving into the neighborhood; so were the Japanese. Many white residents complained that the first newcomers were middle class, but that now, in the mid-1920's, poorer minorities were moving in. Some claimed that this was due to the fall in house prices as whites fled the area (Lapp, *Afro-Americans*, pp. 32–52).
83. For a discussion of New York City, New Rochelle (N.Y.), and New Haven (Conn.), see Ment, "School Segregation." For other studies on segregation during this period, see Homel, *Down from Equality*; and Mohraz, *Separate Problem*.
84. Caughey and Caughey, *Segregation*, details the events leading to the segregation order.
85. Miller, "Restrictive Covenants," pp. 388–91.
86. *California Eagle*, Oct. 1, 1926, p. 1.
87. Ibid., March 18, 1927, p. 6.

88. Ibid., March 21, 1924, p. 10, March 28, 1924, pp. 10–11, Feb. 10, 1928, p. 6.

89. I have borrowed the term "significance of race" from chap. 7 of Katznelson and Weir, *Schooling for All.*

90. These themes are developed in the following works: Higham, *Strangers*; Kolko, *Triumph of Conservatism*; and Wiebe, *Search for Order.*

91. For another point of view, see McDonald, *Urban Fiscal Policy,* especially pp. 262–82; and Peterson, *Politics of School Reform.* See also Rogers, "In Search of Progressivism."

Chapter Five

EPIGRAPH: Snapp, "Our Public Schools," *Los Angeles Times,* May 17, 1923, sec. 2, p. 4.

1. Tyack, *One Best System,* pp. 128, 196–97. Tyack distinguishes between political-educational "administrative progressives" and "pedagogical progressives," his term for the philosophers and psychologists who translated Dewey's ideas into practical classroom methods.

2. *Minutes,* 39: 200, 41: 236. Briggs believed in making school facilities available to immigrants. In July 1924 she told the board that this kept Mexicans in touch with the school, something that was especially important since there was so "much unemployment among Mexicans in San Pedro" (*Minutes,* 43: 422).

3. *Minutes,* 41 (Feb. 4, 1924). When the board turned down the petitions, its justification was that neither group had affiliations with the evening school. But neither did the Benefica Recreativa Sociedad or the Mexican Blue Cross, another group that successfully worked through the principal's office (*Minutes,* 37: 346, for the Mexican Blue Cross).

4. Ibid., 39: 200.

5. Ibid., 38: 276, 41: 7, 42: 374, 43: 97.

6. Ibid., 38: 198.

7. Ibid., 39: 200. Robinson, "Special Correspondence," is the one who made the Polytechnic claim, but his figure of 5,000 is much too high. According to the 1924–25 *Auditor's Annual Financial Report,* Polytechnic's evening school enrollment, including special day classes, was 2,530. If this was not the largest enrollment in the nation, it was certainly the largest in the city.

8. *Minutes,* 43: 162.

9. K. Jackson, *Ku Klux Klan,* especially chap. 13; *LAT,* April 25, 1922.

10. *Minutes,* 40: 389, 424.

11. Vorspan and Gartner, *Jews in Los Angeles,* pp. 166–70.

12. *LAT,* June 1, 1923, sec. 2, p. 21, June 5, 1923, sec. 2, p. 1. The largest Orthodox institution on the West Coast, located in Boyle Heights, had four downtown classrooms for instruction in history

and Hebrew. According to the *Los Angeles Times*, this instruction would not interfere with public school attendance. Another congregation built a synagogue and a community center with a dining hall large enough to feed 200 children free lunches; it also had a dance hall.

13. Board, *Auditor's Annual Financial Report*, 1925, pp. 9, 21, 30. In 1925 the department spent $12,714.69, less than it spent in 1924. The department's share of the district's total operating budget also declined, from 8 percent in 1923–24 to 5 percent in 1924–25. Greater fiscal conservatism as the 1920's wore on may explain the drop in spending, but more likely, the system simply ran more economically after the initial expenditures.

14. Cremin, *Transformation*, p. 192.

15. Frederick Winslow Taylor, *The Principles of Scientific Management* (1911). Taylorism, or Scientific Management, became the theory behind much of progressive education. See Callahan, *Education*, on the implementation of Taylorism in public schooling.

16. Cremin, *Transformation*; Hines, "What Los Angeles Is Doing." Cremin draws the First World War as the line of demarcation between the earlier reform aspects of progressive education and the later pragmatism he associates with the Progressive Education Association.

17. Rothman, *Conscience*, p. 125.

18. Martin, *Manual*, p. 7.

19. Hendricks, *California Education*, p. 17.

20. Gould, *Mismeasurement of Man*, p. 151. For a discussion of IQ testing by teachers and administrators in England, see Sutherland, "Measuring Intelligence." Mental testing challenged English concepts of class rather than race at a time when England had few nonwhite residents.

21. Kevles, "Testing the Army's Intelligence." Krutch, *More Lives Than One*, pp. 87–92, describes the author's experiences in the U.S. Army Psychological Branch testing recruits.

22. Kevles, "Testing the Army's Intelligence," p. 580; Purcell, *Crisis*, p. 100.

23. Fass, "I.Q.," p. 445.

24. Purcell, *Crisis*, pp. 98, 100.

25. Cremin, *Transformation*, p. 188.

26. Leo Kanner, *A History of the Care and Study of the Mentally Retarded* (Springfield, Ill.: Charles C. Thomas, 1967), pp. 114–15.

27. Board, *Annual Report, 1900–1901*, pp. 103–4.

28. Board, *Auditor's Annual Financial Report, 1929*, pp. 34–37. Teachers' salaries did not decline during this period, but they did not rise either. High school teachers' annual base rate increased 50 percent between 1916 and 1920, rising from $1,200 in 1916–17 to $1,400 in 1918–19 and $1,800 in 1919–20. From 1920 to 1930 the rate remained unchanged. On the other hand, the high school principals' minimum

salary increased 75 percent during this period, and that of elementary teachers and principals even more: 82.29 percent for the teachers and 103.13 percent for the principals. In part the disparity in increases may owe to the elementary teachers' initial low rate of $768 in 1916. Even though their salaries climbed faster than those of the high school teachers over the 14-year period, their minimum at the end, $1,400, was still $400 below what the high school teachers earned. Since the principals' salaries depended on the size of the school, elementary principals often made considerably less than their high school counterparts.

29. Tyack, *One Best System*, pp. 144, 163; Callahan, *Education*, pp. 79–80, 210. Bobbitt was a pioneer in the development and use of the school survey, in particular as it related to curriculum. Before he arrived in Los Angeles, he had directed surveys in several other cities, including Denver. (Longstreet, "Bobbitt").

30. Cremin, *Transformation*, p. 200.

31. J. Franklin Bobbitt, "Curriculum Re-Examination in Los Angeles," *High School Research Bulletin*, 2 (Feb. 5, 1923): 1.

32. See Cott, *Modern Feminism*, pp. 243–67, for a discussion of the 1920's peace initiatives.

33. Board, *Courses of Study, 1928*, pp. 158–271.

34. *Bulletin*, 2 (2): 4.

35. Ibid., p. 2, 2 (4): 4.

36. Hall published his famous work *Adolescence* in 1904.

37. On Lewis Terman, see Sears, "Terman," pp. 626–27; Chapman, *Schools as Sorters*; and Minton, *Terman*.

38. Terman et al., *Intelligence Tests*; *Bulletin*, 8 (1): 13. Sutherland had been brought out from Yale University to direct educational research.

39. Terman, *Intelligence of School Children*, p. 73. Terman dedicated his first book, *Measurement of Intelligence* (1916), to the memory of Binet, who had died in 1911. The concept of the intelligence quotient had been used by the German psychologist William Stern, but Terman introduced the term into the language (Kevles, *Eugenics*, p. 79).

40. Dewey, "Mediocrity," p. 36.

41. Lippmann, "Future," p. 10.

42. Terman, "Great Conspiracy," p. 120.

43. Cravens, *Triumph*, pp. 157–59, 253–55 (early critics of the hereditarian theories like the social scientist Franz Boas and the biologist Thomas Hunt Morgan of Columbia University are discussed on pp. 229–51); Purcell, *Crisis*, p. 98; Cloud, *Education*, p. 160; Fass, "I.Q."; Johanningmeier, "Bagley," pp. 39–41. Before joining Columbia, Bagley had taught at the University of Illinois, where he co-founded the *Journal of Educational Psychology* in 1910. In later life, he lost interest in science and decided that teaching was an art, not an applied science. In 1969 Arthur R. Jensen of the University of California, Berkeley, revived

part of the hereditarian argument with his allegations that inherited traits might make for differences in the IQs of whites and blacks in this country ("How Much Can We Boost I.Q.?").

44. Sowell, *American Ethnic Groups*, pp. 207–13.

45. K. Young, *Mental Differences*, pp. 59–60.

46. Sowell, *American Ethnic Groups*, pp. 207–8.

47. *Bulletin*, 10 (4): 6–8. This was the only study published in the *Bulletin* during the 1920's that covered Jewish children as such. It compared the artistic abilities of Jewish, Japanese, Mexican, Molokan, and "mixed" (Chinese, Irish, Italian, Spanish-American, Syrian, and "American") children. The author noted that Jewish children were "chosen" for the survey "inasmuch as they represent a high standard of intelligence, and some relationship between intelligence and art ability is thought to exist" (p. 6). For the study on black children, see *Bulletin*, 3 (2): 2–3.

48. K. Young, *Mental Differences*, p. 60.

49. Ibid., p. 63. Ironically, Young notes that once San Francisco Chinese children learned English, "they forge[d] ahead in their school work."

50. Higham, *Strangers*, p. 314; U.S. Congress, "House Hearings Before the Committee on Immigration and Naturalization." One of the committee's "expert" witnesses was Harry Laughlin, head of the Eugenics Record Office, the arm of the Eugenics Research Association. As Higham notes, Rep. Albert Johnson of Washington, an avowed restrictionist with strong anti-Jewish and anti-Japanese feelings, who steered the immigration legislation through the House, had been elected president of the Eugenics Research Association in 1923.

51. Gonzales, "System of Public Education."

52. *Bulletin* 8 (1): 10–12; Sterry, "Neighborhood School."

53. Cubberley, *Public Education*, pp. 485–86.

54. Tyack, *One Best System*, pp. 208–16, uses examples from a few testing programs but relies on the views of school officials and not those of classroom teachers. See also Clarence Karier, "Testing for Order and Control in the Corporate State," in Karier et al., *Roots of Crisis*, pp. 108–37; Fass, "I.Q."; Gonzales, "System of Public Education"; and Romo, *East Los Angeles*. Karier relies on the work of well-known psychologists like Terman, Edward Thorndike, and Henry Goddard, but does not consider what went on in the classroom. Fass criticizes testing on a broad level but does not investigate any particular program. Gonzales, "System of Public Education," draws different conclusions from a narrow selection of sources in arguing that racism blinded educators so that they never questioned IQ tests. Romo, p. 123, notes that IQ tests were "generally administered in English to Mexican children," simply overlooking the sources showing that testers often administered tests in Spanish.

55. *SJ*, Jan. 23, 1922: 3, 6. Mossman, demonstrating her unending faith in her profession, wrote: "We want each child to build himself an unshakable *foundation* so that he will attack all future problems, confidently, courageously, and joyously."

56. Kilpatrick, *Project Method*, pp. 5, 13.

57. Tyack, *One Best System*, p. 197; Spring, *American School*, pp. 176–77.

58. *Bulletin*, 4 (7): 8. Raybold states the tests were given in the fall of 1925, but that is no doubt a misprint for 1924, since the *Bulletin* is dated June 15, 1925.

59. Ibid. Rudolph Pintner authored several intelligence and performance tests; most likely the one Raybold administered in 1924 was the standard Pintner-Cunningham. Pintner had used his Pintner Non-language Group Test on foreign children and published the results in 1922 (Pintner and Keller, "Intelligence Tests"). In 1930 he published the Non-language Primary Mental Test for use on deaf children in kindergarten through 2d grade, with directions administered in pantomime, and he established the test's validity by correlations with the Stanford-Binet and the Pintner-Cunningham. Cravens notes that Samuel C. Kohs, "at some point in the late 1910s and early 1920s, as he moved away from prospectives of men such as [Henry] Goddard, [G. Stanley] Hall, [Frederick] Kuhlmann, and [Lewis] Terman," had begun to doubt the "hereditarian theory of crime and the whole thrust of early twentieth-century biology and psychology as he learned it in graduate school" (*Triumph*, p. 249).

60. *Bulletin*, 4 (7): 8. I am indebted to Pamela Aschbacher for her knowledge of and insight into IQ testing, and to Francis X. Callahan for his assistance with correlation coefficients and coefficient determination. Raybold's clumsy use of the data was probably due to the lack of sophistication in the discipline.

61. I thank Martin Ridge for sharing his knowledge of the difficulties in determining the criteria of "limited English speakers."

62. *Bulletin*, 5 (2): 2–14; Romo, "Mexican Workers," pp. 95–97.

63. D. Moore, *At Home*, p. 90.

64. *Bulletin*, 5 (2): 13.

65. In 1935 Manuel, a professor of educational psychology, published his findings on the Mexican child's performance on the Spanish and English editions of the Stanford-Binet. Sensitive to some of the difficulties the children of Mexican heritage had in the often hostile environment of public schools, Manuel and his staff, including George I. Sánchez, one of the first Mexican Americans to criticize the conclusions drawn from conventional testing, had rejected the two commonly used Spanish translations of the 1916 Stanford Revision because neither fit the needs of their subjects. They felt that their translation closely followed the English version but made allowances for

the language differences so as to achieve a better fit with the dialect used by Mexicans living in their state.

66. *Bulletin*, 5 (2): 13.

67. Ibid. The schools continued to use translated tests until at least 1930: *Bulletin*, 10 (5): 4.

68. Ibid., 5 (4): 9.

69. Ibid., 6 (3): 10–13, 15.

70. Ibid., p. 13.

71. Ibid.

72. Ibid., p. 15.

73. Carl Wittke, the dean of American Immigration historians, accepted Kallen's theories on pluralism and incorporated them into his best-known work, *We Who Built America* (1939). For later studies, see Mann, *One and Many*; and Powell, "Cultural Pluralism." See also Wish, "Wittke." I am indebted to Steven L. Schlossman, who helped me find several sources on cultural pluralism, and to my father, Rudolph Rosenberg, whose conversations about Horace Kallen and cultural pluralism proved invaluable.

74. *Bulletin*, 7 (6): 13–15.

75. Ibid., 8 (1): 10–12.

76. Ibid., 8 (7): 8.

77. Schmitt, "Binet-Simon Test." Schmitt had worked as a psychologist at the Chicago Juvenile Psychopathic Institute and was familiar with many of the early testing controversies before she came to Los Angeles.

78. *Bulletin*, 11 (3): 40–42.

79. Ibid., 3 (2): 2–3, 11 (1): 65.

80. *Sixteenth Census* (1940), 2 (*Population*): 132. The figures rose from 7,599 in 1910, to 15,579 in 1920, to 38,894 in 1930 (*Thirteenth Census*, 2 [*Population*]: 185; *Fourteenth Census*, 3 [*Population*]: 125; *Fifteenth Census*, 3 [*Population*]: 287).

81. DeGraaf, "Negro Migration"; DeGraaf, "City of Black Angels."

82. *Bulletin*, 3 (2): 2–3.

83. Ibid., 11 (1): 65.

84. Wynn, *Negro Who's Who*, p. 128; Hendricks, "Public Policy."

85. Whitaker, "Gifted Negro Children," p. 82. Whitaker was a talented pianist and performed throughout the Los Angeles area. Her husband, Leon, was a graduate of the University of California's Boalt Hall, where he was on the Law Review. He died shortly after his appointment to the District Attorney's Office, in 1931, at the age of 26. The *California Eagle* ran articles about the talented young couple from 1926 until Leon's death. Hazel continued to appear in the paper because of her innovative teaching at Jefferson High School.

86. For a comprehensive account of black school segregation in California, see Hendricks, "Public Policy." See McClenahan, *Urban*

Neighborhood, p. 92, for a discussion of the area around Jefferson High.

87. Westin, "Implications"; Richardson, "Negro Girl Graduates."

88. Dudden, *Serving Women*, pp. 1, 239. By the beginning of the 19th century more women worked in domestic service than in any other occupation. Social scientists, college-educated home economists, and social reformers such as Lillian Wald and Frances Kellor advocated training schools for servants—at the time typically single women, most often immigrants, who lived in the household. Though the immigration acts of the 1920's cut off the main source of supply, another arose with the movement of blacks into northern cities. But this was a new type of domestic, a live-out servant who often continued to work after marriage and who maintained her own home. Los Angeles schools reflected that change and considered domestic training a realistic course of study for black girls (Cowan, *More Work*, pp. 119–50).

89. *Bulletin*, 11 (5): 65.

90. *Fifteenth Census* (1930), 3 (part 1): 266.

91. K. Jackson, *Ku Klux Klan*, p. 190. Three prominent Angelenos were named as Klan members: U.S. Attorney Joseph Burke, Chief of Police Louis D. Oaks, and Sheriff William Traeger. But none had Johnson's stature.

92. *SJ*, Jan. 17, 1927: 30.

93. Dorn, *Diploma Disease*, pp. 40, 44.

94. Modell, *Racial Accommodation*, p. 127.

95. *Minutes*, 22: 40, 72, 33: 263.

96. Reisler, *Sweat of Their Brow*, pp. 12, 24–31, 203, 265. In 1917 the tax was $8.00; in 1924 a visa fee raised the tax to $10.00 per person. Hoffman, *Unwanted Mexican-Americans*, pp. 28–30. Hoffman notes that the American Federation of Labor called for the restriction of Mexican immigration, but to no avail.

97. Hendricks, "Public Policy," pp. 173–80.

98. Romo, "Mexican Workers," p. 28.

99. *Bulletin*, 10 (4): 6–8. Testers themselves can play a crucial role in the test scores. Studies conducted in England, for example, note that blacks score much higher when tested by black instructors. But the reasons why some ethnic groups are able to perform well under adverse conditions is difficult to assess. In the 1920's many ethnic groups felt the sting of discrimination but perhaps none so strongly as the California Japanese, who tested well. See Watson, "Can Racial Discrimination Affect I.Q.?"

100. Reynolds, "Education of Spanish-Speaking Children," pp. 34–38.

101. Ridge, "Bilingualism."

102. Not all would agree with my assessment. For a different view, see Gonzales, "System of Public Education," pp. 135–81. Gonzales takes the position that Los Angeles educators' racism so blinded them that

they never questioned the validity of standard IQ tests for Spanish-speaking children; neither does he mention the use of IQ tests given in Spanish.

103. *SJ*, April 27, 1925: 34–35.

104. *Los Angeles Examiner*, May 27, 1927, sec. 1, p. 3.

105. Reynolds, "Education of Spanish-Speaking Children," pp. 46–47. Reynolds may have been familiar with the work of educators at the University of Texas.

106. Tyack notes that Progressives refused to abandon their notions of scientific education (*One Best System*, pp. 182–92).

Chapter Six

EPIGRAPH: Adamic, *Laughing in the Jungle*, p. 219.

1. P. Young, "Social Settlements," p. 64.

2. Ibid., pp. 65–66.

3. *SJ*, Oct. 13, 1930: 42.

4. *SJ*, Jan. 21, 1935: 12. School savings banks had been introduced as early as 1900. (Board, *Annual Report, 1900–1901*, pp. 60–61). The Depression made bankers like Morehouse feel that they must reinforce the savings concept.

5. Los Angeles City Schools, *Reliable Recipes in Large Quantities*, p. 34. The tested recipes were submitted by members of the Cafeteria Club of the Secondary Schools; four teachers, from Belvedere Junior High, Bancroft Junior High, Eagle Rock High, and the Frank Wiggins Trade School, made up the research team.

6. *SJ*, Oct. 22, 1934: 28.

7. Board, *Annual Report, 1902–1903*, pp. 104–7. The modern Head Start programs are another manifestation of educators' belief that schools can do a better job educating poor children than families, if given the chance at the earliest age.

8. *SJ*, Oct. 15, 1934: 16.

9. *SJ*, Oct. 22, 1933: 14. Between 1927 and 1933 the annual budget for the schools had declined by almost $7.5 million, even though the average daily attendance had risen by 25,000 (*SJ*, Feb. 13, 1933: 8).

10. Bean, *California*, p. 410; *SJ*, Feb. 13, 1933: 19, May 22, 1933: 14–15; AB 356, *Statutes of California and Amendments to the Codes* (Sacramento, 1933), p. 1011.

11. Cloud, *Education*, p. 197.

12. Saloutos, *They Remember America*; Saloutos, "Exodus"; Rolle, *Italian Americans*. Italians appropriated the word "Golondrinas" from Spanish.

13. Rolle, *Italian Americans*, p. 47.

14. *LAT*, May 10, 1923, sec. 2, p. 11. According to Juan Gómez-Quiñones, Villareal had a long history as an activist and had ties to the Mexican consulate in Los Angeles. He had established the Union

Constitucionalista de Obreros Mexicanos in Los Angeles during the early 1920's. ("First Steps.")

15. R. Allen, "One of Hoover's Friends." The term "alien baiting" is from Louis Adamic, who wrote extensively about the immigrant experience ("Aliens and Alien Baiters," *Harper's Magazine,* Nov. 1936: 567–85).

16. *Report of Governor C. C. Young's Fact Finding Committee* (San Francisco, 1930), pp. 190–91.

17. Bogardus, *Mexican-Americans,* p. 90.

18. Hoffman, *Unwanted Mexican-Americans,* p. 172. Hoffman's title implies that U.S. officials directed their repatriation efforts at Mexican Americans and not Mexican nationals.

19. U.S. Dept. of Labor, *Annual Report of the Commissioner General of Immigration* (Washington, D.C., 1932), p. 2.

20. Miguel E. Bracho, "Data," 1934, tr. J. Vargas, pp. 1–14, John Anson Ford Collection, box 65, HL.

21. Gamio, *Mexican Immigration,* pp. x, 242.

22. Bracho, "Data," as cited in n. 20 above, p. 10.

23. Ibid., p. 14.

24. Ibid., p. 11.

25. Hoffman, *Unwanted Mexican-Americans,* pp. 152–64; Townsend, Lázaro Cárdenas, pp. 307–8.

26. John Anson Ford to Staff, Dec. 24, 1941, Ford Collection, box 65, HL.

27. William Burk to Herman Stark, Dec. 1, 1941, John Anson Ford Collection, box 65, HL.

28. Ibid.; Burk, "Notes on the Mexican Population." The council's population estimates are low: 36,000 Mexicans in a total county population of 230,000. The city schools had 48,748 Mexican students in 1938, according to the *Nationality or Racial Background Survey.*

29. John Anson Ford to Vierling Kersey, Nov. 21, 1941, Ford Collection, box 65, HL.

30. Vierling Kersey to John Anson Ford, Dec. 1, 1941, ibid. For a discussion of Mexicans and manual labor, see Monroy, "Like Swallows at the Old Mission."

31. Shuji Fujii to John Anson Ford, Aug. 10, 1938, Ford Collection, box 65, HL. Examples of ethnic groups expressing their desires to elected officials abound in this collection.

32. Svensrud, "Attitudes," p. 25. Svensrud was a graduate student of Emory Bogardus at the University of Southern California. See also Fukuoka, "Mutual Life and Aid."

33. Svensrud, "Attitudes," p. 264.

34. John Anson Ford to Shuji Fujii, Aug. 19, 1938, Ford Collection, box 65, HL.

35. Board, *Nationality or Racial Background Survey*, 1938.

36. *SJ*, Jan. 21, 1935: 31.

37. Board, "Statement Regarding Use of School Buildings for Civic Centers." All Japanese-language schools were closed in December 1941. Kersey reported on December 10, 1941, that he was monitoring "any maladjustment throughout the city and that he was checking for any abnormal attendance." Assemblies had been held in all schools in order to "properly" inform students of the emergency. He urged that normal relations continue and declared that "good conduct of the young Japanese [would] be sufficient evidence of good citizenship." During this crisis Kersey attended a Public Relations Committee meeting with various other heads of agencies, including Robert Sproul, chancellor of the University of California, and Norman Chandler, editor and publisher of the *Los Angeles Times*. (See "Report from the Minutes of the Anti-Axis Committee Meetings Held During the Week of December 22, 1941," and other materials in John Anson Ford Collection, box 65, HL.)

38. Tom, "Chinese in Community Life," pp. 108–9.

39. Board, "Statement Regarding Use of School Buildings for Civic Centers."

40. Lothrop, "Squardo al Passato." It seems unlikely that all Italian schools fostered Fascism, although some did. The Italian government sponsored the Dante Alighieri societies, which ran many of the earlier Italian-language classes; the government certainly mixed politics in with language some of the time.

41. George M. Crawford, secretary and business manager, San Diego City Schools, to Secretary of the Los Angeles Board of Education, n.d., Use of Schools, Letters, and Rules folder, Board, Office of the Secretariat.

42. Frank A. Bouelle to Superintendent Worth McClure, Seattle Public Schools, Oct. 29, 1934, in ibid.

43. Beach Vasey, deputy county counsel, to Assistant Superintendent C. L. Craig, May 29, 1940, County Counsel Opinion folder, Board, Office of the Secretariat.

44. Board, *Nationality or Racial Background Survey*. The board no longer used the designation neighborhood or semineighborhood to identify schools whose student bodies contained a large proportion of first- or second-generation children.

45. See McClenahan, *Urban Neighborhood*. McClenahan wrote a thoughtful study of the Jefferson High School district and community attitudes toward black and Japanese newcomers.

46. For a study of New York City, see Ment, "School Segregation." See also Meier and Rudwick, "Negro Boycotts"; Mohraz, *Separate Problem*; and Homel, *Down from Equality*. None of these studies makes much mention, if any, of African Americans in the West.

47. Board, *Teacher Directory*, 1927–1928, p. 447, 1931–1932, p. 258. In 1927 35 of the 133 custodians employed by the board were black (*California Eagle*, April 29, 1927, p. 7).

48. Wynn, *Negro Who's Who*, p. 37; Board, *Nationality or Racial Background Survey*, 1938.

49. The reform of city government in 1903 had eliminated the ward system in Los Angeles, and with it the likelihood that a black would be elected to the City Council. Chicago, by contrast, had elected two black aldermen by 1918 (Mohraz, *Separate Problem*, p. 21).

50. In 1934 Augustus F. Hawkins, a Democrat, replaced Roberts (*California Eagle*, Nov. 10, 1938, p. 1). Roberts's defeat represented the movement of African Americans away from the party of Lincoln and to the party of Franklin D. Roosevelt. Five of the nine black newspapers in California in 1916–17 were in Los Angeles (Lapp, *Afro-Americans*, p. 40).

51. Covington, "Color Line," p. 236; V. E. Thurman, ed., *Who's Who in the New Deal* (Los Angeles: New Deal Historical Society, 1938); *California Blue Book and State Roster* (Sacramento, 1938), p. 277.

52. Covington, "Color Line," p. 238. The *California Eagle* announced that Covington was the first "Negro" submitted as a grand juror (Dec. 8, 1938, p. 1).

53. Wynn, *Negro Who's Who*, p. 46; Miller, "Restrictive Covenants," pp. 388–91. Miller also wrote for the *California News* and the *Los Angeles Sentinel*.

54. Loren Miller to Board of Education, 1934, Board, Racial File.

55. Board, Superintendent's Conference Folder, May 29, 1924.

56. Cremin, *American Education*, pp. 119–21. Cremin reminds us that by 1900 black leaders, excluded from the voting polls and public office, demanded power in black institutions, namely colleges, churches, and schools.

57. Board, *Nationality or Racial Background Survey*, 1938; Tom, "Chinese in Community Life," pp. 106–7. Tom, writing in 1944, noted that Chinese students preferred Polytechnic High because "many American-born Chinese boys of today realize that it is better for them to have some technical knowledge than that of liberal arts, for a Chinese with technical ability can find a job more easily. They also realize that if they cannot secure employment here, they can go back to China because technical men are badly needed there."

58. Board, *Nationality or Racial Background Survey*, 1938. On Tom Bradley, see *San Francisco Chronicle*, Oct. 6, 1986, sec. 1, pp. 1, 8. A few African Americans flexed their muscles in areas where they had no majority. In the spring of 1939 the executive secretary of the Women's Political Study Council, Becky Hill, had been able to block an attempt by the girls' vice-principal at Manual Arts High to segregate black graduates during commencement. As we have seen, Manual did not

have that many black students: 128 in a student body of 3,390. Thanks to Hill's efforts, black and white graduates sat side by side during the activities (*California Eagle*, March 2, 1939, p. 8).

59. See, for example, Graelser, "Study of Attendance"; Westin, "Guidance of High School Pupils"; and Richardson, "Negro Girl Graduates."

60. Board, *Nationality or Racial Background Survey*, 1938. The other minority groups were the Mexicans (417), Japanese (117), and Chinese (39). The rest of the students were classified as English, which meant of English-speaking background (86), Italian (55), Polish (26), Jewish (25), German (19), Armenian (9), French (6), Greek (5), Russian (2), Hungarian (1), Dutch (1), and "other" (4).

61. *California Eagle*, April 13, 1939, p. 1, April 27, 1939, p. 1.

62. Ibid., April 16, 1939, p. 7.

63. The hypothesis that some black elites favored segregation to feather their own nests continues to stir up controversy. Both Homel, *Down From Equality*, and Mohraz, *Separate Problem*, mention the issue but have different opinions about the validity of the charge.

64. Board, *Teachers Directory* for the years 1933–39. The letters and petitions to the Board on the appointment of Senola Reeves are in the Board's Racial File.

65. Archie Hairston was the Jefferson evening school counselor (*California Eagle*, Dec. 22, 1938; Wynn, *Negro Who's Who*, p. 33).

66. *California Eagle*, Feb. 2, 1939, p. 1A; Board, *Teachers Directory*, 1938–39.

67. In 1984 the Smithsonian Institution's Air and Space Museum displayed *Black Wings* in its exhibition on "Black Aviators." At about the same time as Jefferson offered this course, the National Association for the Advancement of Colored People urged that the government include "Negroes [in its] plan to train 20,000 college students as civilian pilots" (*California Eagle*, Jan. 5, 1939, p. 1). Besides Los Angeles and Tuskegee, black aviators trained in Chicago.

68. "Private Survey on Negro Teachers" (conducted by John Anson Ford). A table in Tyack, *One Best System*, p. 226, shows the Negro population in 12 northern cities in 1930 and the number of black teachers employed in each. For Los Angeles, he lists "about 54," which is higher than one might suppose from Ford's private survey. Tyack drew his data from Doxey A. Wilkerson, "The Negro in American Education: A Research Memorandum for the Carnegie-Myrdal Study, 'The Negro in America'" (3 vols., 1940).

Conclusion

EPIGRAPH: "Cultural Future of Los Angeles," radio talk, Oct. 5, 1932, Louise Ward Watkins Collection, box 14, HL.

1. Louise Ward to Charles Thompson, Jan. 5, 1906, ibid., box 1.

2. Wiebe, *Search for Order*.

3. Saum, *Popular Mood*, pp. 145–52.

4. Many scholars trace the theme's origin to Benjamin Franklin's autobiography. For criticism of Franklin on this score, see the comments of Leo LaMay and Paul Zall, editors of the 1986 edition of that work. The theme was elaborated by Ellwood Cubberley, *Public Education*; and Lawrence Cremin's work tends to reinforce it in a more sophisticated way.

5. The revisionist work most often cited is Katz, *Irony of Early School Reform*. For a fuller list of works in this vein, see n. 3 of the Introduction, above.

6. Foremost among these studies is Tyack, *One Best System*. See also Peterson, *Politics of Reform*.

7. Higham, *Strangers*, p. 237.

8. Sterry, "Social Attitudes," p. 331; Yee and Yee, "Chinese Baseball Team."

9. Marcus Foster, superintendent of the Oakland public schools in the 1970's, was assassinated by members of the radical Symbionese Liberation Army. Foster had made a fine reputation for himself in Philadelphia before coming to Oakland. One of his most successful measures as principal of Philadelphia's beleaguered black Gratz High School was to build up the school's vocational education program. Though he also introduced rigorous college preparatory classes, he saw most of his students in need of good vocational training. (Tyack and Hansot, *Managers of Virtue*, p. 236.)

10. Bodnar, "Schooling and the Slavic American Family." Bodnar notes (p. 79): "It was in the home rather than the schoolroom that decisions affecting school attendance were usually made. When confronted with the realities of economic survival in America, immigrant parents and their children made crucial but often different decisions about career goals."

11. *LAT*, June 20, 1986, sec. 2, p. 14. The article was written by Pamela Moreland.

Bibliography

A Note on the Sources

The list of references that follows contains works that I found indispensable for the study. For more detailed information on some sources, the reader will want to consult the Notes.

Three institutions house the majority of the primary material I used: the Los Angeles Board of Education, the Research Library and the Education and Psychology Library at the University of California, Los Angeles, and the Henry E. Huntington Library, San Marino, California. Most Board of Education documents are in manuscript form (e.g., the auditor's annual financial reports and the 1938 Nationality or Racial Background Survey). The minutes of the Board of Education are on microfilm, and some are also available in manuscript. The UCLA libraries house printed Los Angeles School District material, including the *School Journal* from 1917 to 1950 and the Department of Psychology and Education's *Educational Research Bulletin* from 1922 to 1932. At Special Collections I consulted the California Ephemeral, Cornelius Cole, John Randolph and Dora Haynes, and Katherine Philips Edson collections. In the Huntington Library, the collections I found most helpful were the Clara Bradley Burdette, Caroline Severance, and John Anson Ford papers, but the Louise Ward Watkins and Margaret Collier Graham papers and the Ephemeral Collection of Friday Morning Club Scrapbooks were also rich sources of information.

References

Acuña, Rudolfo. *Occupied America*. 2d ed. New York: Harper & Row, 1981.

Adamic, Louis. *Laughing in the Jungle: The Autobiography of an Immigrant in America*. New York: Harper Bros., 1932.

Allen, Ann Taylor. "'Let Us Live with Our Children': Kindergarten Movements in Germany and the United States, 1840–1914," *History of Education Quarterly*, 28 (Spring 1988): 23–48.

Allen, Robert S. "One of Mr. Hoover's Friends," *The American Mercury*, 25 (Jan. 1932): 53–62.

Balderrama, Francisco E. *In Defense of La Raza*. Tuscon: Univ. of Arizona Press, 1982.

Bancroft, Irving R., comp. *Health Supervision in Los Angeles City Schools*. Los Angeles Board of Education pamphlet, June 25, 1917.

Bartlett, Dana. *Better City*. Los Angeles: Nuener Press, 1909.

Bary, Valeska, and Frances Cahn. *Welfare Activities of Federal, State, and Local Governments in California, 1850–1934*. Berkeley: Univ. of California Press, 1936.

Baughman, Ruby. "Elementary Education for Adults," *American Academy of Political and Social Science Annals*, 29 (Jan. 1921): 161–68.

———, comp. *Elementary Adult Education*. Los Angeles Board of Education pamphlet, publication 27, Nov. 1919.

Beale, Howard K. *Are Teachers Free?* New York: Scribner's, 1936.

Bean, Walton. *California: An Interpretive History*. Berkeley: Univ. of California Press, 1973. Originally published in 1968.

Beck, Nicholas Patrick. "The Other Children: Minority Education in California Public Schools from Statehood to 1890." Ph.D. diss., Univ. of California, Los Angeles, 1975.

Bettinger, M. C. "Twenty-Five Years in the Schools of Los Angeles," *Historical Society of Southern California*, 8–9 (1909–10): 67–75.

Blair, Karen. *The Clubwoman as Feminist: True Womanhood Redefined, 1868–1914*. New York: Holmes & Meir, 1980.

Bobbitt, Franklin. *Curriculum-Making in Los Angeles*. Chicago: University of Chicago Press, 1922.

Bodnar, John. "Schooling and the Slavic American Family, 1900–1940," in Bernard J. Weiss, ed., *American Education and the European Immigrant, 1840–1940*, pp. 78–95. Urbana: Univ. of Illinois Press, 1982.

Bogardus, Emory S. *The Mexicans in the United States*. New York: Arno Press and the *New York Times*, 1970. Originally published in 1934 by the University of Southern California Press.

Bottles, Scott L. *Los Angeles and the Automobile: The Making of the Modern City*. Berkeley: Univ. of California Press, 1987.

Bowles, Samuel, and Herbert Gintis. *Schooling in Capitalistic America: Educational Reform and the Contradictions of Economic Life*. New York: Basic Books, 1976.

Braitman, Jacqueline R. "A California Stateswoman: The Public Career of Katherine Philips Edson," *California History*, 65 (June 1986): 82–95.

Briggs, L. B. R. "Some Old-Fashioned Doubts About New-Fashioned Education," *Atlantic Monthly*, Oct. 1900: 463–70.

Bryan, Mary de Garmo. *The School Cafeteria*. New York: Croft, 1946.

Bullert, Gary. *The Politics of John Dewey*. Buffalo, N.Y.: Prometheus Books, 1983.

Bunker, Frank Forest. *The Junior High School Movement—Its Beginning*. Washington, D.C.: Roberts Co., 1935.

Burk, William. "Some Notes on the Mexican Population in Los Angeles County." Dec. 1941. John Anson Ford Collection, box 65, Huntington Library, San Marino, Calif.

Byington, Margret. *Homestead: The Household of a Mill Town.* New York: Sage Foundation, 1910.

California Commission of Immigration and Housing (CCIH). *The Home Teacher.* Sacramento, 1916.

———. *Report.* Sacramento, 1915.

Callahan, Raymond E. *Education and the Cult of Efficiency.* Chicago: Univ. of Chicago Press, 1962.

Camarillo, Albert. *Chicanos in the Changing Society: From Mexican Pueblo to American Barrio in Santa Barbara and Southern California, 1848–1930.* Cambridge, Mass.: Harvard Univ. Press, 1979.

Carstensen, Vernon. "Walter Albert Jessup," in *Dictionary of American Biography,* supplement 3, pp. 386–88.

Caughey, John, and LaRee Caughey. *Segregation on Our Doorstep.* Los Angeles: Quail Books, 1966.

Chan, Sucheng. *This Bittersweet Soil: The Chinese in California Agriculture, 1860–1910.* Berkeley: Univ. of California Press, 1987.

Chapman, Paul D. *Schools as Sorters: Lewis M. Terman, Applied Psychology, and the Intelligence Testing Movement, 1890–1988.* New York: New York Univ. Press, 1988.

Chase, Amanda Mathews. "The Explosions of Tommaso." *OutWest Magazine,* 43 (March 1916): 139–42.

Cleland, Robert Glass, and Frank B. Putnam. *Hellman and the Farmers and Merchant Bank.* San Marino, Calif.: Huntington Library Press, 1965.

Clifford, Geraldine Joncich. " 'Daughters into Teachers,' " in Alice Prentice and Marjorie R. Theobold, eds., *Women Who Taught: Perspectives on the History of Women and Teaching,* pp. 115–35. Toronto: University of Toronto Press, 1991.

Cline, Scott. "Creation of an Ethnic Community: Portland Jewry, 1851–1866," *Pacific Northwest Quarterly,* 76 (April 1985): 52–60.

Cloud, Roy. *Education in California.* Stanford, Calif.: Stanford Univ. Press, 1952.

Cohen, Ronald. *Children of the Mill: Schooling and Society in Gary, Indiana, 1906–1960.* Bloomington: Indiana University Press, 1990.

Cohen, Ronald, and Raymond Mohl. *The Paradox of Progressive Education: The Gary Plan and Urban Schooling.* Port Washington, N.Y.: Kennikat Press, 1979.

Cott, Nancy. *The Grounding of Modern Feminism.* New Haven, Conn.: Yale Univ. Press, 1987.

Covello, Leonard, and G. D'Agostino. *The Heart Is the Teacher.* New York: McGraw Hill, 1958.

Covington, Floyd C. "Where the Color Line Chokes," *Sociology and Social Research,* 20 (Jan.–Feb. 1936): 236–41.

Cowan, Ruth Schwartz. *More Work for Mother: The Ironies of Household Technology from Open Hearth to the Microwave.* New York: Basic Books, 1983.
Cravens, Hamilton. *The Triumph of Evolution: American Scientists and the Heredity-Environment Controversy, 1900–1941.* Philadelphia: Univ. of Pennsylvania Press, 1978.
Cremin, Lawrence. *American Education: The Metropolitan Experience, 1876–1980.* New York: Harper & Row, 1988.
———. *The Transformation of the School: Progressive American Education, 1876–1957.* New York: Random House, 1961.
Cuban, Larry. *How Teachers Taught: Constancy and Change in the American Classroom, 1890–1980.* New York: Longman, 1984.
Cubberley, Ellwood P. *Public Education in the United States.* Boston: Houghton Mifflin, 1934.
Daniels, Roger. *The Politics of Prejudice: The Anti-Japanese Movement in California and the Struggle for Exclusion.* Berkeley: Univ. of California Press, 1962.
Davis, Lenwood G. *The Black Woman in American Society: A Selected Annotated Bibliography.* Boston: Hall & Co., 1975.
Dean, Arthur. *Our Schools in War Time and After.* Boston: Ginn, 1918.
DeGraaf, Lawrence. "The City of Black Angels: Emergence of the Los Angeles Ghetto, 1890–1930," *Pacific Historical Review,* 39 (1970): 323–52.
———. "Negro Migration to Los Angeles, 1930–1950." Ph.D. diss., Univ. of California, Los Angeles, 1962.
D'Emilio, John, and Estelle Freedman. *Intimate Matters: A History of Sexuality in America.* New York: Harper & Row, 1988.
Deverell, William F. "The Los Angeles 'Free Harbor Fight,' " *California History,* 70 (1991): 12–29.
Dewey, John. *Enlistment for the Farm: A Message on How Schoolchildren Can Aid the Nation. Columbia War Papers,* 1 (1917).
———. "Mediocrity Versus Democracy," *The New Republic,* 33 (Dec. 6, 1922): 35–37.
Dorn, Ronald. *The Diploma Disease.* Berkeley: Univ. of California Press, 1976.
Dudden, Faye E. *Serving Women: Household Service in Nineteenth-Century America.* Middletown, Conn.: Wesleyan Univ. Press, 1983.
Dumenil, Lynn. " 'The Insatiable Maw of Bureaucracy': Antistatism and Education Reform in the 1920s," *Journal of American History,* 77 (Sept. 1990): 499–524.
Dumke, Glenn S. *The Boom of the Eighties in Southern California.* San Marino, Calif.: Huntington Library Press, 1944.
Eales, John. "A Brief General History of the Los Angeles School System." Ph.D. diss., Univ. of California, Los Angeles, 1956.
Edson, Saker Kenningson. *Pushing the Limits: The Female Administrative Aspirant.* Albany: State Univ. of New York Press, 1988.

Erickson, David A., and Theodore L. Reller, eds. *The Principal in Metropolitan Schools*. Berkeley: McCutchan Co., 1979.
Ewen, Elizabeth. *Immigrant Women in the Land of Dollars: Life and Culture on the Lower East Side, 1890–1925*. New York: Monthly Review Press, 1985.
Fass, Paula. "The I.Q.: A Cultural and Historical Framework," *American Journal of Education*, 88 (Aug. 1980): 431–58.
———. *Outside In: Minorities and the Transformation of American Education*. New York: Oxford Univ. Press, 1989.
Fogelson, Robert. *The Fragmented Metropolis: Los Angeles, 1850–1930*. Cambridge, Mass.: Harvard Univ. Press, 1967.
Ford, John Anson. *Thirty Explosive Years in Los Angeles County*. San Marino, Calif.: Huntington Library Press, 1961.
Freedman, Estelle. "Separatism as Strategy: Female Institution Building and American Feminism, 1870–1930," *Feminist Studies*, 5 (Fall 1979): 512–29.
Freeman, Sherman. "Board of Education–Superintendent Relationships in the Los Angeles School System, 1853–1920." Ph.D. diss., Univ. of California, Los Angeles, 1951. 2 vols.
Friday Morning Club. *Directory*, 1891–1941. Huntington Library, San Marino, Calif.
———. "Mary S. Gibson, Pioneer," Obituary, 1930. Huntington Library, San Marino, Calif.
———. Scrapbooks. Ephemera Collection, Huntington Library, San Marino, Calif.
———. "Caroline Severance, Pioneer," Obituary, 1925. Huntington Library, San Marino, Calif.
Friedricks, William B. "Capital and Labor in Los Angeles: Henry E. Huntington vs. Organized Labor, 1900–1920," *Pacific Historical Review*, 59 (Aug. 1990): 375–95.
Frost, Richard H. *The Mooney Case*. Stanford, Calif.: Stanford Univ. Press, 1968.
Fukuoka, Fumika. "Mutual Life and Aid Among the Japanese in Southern California with Special Reference to Los Angeles." M.A. thesis, Univ. of Southern California, 1937.
Galarza, Ernesto. *Barrio Boy*. South Bend, Ind.: Univ. of Notre Dame Press, 1971.
Gamio, Manuel. *Mexican Immigration to the United States: A Human Migration and Adjustment*. New York: Dover, 1971.
García, Mario T. *Mexican Americans: Leadership, Ideology, and Identity, 1930–1960*. New Haven, Conn.: Yale Univ. Press, 1989.
Geltner, Sandra O. "Common Schools in Los Angeles, 1850–1900." Ph.D. diss., Univ. of California, Los Angeles, 1974.
Gibson, Mary S. "Schools for the Whole Family," *Survey Graphic*, June 1926: 301–3.

———, comp. *A Record of Twenty-Five Years of the California Federation of Women's Clubs, 1900–1925*. Los Angeles: General Federation of Women's Clubs, 1927.

———. *A Suggested Program for Americanization, 1918–1920*. Clara Bradley Burdette Collection, pamphlet box 43, Huntington Library, San Marino, Calif.

Glassberg, David. "Restoring a 'Forgotten Childhood': American Play and the Progressive Era's Elizabethan Past," *American Quarterly*, 32 (1980): 352–68.

Gómez-Quiñones, Juan. "The First Steps: Chicano Labor Conflict and Organizing, 1900–1920," in Manuel P. Servin, ed., *An Awakened Minority: The Mexican-Americans*, 2d ed., pp. 79–113. Beverly Hills, Calif: Glencoe Press, 1974.

Gonzales, Gilbert. "The System of Public Education and Its Functions Within the Chicano Communities, 1920–1933." Ph.D. diss., Univ. of California, Los Angeles, 1974.

Gordon, Mary M. "Patriots and Christians: A Reassessment of Nineteenth-Century School Reforms," *Journal of Social History*, 11 (Summer 1978): 554–73.

Gould, Stephen J. *The Mismeasurement of Man*. New York: Norton, 1981.

Graelser, Lillian Kernaghan. "A Study of Attendance at Thomas Jefferson High School." M.A. thesis, Univ. of Southern California, Los Angeles, 1938.

Greer, Colin. *The Great School Legend: A Revisionist's Interpretation of American Public Education*. New York: Basic Books, 1972.

Grob, Gerald. *Mental Illness and American Society, 1875–1940*. Princeton, N.J.: Princeton Univ. Press, 1983.

Guinn, James M. "The Beginnings of the School System of Los Angeles," *Historical Society of Southern California*, 8–9 (1911): 195–207.

———. *A History of California and an Extended History of Its Southern Coast Counties. Also Containing Biographies of Well-Known Citizens of the Past and Present*. 3 vols. Los Angeles: Historic Record Co., 1915.

Hanson, Marilyn J. "History of the Kindergarten Movement in California, 1863–1920." Ph.D. diss., Univ. of California, Los Angeles, 1971.

Hapgood, Norman. *Professional Patriots*. New York: Albert & Charles Boni, 1927.

Hays, Samuel. "The Politics of Reform in Municipal Government in the Progressive Era," *Pacific Northwest Quarterly*, 55 (Oct. 1964): 157–69.

Hendricks, Irving. *California Education: A Brief History*. San Francisco: Boyd & Fraser, 1980.

———. "Public Policy Toward the Education of Non-White Minority

Group Children in California, 1849–1940." National Institutes of Education Project NE-G-003-0082, Univ. of California, Riverside, 1975.

Herman, David George. "Neighbors on the Golden Mountain: The Americanization of Immigrants in California." Ph.D. diss., Univ. of California, Berkeley, 1981. 2 vols.

Higham, John. *Strangers in the Land: Patterns of American Nativism, 1860–1925*. New Brunswick, N.J.: Rutgers Univ. Press, 1955.

Hines, Harlen C. "What Los Angeles Is Doing with the Results of Testing," *Journal of Educational Research*, 5 (Jan. 1922): 45–47.

Hoffman, Abraham. *Unwanted Mexican-Americans in the Great Depression: Repatriation Pressure*. Tucson: Univ. of Arizona Press, 1974.

Hogan, David J. *Class and Reform: School and Society in Chicago, 1880–1930*. Philadelphia: Univ. of Philadelphia Press, 1985.

Homel, Michael W. *Down from Equality: Black Chicagoans and the Public Schools, 1920–1941*. Urbana: Univ. of Illinois Press, 1983.

Hundley, Norris, Jr. "Susan Miller Dorsey," in Barbara Sicherman, Carol Hurd Green, et al., eds., *Notable American Women, 1607–1950*, pp. 375–77. Cambridge, Mass.: Harvard Univ. Press, 1980.

Huthmacher, J. Joseph. "Urban Liberalism and the Age of Reform," *Mississippi Valley Historical Review*, 44 (Sept. 1962): 321–44.

Jackson, George. "A History of the Adult Education Program in the Los Angeles Public Schools." Ph.D. diss., Univ. of California, Los Angeles, 1957.

Jackson, Kenneth T. *The Ku Klux Klan in the City, 1915–1930*. New York: Oxford Univ. Press, 1967.

Jensen, Arthur R. "How Much Can We Boost I.Q. and Scholastic Achievement?," *Harvard Educational Review*, 33 (Winter 1969): 1–123.

Jensen, Joan M. "After Slavery: Caroline Severance in Los Angeles," *Southern California Quarterly*, 48 (June 1966): 175–86.

Jessup, Walter, and Albert Shiels. "Report of the Advisory Committee of the Board of Education." Los Angeles, 1916.

Johanningmeier, Edwin V. "Bagley," in *Dictionary of American Biography*, supplement 4.

Kaestle, Carl. *Pillars of the Republic: Common Schools and American Society, 1780–1860*. New York: Hill & Wang, 1983.

Kallen, Horace. *Culture and Democracy in the United States: Studies in Group Psychology of the American Peoples*. New York: Boni & Liveright, 1924.

———. "Democracy vs. the Melting Pot: A Study of American Nationality," *The Nation* (2 parts), 100 (Feb. 18 and 25, 1915): 190–94, 217–20.

Karier, Clarence, Paul C. Violas, and Joel Spring. *Roots of Crisis: Ameri-*

can Education in the Twentieth Century. Chicago: Univ. of Chicago Press, 1973.
Kasson, John F. *Amusing the Millions: Coney Island at the Turn of the Century*. New York: Hill & Wang, 1985.
Katz, Michael. *The Irony of Early School Reform: Educational Innovation in Mid-Nineteenth Century Massachusetts*. Cambridge, Mass.: Harvard Univ. Press, 1968.
Katznelson, Ira, and Margaret Weir. *Schooling for All: Class, Race, and the Decline of the Democratic Ideal*. New York: Basic Books, 1985.
Kawasaki, Kanichi. "The Japanese Community of East San Pedro, Terminal Island, California." M.A. thesis, Univ. of Southern California, 1931.
Kelley, Lawrence C. *The Assault on Assimilation: John Collier and the Origins of Indian Policy Reform*. Albuquerque: Univ. of New Mexico Press, 1983.
Kennedy, Mrs. M. C., ed. *California Congress of Mothers*. Los Angeles: California Congress of Mothers, 1931.
Kenner, Leo. *A History of the Care and a Study of the Mentally Retarded*. Springfield, Ill.: Charles C. Thomas, 1967.
Kerber, Linda. "Separate Spheres, Female Worlds, Woman's Place: The Rhetoric of Women's History," *Journal of American History*, 75 (June 1988): 9–39.
Kevles, Daniel J. *In the Name of Eugenics: Genetics and the Use of Human Heredity*. New York: Knopf, 1985.
———. "Testing the Army's Intelligence: Psychologists and the Military in World War I," *Journal of American History*, 55 (Dec. 1969): 565–81.
Kilpatrick, William Heard. *The Project Method*. New York: Columbia Univ. Press, 1918.
Kingston, Maxine Hong. *China Men*. New York: Knopf, 1980.
———. *The Woman Warrior*. New York: Knopf, 1976.
Kirschner, Don S. *The Paradox of Professionalism: Reform and Public Service in Urban America, 1900–1940*. Westport, Conn.: Greenwood Press, 1986.
Kluger, Richard. *Simple Justice: The History of Brown v. Board of Education and Black America's Struggle for Equality*. New York: Random House, 1975.
Kolko, Gabriel. *Triumph of Conservatism: A Reinterpretation of American History, 1900–1916*. New York: Free Press, 1977.
Krause, Corinne A. *Grandmothers, Mothers, and Daughters: Oral Histories of Three Generations of Ethnic American Women*. Boston: Twayne, 1991.
Krutch, Joseph Wood. *More Lives Than One: An Autobiography*. New York: Sloan Association, 1962.

Lapp, Rudolph M. *Afro-Americans in California*. San Francisco: Boyd & Fraser, 1987.
Lazerson, Marvin. *Origins of the Urban School: Public Education in Massachusetts, 1870–1915*. Cambridge, Mass.: Harvard Univ. Press, 1971.
Lazerson, Marvin, and W. Norton Grubb. *American Education and Vocationalism: A Documentary History, 1870–1970*. New York: Teacher College Press, 1974.
Levenstein, Harvey. "The New England Kitchen and the Origins of Modern Eating Habits," *American Quarterly*, 32 (1980): 369–86.
Lippmann, Walter. "A Future for the Tests," *The New Republic*, 33 (Nov. 29, 1922): 9–11.
Longstreet, Wilma. "John Franklin Bobbitt," in John F. Ohes, ed., *Biographical Dictionary of American Educators*, pp. 443–44. Westport, Conn.: Greenwood Press, 1978.
Los Angeles Settlement Association. Pamphlet, [1905]. University Research Library, Univ. of California, Los Angeles.
Lothrop, Gloria Ricci. "Uno Squardo al Passato: A Backward Look at an Italian Household During Depression Days," *Pacific Historian*, 27 (Winter 1983): 38–47.
Lou, Raymond. "The Chinese American Community of Los Angeles, 1870–1900: A Case of Resistance, Organization, and Participation." Ph.D. diss., Univ. of California, Los Angeles, 1982.
Lynd, Robert, and Helen M. Lynd. *Middletown: A Study in Contemporary American Culture*. New York: Harcourt Brace, 1929.
McClenahan, A. Bessie. *The Changing Urban Neighborhood*. Los Angeles: Univ. of Southern California Press, 1929.
McClymer, John F. "The Federal Government and the Americanization Movement, 1915–1924," *Prologue*, Spring 1978: 24–29.
McCoy, W. T., and G. W. Tanner. *Report of the Better School Service of the National Federation of Teachers*. N.p.: Jan. 1921.
McDonald, Terrence J. *Parameters of Urban Fiscal Policy: Socioeconomic Change and Political Culture in San Francisco, 1860–1906*. Berkeley: Univ. of California Press, 1986.
McGregor, Georgette Foster. "Education Career of Susan Miller Dorsey." Ph.D. diss., Univ. of California, Los Angeles, 1949.
McLean, Kathryn Anderson. *Mama's Bank Account*. New York: Harcourt Brace, 1943.
Maidenberg, Harry F. "Do You Remember? Cafes, Grills, Lunch Wagons, Tamale Wagons" (Los Angeles: Harry Karstens, n.d.). Ephemera Collection, Educational File, Huntington Library, San Marino, Calif.
Mann, Arthur. *The One and the Many: Reflections on the American Identity*. Chicago: Univ. of Chicago Press, 1979.
Martin, M. Francis, comp., *Manual for Development Schools and Rooms*. Los Angeles Board of Education publication. Sept. 1927.

Matthews, Glenna. *Just a Housewife: The Rise and Fall of Domesticity in America*. New York: Oxford Univ. Press, 1987.

Meier, August, and Elliot Rudwick. "Negro Boycotts of Jim Crow Schools in the North, 1897–1925," *Integrated Education*, 5 (Aug.–Sept. 1967): 61–65.

Ment, David. "Patterns of School Segregation, 1900–1940: A Comparative Study of New York City, New Rochelle, and New Haven," in Ronald K. Goodenow and Diane Ravitch, eds., *Schools in Cities: Consensus and Conflict in America Education History*, pp. 67–110. New York: Holmes & Meier, 1983.

Miller, Loren. "Scotching Restrictive Covenants," in John Caughey and LaRee Caughey, eds., *Los Angeles: Biography of a City*, pp. 388–91. Berkeley: Univ. of California Press, 1977.

Minton, Henry. *Lewis M. Terman: Pioneer in Educational Testing*. New York: Univ. of New York Press, 1988.

Modell, John. *The Economics and Politics of Racial Accommodations: The Japanese of Los Angeles, 1900–1942*. Urbana: Univ. of Illinois Press, 1977.

Mohraz, Judy Jolley. *The Separate Problem: Case Studies of Black Education in the North, 1900–1930*. Westport, Conn.: Greenwood Press, 1979.

Monkkonen, Eric. *The Dangerous Class: Crime and Poverty in Columbus, Ohio, 1860–1885*. Cambridge, Mass.: Harvard Univ. Press, 1975.

Monroy, Douglas. "Like Swallows at the Old Mission: Mexicans and the Racial Politics of Growth in Los Angeles in the Interwar Period," *Western Historical Quarterly*, 14 (Oct. 1983): 435–58.

Moore, Debra Dash. *At Home in America: Second Generation New York Jews*. New York: Columbia Univ. Press, 1981.

Moore, Ernest C. "Fundamental Concepts Underlying Junior College Education," *California Quarterly of Secondary Education*, 4 (Oct. 1928): 9–14.

———. "John H. Francis: Inventor and Father of the Junior High School," *California Quarterly of Secondary Education*, 2 (June 1927): 302.

Moore, Willard Burgess. *Molokan Oral Tradition*. Berkeley: Univ. of California Press, 1973.

Morantz-Sanchez, Regina. *Sympathy and Science: Women Physicians in American Medicine*. New York: Oxford Univ. Press, 1985.

Mowry, George. *The California Progressives*. Berkeley: Univ. of California Press, 1951.

National Education Association (NEA). *Report of the Committee on Salaries, Tenure, and Pensions of Public School Teachers in the United States*. N.p.: July 1905.

Newmark, Harris. *Sixty Years in Southern California*. New York: Knickerbocker Press, 1926.

Ostrom, Robert. "Los Angeles School Board Politics: An Analysis of Non-Partisanship in the Los Angeles City Board of Education." M.A. thesis, Univ. of California, Los Angeles, 1945.

Oxnam, Bromley G. "The Mexican in Los Angeles from the Standpoint of the Religious Forces of the City," *Annals of the American Academy of Political and Social Sciences*, 43 (Jan. 1921): 130–33.

Pascoe, Peggy. *Relations and Rescue: The Search for Female Authority in the American West, 1874–1939*. New York: Oxford Univ. Press, 1990.

Peterson, Paul E. *The Politics of School Reform, 1870–1940*. Chicago: Univ. of Chicago Press, 1985.

Pintner, Rudolph, and Ruth Keller. "Intelligence Tests of Foreign Children," *Journal of Education Psychology*, 13 (April 1922): 214–22.

Powell, James Henry. "The Concept of Cultural Pluralism in American Society, 1915–1965." Ph.D. diss., Notre Dame Univ., 1971.

"Private Survey on Negro Teachers in Los Angeles Public Schools," 1945. John Anson Ford Collection, box 65, Huntington Library, San Marino, Calif.

Purcell, Edward A. *The Crisis of Democratic Theory and the Problem of Value*. Lexington: Univ. of Kentucky Press, 1978.

Putnam, Jackson K. *Modern California Politics, 1917–1980*. San Francisco: Boyd & Fraser, 1980.

Reid, Robert L., ed. *Battleground: The Autobiography of Margaret A. Haley*. Urbana: Univ. of Illinois Press, 1982.

Reisler, Mark. *By the Sweat of Their Brow: Mexican Immigrant Laborers in the United States, 1900–1940*. Westport, Conn.: Greenwood Press, 1976.

Reller, Theodore L. *The Development of the City Superintendency of Schools in the United States*. Philadelphia: Self-published, 1935.

"Report from the Minutes of the Anti-Axis Committee Meetings Held During the Week of December 22, 1941." John Anson Ford Collection, box 65, Huntington Library, San Marino, Calif.

Reynolds, Anne. "The Education of Spanish-Speaking Children in Five Southwestern States," U.S. Dept. of the Interior, Office of Education *Bulletin* 7 (1933): 1–60.

Richardson, Adeline C. "A Follow-up Study of Negro Girl Graduates of a Los Angeles High School." M.A. thesis, Univ. of Southern California, 1941.

Ridge, Martin. "Bilingualism—California's New Past," *Southern California Historical Society*, 66 (May 1983): 47–60.

Roberts, Edwards. *With the Invaders: Glimpses of the Southwest*. San Francisco: Carson, 1885.

Robinson, Alcyon. "Special Correspondence: Los Angeles School System," *School and Society*, 58 (June 2, 1923): 609–12.

Robinson, W. W. *Land in California*. Berkeley: Univ. of California Press, 1948.

Rogers, Daniel. "In Search of Progressivism," *Reviews in American History*, 10 (Dec. 1982): 113–32.

Rolle, Andrew. *California: A History*. Arlington Heights, Ill.: AHM Publishing Co., 1978.

———. *The Italian Americans: Troubled Roots*. New York: Free Press, 1980.

Rolvaag, O. E. *Giants in the Earth: A Saga of the Prairie*. New York: Harper Bros., 1927.

Romo, Ricardo. *East Los Angeles: History of a Barrio*. Austin: Univ. of Texas Press, 1983.

———. "Mexican Workers in the City: Los Angeles, 1915–1930." Ph.D. diss., Univ. of California, Los Angeles, 1975.

Rossiter, Margaret. *Women Scientists in America: Struggles and Strategies to 1940*. Baltimore: Johns Hopkins Univ. Press, 1982.

Rothman, David. *Conscience and Convenience: The Asylum and Its Alternatives in Progressive America*. Boston: Little, Brown, 1980.

Ruddy, Ella Giles, ed. *The Mother of Clubs: Caroline M. Seymour Severance*. Los Angeles: Baumgardt Publishing Co., 1906.

Ruiz, Vicki. *Cannery Women, Cannery Lives: Mexican Women, Unionization, and the California Food Processing Industry, 1930–1950*. Albuquerque: Univ. of New Mexico Press, 1987.

Saloutos, Theodore. "Exodus, U.S.A.," in O. Fritiof Ander, ed., *In the Trek of the Immigrants: Essays Presented to Carl Wittke*, pp. 197–215. Rock Island, Ill.: Augustana College Library, 1964.

———. *They Remember America: The Story of the Repatriated Greek Americans*. Berkeley: Univ. of California Press, 1956.

Sánchez, George J. "The Historic Roots of 'English Only': Americanization and the Mexican American, 1915–1930." Paper presented at the annual meeting of the Organization of American Historians, Reno, Nev., 1988.

San Miguel, Guadalupe. *Let All of Them Take Heed: Mexican Americans and the Campaign for Educational Equality in Texas, 1910–1981*. Austin: Univ. of Texas Press, 1987.

Sargent, Harry. "The History of Secondary Education in the City of Los Angeles." Unpublished manuscript, Los Angeles Board of Education, 1955.

Saum, Lewis O. "'Astonishing the Natives': Bringing the Wild Wild West to Los Angeles," *Montana*, 38 (Summer 1988): 2–13.

———. *The Popular Mood of America, 1860–1890*. Lincoln: Univ. of Nebraska Press, 1990.

Schiesl, Martin. "Progressive Reform in Los Angeles Under Mayor Alexander, 1909–1913," *California Historical Quarterly*, 54 (1974): 37–56.

Schlossman, Steven L. *Love and the American Delinquent: The Theory and Practice of Progressive Juvenile Justice, 1825–1920*. Chicago: Univ. of Chicago Press, 1977.

Schmitt, Clara. "The Binet-Simon Test of Mental Ability. Discussion and Criticism," *The Pedagogical Seminary*, 9 (June 1912): 186–200.

Schultz, Stanley. *The Culture Factory: The Boston Public Schools, 1789–1860*. New York: Oxford Univ. Press, 1973.

Sears, Robert R. "Lewis Madison Terman," in *Dictionary of American Biography*, supplement 6.

Sedlak, Michael W., and Steven Schlossman. "The Public School and Social Services: Reassessing the Progressive Legacy," *Educational Theory*, 35 (1985): 371–83.

Shapiro, Laura. *Perfection Salad: Women and Cooking at the Turn of the Century*. New York: Farrar, Straus, & Giroux, 1986.

Shapiro, Michael Steven. *Child's Garden: The Kindergarten Movement from Froebel to Dewey*. University Park: The Pennsylvania State University Press, 1983.

Shiels, Albert, comp., *Los Angeles City Schools and the War*. Pamphlet, Los Angeles Board of Education publication 10, Feb. 1918.

Shippey, Lee. "Los Angeles," in Alice Hunt Barlett, ed., *The Anthology of Cities*, p. 135. London: Erskine MacDonald, 1927.

Sinclair, Upton. *The Goslings: A Study of American Schools*. Pasadena, Calif.: Self-published, 1924.

Sklar, Kathryn Kish. "Hull House in the 1880's: A Community of Women Reformers," *Signs: Journal of Women in Culture and Society*, 10 (Summer 1985): 658–77.

Smith, Joan K. *Ella Flagg Young: Portrait of a Leader*. Ames, Iowa: Educational Studies Press and the Iowa State University Research Foundation, 1979.

Sokaloff, Lillian. "The Russians in Los Angeles," *Studies in Sociology*, 3 (March 1918): 1–16.

Sowell, Thomas, ed. *American Ethnic Groups*. N.p.: Urban Institute, 1978.

Spalding, William A., comp. *History and Reminiscences: Los Angeles, City and County*. 3 vols. (Vols. 2–3 are biographical compilations.) Los Angeles: Fintrell & Sons, 1931.

Splitter, Henry Winfred. "Education in Los Angeles, 1850–1900," *The Historical Society of Southern California Quarterly*, 33 (Sept. 1951): 226–44.

Spring, Joel. *The American School: Varieties of Historical Interpretation of the Foundations and Development of American Education, 1642–1985*. New York: Longman, 1986.

Starr, Harris Elwood. "Horatio Stebbins," in *Dictionary of American Biography*, vol. 17, pp. 549–50.

Starr, Kevin. *Americans and the California Dream, 1850–1915*. New York: Oxford University Press, 1973.

———. *Inventing the Dream: California Through the Progressive Era*. New York: Oxford University Press, 1985.

"Statement Regarding Use of School Buildings for Civic Centers, During 1937–1938, and Requests to Eliminate Fees for Use of School Buildings." Unpublished manuscript, Los Angeles Board of Education, 1937.

Sterry, Nora. "Housing Conditions in Chinatown, Los Angeles," *Journal of Applied Sociology*, 7 (Nov.–Dec. 1922): 71–75.

———. "The Neighborhood School," *California Quarterly of Secondary Education*, 2 (Jan. 1927): 117–23.

———. "Social Attitudes of Chinese Immigrants," *Journal of Applied Sociology*, 7 (July–Aug. 1923): 325–33.

Stimson, Grace H. *Rise of the Labor Movement.* Los Angeles: Univ. of California Press, 1955.

Stoddart, Bessie. "Recreative Centers of Los Angeles, California," *Annals of the American Academy of Political and Social Science*, 35 (Jan.–May 1910): 426–35.

Sutherland, Gillian. "Measuring Intelligence: English Local Education Authorities and Mental Testing, 1919–1939," in J. V. Smith and D. Hamilton, eds., *The Meritocratic Intellect: Studies of the History of Educational Research*, pp. 79–95. Aberdeen, Scotland: Aberdeen Univ. Press, 1980.

Svensrud, Marian. "Attitudes of the Japanese Towards Their Language Schools," *Sociology and Social Research*, 17 (Jan.–Feb. 1933): 259–64.

Swift, Fletcher Harper. *Emma Marwedel, 1818–1893: Pioneer of the Kindergarten in California.* Berkeley: Univ. of California Press, 1931.

Tan, Amy. *The Joy Luck Club.* New York: Random House, 1989.

Taylor, Paul. *An American-Mexican Frontier.* Chapel Hill: Univ. of North Carolina Press, 1944.

Terman, Lewis. "The Great Conspiracy," *New Republic*, 33 (Dec. 27, 1922): 116–20.

———. *Intelligence of School Children.* Boston: Houghton Mifflin, 1919.

———. *Measurement of Intelligence.* Boston: Houghton Mifflin, 1916.

Terman, Lewis M., Virgil E. Dickson, A. H. Sutherland, Raymond H. Franger, C. R. Tupper, and Grace Fernald. *Intelligence Tests and Social Reorganization.* Yonkers-on-Hudson, N.Y.: World Book Co., 1922.

Tom, Kim Fong. "Participation of Chinese in Community Life in Los Angeles." M.A. thesis, Univ. of Southern California, 1944.

Townsend, William Cameron. *Lázaro Cárdenas: Mexican Democrat.* Ann Arbor, Mich.: George Wahr Publishing Co., 1952.

Troen, Selwyn. *The Public and the Schools: Shaping the St. Louis System, 1838–1920.* Columbia: Univ. of Missouri Press, 1975.

Tuchman, Barbara. *The Zimmermann Telegram.* New York: Dell, 1965.

Tyack, David. *The One Best System: A History of American Urban Education*. Cambridge, Mass.: Harvard Univ. Press, 1974.

Tyack, David, and Elisabeth Hansot. *Managers of Virtue: Public School Leadership in America, 1820–1980*. New York: Basic Books, 1982.

United States Congress. "House Hearing Before the Committee on Immigration and Naturalization, Europe as an Emigrant-Exporting Continent and the United States as an Immigrant-Receiving Nation and Re-Examination of Previous Researches." 68th Cong., 1st Sess. Published as *Analysis of America's Modern Melting Pot*. Washington, D.C., 1924.

———. *Reports* of the Commission of Immigration. Washington, D.C., 1911. This work is based on 1908 data.

Urban, Wayne. *Why Teachers Organize*. Detroit: Wayne State Univ. Press, 1982.

Violas, Paul C. *The Training of the Urban Working Class: A History of Twentieth-Century American Education*. Skokie, Ill: Rand McNally, 1978.

Von Brauchitsch, Dennis M. "The Ku Klux Klan in California, 1921–1924." M.A. thesis, Sacramento State College, 1967.

Vorspan, Max, and Lloyd P. Gartner. *History of the Jews in Los Angeles*. San Marino, Calif.: Huntington Library Press, 1970.

Walkowitz, Daniel J. "The Making of a Feminine Professional Identity: Social Workers in the 1920s," *American Historical Review*, 95 (Oct. 1990): 1051–1075.

Warner, J. J., Benjamin Hayes, and J. P. Widney. *An Historical Sketch of Los Angeles County*. Los Angeles: O. W. Smith, 1936. Originally published in 1876.

Waterman, S. D. *A History of Berkeley Schools*. Berkeley, Calif.: Professional Press, 1918.

Watson, Peter. "Can Racial Discrimination Affect I.Q.?," in Ken Richardson and David Spears, eds., *Race and Intelligence: The Fallacies Behind the Race-I.Q. Controversy*, pp. 56–67. Baltimore: Pelican Books, 1972.

Westin, Saul O. "Guidance of High School Pupils from Follow-Up Study." M.A. thesis, Univ. of Southern California, 1939.

Weyer, M. Anita. "Joseph Scott: A Life of Service," *Southern California Quarterly*, 48 (Sept. 1966): 241–64.

Whitaker, Hazel Gottschaff. "A Study of Gifted Negro Children in Los Angeles City Schools." M.A. thesis, Univ. of Southern California, 1931.

Wiebe, Robert. *The Search for Order, 1877–1920*. New York: Hill & Wang, 1967.

Wiggin, Kate Douglas Smith. *My Garden of Memory*. Boston: Houghton Mifflin, 1923.

Williams, Marilyn Thornton. "New York City's Public Baths: A Case Study in Progressive Reform," *Journal of Urban History* (Nov. 1980): 49–81.

Williams, R. Hal. *The Democratic Party and California Politics, 1880–1896*. Stanford, Calif.: Stanford Univ. Press, 1973.

Wish, Harvey. "Carl Wittke, Historian," in O. Fritiof Ander, ed., *In the Trek of the Immigrants: Essays Presented to Carl Wittke*, pp. 3–16. Rock Island, Ill.: Augustana College Library, 1964.

Woods, Robert A., and Albert J. Kennedy, eds., *Handbook of Settlements*. New York: Charities Publication Committee, 1911.

Wrigley, Julia. *Class Politics and Public Schools: Chicago, 1900–1950*. New Brunswick, N.J.: Rutgers Univ. Press, 1982.

Wynn, Commodore, ed. *Negro Who's Who in California*. Los Angeles: Negro Who's Who in California, 1948.

Yee, George, and Elsie Yee. "The 1927 Chinese Baseball Team," *Gum Saan Journal* (Chinese Historical Society of Southern California), Dec. 1980: 1–8.

Young, Kimball. *Mental Differences in Certain Immigrant Groups*. Eugene: Univ. of Oregon Press, 1922.

Young, Pauline V. *The Pilgrims of Russian Town*. Chicago: Univ. of Chicago Press, 1932.

———. "The Social Settlements in the Changing City," *Sociology and Social Research*, 20 (Sept.–Oct. 1935): 63–70.

Zenderland, Leila. "Psychological Expertise and Public Education: The Battle Over Intelligence Testing in New York City, 1910–1915." Paper presented at the annual meeting of the Organization of American Historians, Minneapolis, 1985.

Index

In this index an "f" after a number indicates a separate reference on the next page, and an "ff" indicates separate references on the next two pages. A continuous discussion over two or more pages is indicated by a span of page numbers, e.g., "57–59." *Passim* is used for a cluster of references in close but not consecutive sequence. Subentries are ordered by page number rather than alphabetically.

Library of Congress Cataloging-in-Publication Data

Raftery, Judith Rosenberg
Land of fair promise : politics and reform in Los Angeles schools,
1885–1941 / Judith Rosenberg Raftery.
p. cm.
Includes bibliographical references and index.
ISBN 0-8047-1930-6 (alk. paper) :
1. Education—California—Los Angeles—History. 2. Public
schools—California—Los Angeles—History. 3. Educational change—
California—Los Angeles—History. I. Title.
LA245.L6R34 1992
370'.9794'94—dc20
91-26888

This book has been typeset by Tseng Information Systems, Inc.
in 10/12 Trump. It is printed on acid-free paper.